Organizing Visions

Ethics and Intersectionality
An Orbis Series in Theological Ethics

Series Editors
Miguel A. De La Torre
Stacey M. Floyd-Thomas
David P. Gushee

Titles include:

Juan M. Floyd-Thomas, *Critical Race Theology: White Supremacy, American Christianity, and the Ongoing Culture Wars*

Melanie Jones Quarles, *Up Against a Crooked Gospel: Black Women's Bodies and the Politics of Redemption*

Miguel A. De La Torre and Mitri Raheb, eds., *Tear Down These Walls: Decolonial Approaches to Barriers and Liberation*

Gary Dorrien, Charlene Sinclair, and Aaron Stauffer, eds., *Organizing Visions: Social Ethics and Broad-Based Solidarity Activism*

ETHICS AND INTERSECTIONALITY

Organizing Visions

Social Ethics and Broad-Based
Solidarity Activism

Gary Dorrien
Charlene Sinclair
Aaron Stauffer

Editors

ORBIS BOOKS
Maryknoll, New York 10545

Founded in 1970, Orbis Books endeavors to publish works that enlighten the mind, nourish the spirit, and challenge the conscience. The publishing arm of the Maryknoll Fathers and Brothers, Orbis seeks to explore the global dimensions of the Christian faith and mission, to invite dialogue with diverse cultures and religious traditions, and to serve the cause of reconciliation and peace. The books published reflect the views of their authors and do not represent the official position of the Maryknoll Society. To learn more about Maryknoll and Orbis Books, please visit our website at www.orbisbooks.com.

Copyright © 2025 by Gary Dorrien, Charlene Sinclair, and Aaron Stauffer

Published by Orbis Books, Box 302, Maryknoll, NY 10545-0302.

All rights reserved.

All Vatican documents are available at Vatican.va.

Scripture quotations, unless otherwise noted, are from New Revised Standard Version Bible: Catholic Edition, copyright © 1989, 1993 National Council of the Churches of Christ in the United States of America. Used by permission. All rights reserved worldwide.

No part of this publication may be reproduced or transmitted in any form or by any means, electronic or mechanical, including photocopying, recording, or any information storage or retrieval system, without prior permission in writing from the publisher.

Queries regarding rights and permissions should be addressed to: Orbis Books, P.O. Box 302, Maryknoll, NY 10545-0302.

Manufactured in the United States of America

Library of Congress Cataloging-in-Publication Data

Names: Dorrien, Gary J. editor | Sinclair, Charlene editor | Stauffer, Aaron editor
Title: Organizing visions : social ethics and broad-based solidarity activism / Gary Dorrien, Charlene Sinclair, Aaron Stauffer, editors.
Description: Maryknoll, NY : Orbis Books, [2025] | Series: Ethics and intersectionality | Includes bibliographical references and index. |
Identifiers: LCCN 2025019754 (print) | LCCN 2025019755 (ebook) | ISBN 9781626986251 trade paperback | ISBN 9798888660805 epub
Subjects: LCSH: Christian sociology—History—20th century | Faith-based community organizing—History—20th century | Christian ethics—History—20th century | Social ethics—History—20th century | Christian sociology—History—21st century | Faith-based community organizing—History—21st century | Christian ethics—History--21st century | Social ethics—History—21st century
Classification: LCC BT738 .O67 2025 (print) | LCC BT738 (ebook) | DDC 261.8—dc23/eng/20250717
LC record available at https://lccn.loc.gov/2025019754
LC ebook record available at https://lccn.loc.gov/2025019755

To Ernesto Cortés Jr.

Contents

Acknowledgments ix

Introduction: Organizing Visions of Social Ethical Organizers xi
   Gary Dorrien

Part I

1. The Problems and Promise of Radical Social Gospel in
Organizing Movements 3
   Aaron Stauffer

2. Making Ministers or Training Technocrats?
Religious Education for Social Transformation and the
Problems of Professionalized Democracy 22
   Joseph Strife

3. Traditions in Organizing: A Social Catholic Perspective 42
   Nicholas Hayes-Mota

4. National Welfare Rights Organization's Beulah Sanders
at the 1972 National Council of Churches Convention 69
   Carolyn Baker and Colleen Wessel-McCoy

Part II

5. Faith and Labor: Organizing for the Kingdom of God on Earth . . . 85
   K.B. Brower

6. Teaching Community Organizing in Theological Education:
Pedagogical Conundrums and Delights 100
   Cynthia Moe-Lobeda

7. Is, Ought, and How: Intertwining Social Ethics and
Social Movement Theory for Social Change 118
   C. Melissa Snarr

8. In Search of Our Common Treasure: A Womanist Approach
to Antiracism Work 133
   Malinda Elizabeth Berry

9. We Want to Be Loving: The Ethics of Reciprocity in
    Chicago's Response to Venezuelan Asylum Seekers. 149
        Christophe D. Ringer
10. To Be Foils, Not Fooled:
    The Insistent Practice and Insurgent Pedagogy of Christian Social
    Liberation Ethics for Colleagues, Church, and Community 160
        Stacey Floyd-Thomas

Conclusion 189
    Aaron Stauffer
Afterword. 203
    Peter Laarman
Contributors 209
Bibliography 211
Index. 231

Acknowledgments

This book would not have come to be without the support of several individuals and institutions, especially the Highlander Research and Education Center, and its co-executive director Rev. Allyn Maxfield-Steele. Highlander has incubated SEED from the start, as it has so many other movements. We are deeply grateful to the deft editing work of Thomas Hermans-Webster and the entire crew at Orbis Books—this is a perfect house for this book—and to the series editors, Miguel A. De La Torre, Stacey M. Floyd-Thomas, and David P. Gushee.

Introduction

Organizing Visions of Social Ethical Organizers

Gary Dorrien

This book comes from a scrappy group of social ethicists and organizers who believe that academics, organizers, and clerics must forge new ways of working together in interfaith liberationist work. Charlene Sinclair, Aaron Stauffer, and I founded Social Ethics Energizing Democracy (SEED) in July 2022 to create a vehicle for this multifaceted project. Charlene is a veteran leader of organizing efforts to reverse generations of structural racism toward communities of color in the United States. Aaron is a former organizer for the Industrial Areas Foundation (IAF) and Religions for Peace who specializes in church-based community organizing. Both had written doctoral dissertations with me on the history, problems, and possibilities of broad-based interfaith organizing. We said it was time to bring together organizers, pastors involved in organizing, academics who teach social ethics and related subjects, and people with a foot in two or more of these camps. This book, on which Aaron has served as chief editor, exudes the commitment of SEED to faith-based organizing.

I came to this work through the door of solidarity activism, which led me into Episcopal Church ministry at the age of thirty and an academic career at the age of thirty-five. In my twenties, I was an organizer for the Democratic Socialist Organizing Committee (DSOC), which morphed in 1982 into Democratic Socialists of America. In my late twenties and early thirties, I was also an every-week speaker for the Committee in Solidarity with the People of El Salvador and the founder of an Albany, New York, diocesan chapter of the Episcopal Peace Fellowship. I had belatedly joined a church and did not consider an academic career. Before I could join a church, I had to believe that churches could be effective in social justice activism. Later, I made a similar judgment about the academy. I have long argued that breakthrough gains for universal healthcare, economic democracy, and saving the planet occur during periods of liberal ascendancy in solidarity with mass movements. The preconditions fitting this theory of change were lacking for most of my lifetime. They materialized only in recent years, yielding mass movements for justice and eco-justice, but also Right-nationalist movements that repudiate the norms and institutions of liberal democracy.

The Right-nationalist movements vying for power in Europe are mostly racial-ethnic, fueled by their hostility to multiracial liberal democracy, which they call "globalism," charging that Black and Brown migrants are reverse-colonizing the so-called native white Europeans. Right-nationalism in the United States expresses comparable grievances against non-White immigrants and liberal democracy, with three key differences: (1) The United States is a nation of immigrants with a distinctly powerful tradition of civic nationalism based on the claim that the United States is a creedal nation, not the homeland of an ethnic group. (2) Religion plays a much larger role in the United States than in most of Europe. And (3), fusing aspects of (1) and (2), every revival of US American nationalism resurrects the Manifest Destiny myth that America is an exception to history.

Journalist John O'Sullivan contended in 1845 that the United States had a Manifest Destiny to annex the Republic of Texas as a slave state and spread all the way to California and Oregon. God, he maintained, wanted Anglo-Saxon America to be as expansive and powerful as possible. Whig leaders were incredulous at this argument, objecting that Manifest Destiny was brazenly imperialist: Were they to suppose that no nation on earth has a divine right to universal conquest except the universal Yankee nation? The United States has compelled its political candidates ever since to profess their belief in American Exceptionalism, if not outright Manifest Destiny.

A powerful Right-nationalist species of American Exceptionalism has been ascending in American politics since 2011, the same year that a tipping point also occurred on the democratic Left. Barack Obama was elected president in 2008 amid a spectacular financial crash and George W. Bush's massive bailouts of the megabanks. A wildly angry movement calling itself the Tea Party railed against the election of a Black liberal Democrat and the disastrous Bush presidency, challenging the Republican Party establishment for control of the party. Donald Trump perceived in 2011 that, if he could take over the populist-nationalist insurgency, he

INTRODUCTION   xiii

could overtake the Republican Party. He wasn't ready to run for president, but saw his opening, the tipping point on the political Right. Meanwhile, the crash and the bailouts of 2008 yielded tame reactions on the political Left, chastened by the demands of defending Obama, until the Occupy Wall Street explosion of 2011. Masses of people were fed up with being downsized and humiliated. For twenty years, neoliberal capitalist apologists had wielded a devastating slogan, "There is no alternative." Then TINA lost its shutdown power. Occupy Wall Street was a wild, brief, chaotic, turning point, demanding that there must be an alternative to severe inequality, White supremacy, and destroying the planet.[1]

New movements for immigration justice, a raised minimum wage, antiracism, equality, ecojustice, and First Nation peoples' sovereignty swiftly ensued—the Dreamer movement, Fight for $15, Black Lives Matter, the Bernie Sanders presidential nomination campaigns of 2016 and 2020, and the Dakota Access Pipeline protests. The democratic Left had been habituated to a stubborn remnant mode of organizing and an ever-shrinking unionism. Now we rejoiced at witnessing a new era of mass movements. The Bernie campaigns showed that tens of millions of US Americans are committed to universal healthcare, economic justice, abolishing structures of racial, sexual, and cultural denigration, and saving a suffocating planet. The Democratic Party, however, is a corporate powerhouse dominated by economic and cultural elites cut off from the struggles of working-class communities. Thus, it regarded Sanders as a mortal threat to the party, while Sanders spoke a one-key-only language of social democratic humanism that did not break through to Black and Hispanic voters. The estrangement of the Democratic Party from its own former base in the working class played a large role in electing Trump to the presidency in 2016, and a larger one in 2024.

The contributors to this book are scholar-activists who are committed to comprehending the historical roots and legacies of our work, including its ongoing historical trajectories. Many of us teach social ethics, a field founded in the 1880s by the social gospel movement, which argued that Christians are morally obligated to support movements for justice and peace. The emphasis of the social gospel on social justice organizing was

---

[1] This section on anti-neoliberal turning points adapts material from Gary Dorrien, *Social Democracy in the Making: Political and Religious Roots of European Socialism* (New Haven, CT: Yale University Press, 2019), ix–x.

novel in American Christianity. It impelled social gospel academics to invent a field that studied reform movements—social ethics. In subsequent decades, many social ethicists shucked off their field's original emphasis on organizing. Some returned to individualism, or a posited orthodoxy, or both; some said the social gospel attempt to reform society had been hopelessly naïve; and many allowed the Democratic Party establishment to define what was "real" in politics and society. This book imagines a new broad-based solidarity activism that builds on the social gospel, Niebuhrian realist, liberationist, and social Catholic traditions of struggling for justice.

The social gospel arose differently in White Protestant and Black Protestant churches. In White Protestantism, it was primarily an anxious response to the struggle between owners and workers, the rise of trade unionism, and the specter of urban corruption. Union organizers said it was obvious that White Protestant churches would never side with them. It was possible to imagine a Catholic social gospel, since many Catholics joined the unions, but Protestant ministers preached to the capitalist class that paid their salary. This accusation hurt the feelings of social gospel founders Washington Gladden and Richard Ely. They vowed to overcome their class bias, reaching out to working-class communities that despised the Protestant churches. A succeeding generation of social gospel founders led by W. D. P. Bliss, Vida Scudder, Walter Rauschenbusch, and Harry F. Ward took a further step, building a socialist flank alongside the social gospel mainstream.

In Black Protestant churches that advocated a social gospel, there was no choice concerning which issue trumped the others. The Black social gospel was the answer to an anguished question: What would a new abolitionism be? Abolitionism and the Civil War had come and gone; Reconstruction had been forsaken; the Fourteenth and Fifteenth Amendments were eviscerated in much of the South; the United States imposed a racial caste system lacking any parallel in the post-slavery Americas; and a mania of lynching descended on Black Americans. The founders of the Black social gospel—William Simmons, Reverdy Ransom, Alexander Walters, Ida B. Wells-Barnett, Nannie Burroughs, and Adam Clayton Powell Sr.—did not say that America just needed to fulfill its Manifest Destiny. They said the United States must overcome the betrayal of its own faith that all human beings possess God-given dignity. They taught that God cares about the poor, the excluded, the oppressed, and the kingdom of God.

Introduction

Both social gospel movements contained a mainstream of progressive reformers and a flank of socialists. The three founders of social ethics were Ely, an Episcopalian political economist who taught at Johns Hopkins University; Francis Greenwood Peabody, a Unitarian cleric who taught at Harvard Divinity School; and Graham Taylor, a Congregational cleric who taught at Chicago Theological Seminary. All were White progressives, radical only in the way that the social gospel was inherently radical, contending that Christianity operated for centuries with the wrong hierarchy of topics. The church is Christian only when it enlists churches in struggles for justice.[2]

Social Darwinism dominated the emerging social sciences, especially economics and sociology. This situation alarmed Ely and Gladden, driving them in 1885 to create the American Economic Association. The churches needed very much, they said, to accept Darwinian biology, but embracing the Social Darwinist ideology of predatory domination and laissez-faire capitalism was out of play. Morally, Social Darwinism was a non-starter for anyone who preached Matthew 25 sermons about seeing Christ in the faces of the poor. The social gospel founders did not know where to draw the line between Darwinism and Social Darwinism. They debated this issue with anguish, looking for help wherever they could find it, knowing they were out-gunned intellectually by Herbert Spencer and William Graham Sumner, the doyens of Social Darwinism. Meanwhile Ely, Peabody, and Taylor said that applying the social gospel to real-world contexts must be a field of its own. It was not enough to study the Bible or theology from a social gospel perspective. Nobody knows beforehand, or in a library, what the relevant issues and solutions are. Peabody reasoned that the reform movements reveal where the places of suffering and injustice exist in society.

Peabody's courses focused on movements for temperance, urban reform, and the rights of workers, Black Americans, and Native Americans. His method had three steps—observation, generalization, and correlation.

---

[2] This section on the social gospel origin of social ethics adapts and capsulizes my work on this subject in numerous books, especially Gary Dorrien, *Social Ethics in the Making: Interpreting an American Tradition* (Malden, MA: Wiley-Blackwell, 2009), 1–5; Dorrien, *The New Abolition: W. E. B. Du Bois and the Black Social Gospel* (New Haven, CT: Yale University Press, 2015), 2–5; and Dorrien, *Over from Union Road: My Christian-Left-Intellectual Life* (Waco, TX: Baylor University Press, 2024), 184–85.

Description and analysis are important, Peabody said, but merely academic. Solutions are good, but piecemeal. Social ethics aimed to grasp the ethical character and principles of society as a whole, employing the tools of the newfound social sciences to serve this purpose, binding social ethics to social science. Ely, Peabody, and Taylor were middle-class idealists who cringed at having to talk about power and the class struggle. They preferred to talk about democracy, faith, social progress, scientific advancement, peace, the common good, and the way of Jesus. They objected sharply to being called socialists, since socialist radicalism scared and repelled them. Yet in a broad sense of the term, almost the entire US American social gospel tradition was socialist for advocating cooperative ownership and the nationalization of natural monopolies.[3]

Socialism arose in England and France in the 1820s as the idea that workers should be able to work cooperatively with one another instead of being pitted against one another. Society should be organized as a community of producer cooperatives or cooperative guilds. Some contended that the vision of a cooperative society cannot be achieved without strong industrial unions, so various kinds of syndicalism arose contending that worker syndicates should *be* the government. Other new forms of socialism ascribed an important role to the state or conceived socialism itself as state collectivism. Karl Marx condemned all forms of state socialism as a sellout absurdity; meanwhile six kinds of "Marxian" theory arose interpreting Marx as a syndicalist, an anarcho-syndicalist utopian, a radical democrat, a two-house reformist revolutionary (which the German Social Democratic Party called Orthodox Marxism), a Communist, and a guild socialist. Christian socialists variously aligned with these types or espoused their own ethically-based perspectives.[4]

In England and Switzerland, Christian socialism was a major player in the political Left, and socialism was democratic. The leading Christian socialists included John Ludlow and Charles Marson (England), and Leonhard Ragaz and Hermann Kutter (Switzerland). In most of Continental Europe, Christian socialists were marginalized, and Marxists

---

[3] See Dorrien, *Social Ethics in the Making*, 6–59, 60–145; and Dorrien, "Social Ethics for Social Justice: The Legacies of the Social Gospel and a Case for Idealistic Discontent," in *Ethics and Advocacy: Bridges and Boundaries,* ed. Harlan Beckley, Douglas F. Ottati, Matthew R. Petrusek, and William Schweiker (Eugene, OR: Cascade Books, 2022), 106–30.

[4] Dorrien, *Social Democracy in the Making*, 50–79, 114–34.

Introduction

contended that democracy was a bourgeois fraud. Real democracy, according to the Marxian Left, would be achieved only after the proletarian revolution abolished capitalism. In the United States, White religious socialists W. D. P. Bliss, George Herron, Walter Rauschenbusch, Vida Scudder, and Harry Ward, and Black religious socialists Reverdy C. Ransom, George Frazier Miller, W. E. B. Du Bois, George W. Slater, and George W. Woodbey frightened the social gospel founders by accentuating the differences between progressive reform and socialist restructuring. The Christian socialists developed a concept of power as inclusive transformative capacity. Capitalism, they said, is inherently predatory; you cannot reform it by adding cooperatives and social welfare.

Ransom and Woodbey stressed that capitalism was like slavery; in fact, it was the basis of chattel slavery and a form itself of slavery. Du Bois added that democracy and imperialism expanded together because White workers shared the spoils of exploiting people of color. The rule of might grew precisely as democracy spread. The only solution to this miserable picture, Du Bois said, was for the labor and socialist movements to reach all the way to the world's most oppressed people, not stopping with White workers. Some interpreters, past and present, have described the social gospel socialists as the real thing and the reformers as pretenders who thwarted the real thing. But the leading Christian socialists were not ideologues who believed in magical socialism or sought to divide the social gospel movement over this issue; only Woodbey espoused the magical Marxist dogma that socialism is the cure for all social ills. The Christian socialists prized the broadly social Christian movement to which they belonged, and it mattered to them that sin and evil long predated capitalism. On their view, the social gospel was the next Great Awakening movement, this time recovering the social justice teaching of the Bible.[5]

Two intertwined ironies were fateful for the social gospel. The movement's historic figures belonged to its socialist flank, but the movement was defined historically by the sentimentality, moralism, and idealism of its mainstream.

---

[5] W. E. B. Du Bois, "The African Roots of the War," *Atlantic Monthly* 115 (May 1915), 707–14. This discussion capsulizes my extensive discussions in Dorrien, *The New Abolition*, 281–86 and 453–82; and Dorrien, *American Democratic Socialism: History, Politics, Religion, and Theory* (New Haven, CT: Yale University Press, 2021), 42–119. For an original and important source on George Washington Woodbey, see Charles Holm, "'To Be Free from the Slavery of Capitalism' : David Walker, Peter H. Clark, and George Washington Woodbey's Black Socialist Thought," (PhD diss., University of Texas, Austin, 2021).

Social gospel reformers preached a gospel of cultural optimism and a Jesus of middle-class idealism. Many were pacifists who exalted the antiwar issue above all other issues, describing Mohandas Gandhi as the Jesus-figure of the twentieth century. Sometimes they urged Christians to stop talking about class, a degrading concept. In the early 1930s, Reinhold Niebuhr redirected American theology by ridiculing the social gospel on these points. His frosty proto-Marxist polemic, *Moral Man and Immoral Society* (1932), brilliantly skewered the optimism and idealism of the social gospel, while taking for granted its core commitment to social justice activism.

Politics, Niebuhr taught, is about struggling for power. Liberal denials of this truism are stupid, especially the moral idealism of progressive Christianity. Niebuhr contended that Jesus preached an ethic of individual perfectionism that paid no attention to social consequences. Moreover, there is no such thing as a moral group. No human group willingly subordinates its interests to the interests of others; morality belongs to the sphere of individual action. Therefore, the highest good of a Christian social ethic in the social sphere is not love, but justice, which requires a struggle for power. Niebuhr swung the field of social ethics to his language of crisis, paradox, tragedy, and power struggle, trading the Progressive language of progress and ethical idealism for the orthodox-sounding language of sin, redemption, tragedy, and transcendence. He moved simultaneously, as he said, to the socialist left politically and to the neo-orthodox right theologically. Then in the mid-1940s he tacked back to the mainstream of the Democratic Party, taking most of the social ethics field with him. Niebuhr said there was no good reason to remain a democratic socialist because the New Deal achieved most of the socialist agenda while Socialists languished in marginalized irrelevance. A bit later, he refashioned his Christian Realism as a species of Cold War anti-Communism, until the war in Vietnam went very badly and Niebuhr judged that Cold War containment had to be more selective.[6]

The greatest social gospel tradition is the one that arose in Black churches and paved the way to the Civil Rights movement. Black social gospel founders Reverdy Ransom, Alexander Walters, George Slater Jr., and Richard R. Wright Jr. enlisted their churches in the fight for racial justice, building protest organizations. They preached about equality, democracy,

---

[6] Reinhold Niebuhr, *Moral Man and Immoral Society: A Study in Ethics and Politics* (New York: Scribner's, 1932); Niebuhr, *Reflections on the End of an Era* (New York: Scribner's, 1934); Dorrien, *Social Ethics in the Making*, 226–94.

and Jesus loving all the children. Not to enter the social and political struggle for justice was to betray Jesus. The founders passed this faith to the generation of Mordecai Johnson, Benjamin Mays, J. Pius Barbour, and Howard Thurman, who passed it directly to Martin Luther King Jr.

King's teachers showed him that church leaders could combine academic intellectualism, religious faith, and a passion for social justice. In fact, they said, it was imperative for the church to become known for combining these things. Johnson, Mays, Barbour, and Thurman were democratic socialists and anti-colonial internationalists who took for granted that the best versions of the social gospel were democratic socialist and anti-imperialist. King assumed the same thing, never believing it made him unusual. After King was assassinated in 1968, liberation theologies arose in South America, the United States, and South Africa, contending that theology must privilege the questions and experiences of oppressed people of faith.[7]

Acts of solidarity and praxis come first; liberation theology is secondary reflection shaped by the voices of oppressed people. James Cone, the leading founder of Black liberation theology, had begun his academic career in 1965 as a neo-orthodox theologian who bristled that racism was a low-priority topic in his field. He burned with rage at being stuck in a field that merely regurgitated what German theologians said. After King was cut down, Cone imagined a Black theology that fixed on the struggles of Black people to overthrow oppression and dependency.

Cone rejected the liberal commitment to engaging critical disbelief, putting God in question, searching for the historical Jesus, and making claims to ethical universality. White Christianity, he said, is demonic, not something to critically appropriate. If liberation is the essence of the divine nature, God is Black. "Black" names a specific identity group *and* is a symbol of all oppressed people. To be liberated is to become Black with God. Afterward, there arose several kinds of Black theology, including womanist versions that privileged the wisdom and experience of Black women. Social ethicist Katie Cannon founded womanist ethics on novelist Alice Walker's historic definition that a womanist is a Black feminist or feminist of color who is willful and courageous, loves other women and herself, is committed to survival and the wholeness of people, and bears the same relation to feminism that purple has to lavender.[8]

---

[7] Gary Dorrien, *Breaking White Supremacy: Martin Luther King Jr. and the Black Social Gospel* (New Haven, CT: Yale University Press, 2018).

[8] James H. Cone, *Black Theology and Black Power* (New York: Harper & Row,

Catholic versions of the social gospel developed over the same timespan in the nineteenth century as socialism and the Protestant social gospel. In the 1830s, a tradition of social Catholicism responding to socialism began in Europe; in 1891, Pope Leo XIII intervened in it by issuing a historic pro-union encyclical, *Rerum Novarum*. This encyclical launched the papal tradition of Catholic Social Teaching. American Catholicism, however, was slow to develop a Catholic equivalent of the social gospel. Catholic workers streamed into the Knights of Labor and the American Federation of Labor, but Leo XIII's scathing critique of capitalism was jarring, threatening, and out of play in American Catholic seminaries. For twenty-five years, it had no public American Catholic defenders except John A. Ryan, a moral theologian at St. Paul Seminary in Minneapolis and Catholic University of America in Washington, DC. Ryan contended in his first book, *A Living Wage* (1906), that the rights to live and marry inhere in all persons, there is a secondary and derivative right to a living wage, and the United States needed living wage legislation. He advocated an eight-hour workday, a progressive tax on income and inheritance, state government unemployment and health insurance, and national and state government ownership of the railroads and telephone companies.[9]

Ryan waited until 1919 to acquire Catholic company. The National Catholic War Council adopted his program for postwar social reconstruction, and Ryan founded the National Catholic Welfare Council (NCWC), serving for many years as head of its Social Action Department. Meanwhile the labor priest movement of the 1930s and the founding of Dorothy Day's Catholic Worker movement in 1933 broke the mold of an immigrant faith angling for acceptance. Social Catholicism, anchored by papal encyclicals, was now an established third way between unfettered capitalism and atheistic socialism, even in the United States. Catholic

---

1969); Gustavo Gutiérrez, *A Theology of Liberation: History, Politics, and Salvation,* trans. Caridad Inda and John Eagleson (Maryknoll, NY: Orbis Books, 1973); Katie Geneva Cannon, *Black Womanist Ethics* (Atlanta: Scholars Press, 1988); Alice Walker, *In Search of Our Mothers' Gardens: Womanist Prose* (San Diego: Harcourt Brace Jovanovich, 1983); Gary Dorrien, *A Darkly Radiant Vision: The Black Social Gospel in the Shadow of MLK* (New Haven, CT: Yale University Press, 2023), 205–32, 261–333.

[9] John A. Ryan, *A Living Wage* (New York: Macmillan, 1906); Pope Leo XIII, *Rerum Novarum: The Condition of Labor* (1891), in *Catholic Social Thought: The Documentary Heritage,* ed. David J. O'Brien and Thomas A. Shannon (Maryknoll, NY: Orbis Books, 1992), 14–39; Dorrien, *Social Ethics in the Making,* 185–215.

institutions teach their history, ensuring that the papal tradition of Catholic Social Teaching and the broader tradition of social Catholicism will not be forgotten. The same cannot be said of the Protestant social gospel that founded social ethics and was Christian socialist at its best.

Social Ethics and Political Theology

Social ethics, as I conceive it, is a tradition of academic, ecumenical, and public discourse that analyzes the relations of power at multiple sites of exploitation, exclusion, harm, and oppression. It names an academic field, the tradition of social ethical theology that developed within the ecumenical movement, and a tradition of public intellectualism and interfaith activism. The social gospel origins of social ethics and its defining commitment to social justice naturally produced a tradition dominated by progressives, democratic socialists, Niebuhrian realists, and liberationists. But some traditions of social ethics are strongly conservative, ascribing greater importance to religious authority, notably conservative forms of Catholicism and evangelicalism, and some traditions of social ethics are merely academic, spurning the emphasis on activist organizing that founded the field.

The relationships between social ethics and political theology are similarly controverted. Social ethics is a field in the academy, whereas political theology is a subfield boasting a growing interdisciplinary following. There are no irreconcilable differences between these enterprises, but both have a Christian socialist origin, contrary to the Carl Schmitt story that many political theologians somehow prefer. Schmitt was a Nazi legal theorist who despised liberal democracy in standard Nazi fashion. He taught, cynically but interestingly, that all forms of political thinking are ways of renaming theological categories. His scholarly bandwagon—which got rolling in the political theologies of the 1960s, sprawled to multiple fields in the 1980s, and is now a cottage industry—gave theologians an opening to reverse his program: All theology is political, especially when it claims otherwise. This reverse-Schmitt procedure undergirds much creative work in contemporary religious thought, especially in neo-Marxist, Deleuzian, and liberationist forms of political theology. It tracks the displacement of God by the sovereignty of the modern state, which in some renderings gave way to the godly sovereignty of corporate neo-capitalism, capitalist Empire. It importantly counters the isolation of the political from the theological and religious that defined the soulless subjectivity of Enlightenment rationality, which uprooted transcendence from the materiality of life.[10]

But Christian socialists wrote political theology, making some of these very arguments, long before Schmitt, Emanuel Hirsch, and Paul Althaus championed the atrocious idea of fascist theology. Early Christian socialism in England, Germany, Switzerland, the United States, and Canada was a creative response to the social ravages of unfettered nineteenth-century capitalism. In England and North America, it was predominantly cooperative, progressive, social ethical, and pragmatic, usually fusing liberal and democratic elements, with less opposition from ecclesiastical establishments than Christian socialists experienced elsewhere. In Germany, Christian socialism had a stronger ideological and statist character as a consequence of yearning for, and then defending, a unified state. Here, Christian socialists had to fight off a Social Democratic movement that was hostile to religion and established churches that were hostile to trade unions and socialism. Social ethics and political theology, I believe, work best when they live up to the religious socialist traditions from which they arose. To interpret the political theologies formulated by Jürgen Moltmann, Dorothee Sölle, and Johann Baptist Metz in the 1960s and 1970s as a renewal of Schmitt's enterprise is grievously wrong. Moltmann, Sölle, and Metz were Christian democratic socialists who knew what they owed to previous generations of Christian socialism.[11]

Social Ethics Energizing Democracy

In July 2022, Charlene, Aaron, and I convened a two-day gathering of twenty-five founders of SEED. The following January, we conducted two sessions at the Society of Christian Ethics conference in Chicago, where the idea of this book was first broached. Later, there was a weeklong gathering in Nashville, Tennessee, where the book was mapped out. We resisted the

---

[10] This discussion of political theology adapts material from Dorrien, *Social Democracy in the Making*, 2–3.

[11] Jürgen Moltmann, *Religion, Revolution, and the Future*, trans. M. Douglas Meeks (New York: Charles Scribner's Sons, 1969); Dorothee Sölle, *Beyond Mere Obedience: Reflections on a Christian Ethic for the Future* (Minneapolis: Augsburg Press, 1970); Johann Baptist Metz, *Theology of the World*, trans. William Glen-Doepel (New York: Seabury, 1969); Gary Dorrien, *Reconstructing the Common Good: Theology and the Social Order* (Maryknoll, NY: Orbis Books, 1990), 77–100.

INTRODUCTION   xxiii

turf boundaries and stereotypes that keep organizers and academics from working together. Democracy in the United States, we said, always fragile and imperiled in the first place, has entered a new period of acute crisis. White Christian nationalism plays a major role in the mounting danger. Climate change is driving millions of desperate people from places that are no longer habitable. Ranged against a toxic tide of authoritarian nationalism, we see faint and fragmented resistance movements. We need stronger counternarrative voices in the work of social justice organizing, and we need to combat frontline loneliness, supporting those on the front lines doing the work. This book is one of SEED's founding projects.[12]

Aaron Stauffer, reflecting on the contribution of the social gospel to grassroots and labor organizing, describes the remarkable ministry of social gospel stalwart Howard "Buck" Kester in the Southern Tenant Farmers Union (STFU). Born in 1904 to a Virginia tailor who moved the family in 1916 to Beckley, West Virginia, Kester witnessed the labor strife and racism of Beckley, watched his father drift in and out of the Ku Klux Klan, and joined the youth bastions of the social gospel movement as a student at Lynchburg College—the YMCA, the World Student Christian Federation, and the Student Volunteer Movement. He cut his activist teeth in the YMCA, working to integrate YMCA summer camps, and dropped out of Princeton Theological Seminary, because it spurned the social gospel. In 1926 he enrolled at Vanderbilt School of Religion, where he absorbed the social gospel socialism of social ethicist Alva Taylor, who was fired a decade later for being too radical. Kester joined the Socialist Party for its socialism, joined the Fellowship of Reconciliation for its pacifism, and joined the NAACP for its antiracism, writing journalistic reports on lynching for the NAACP. In 1934, he threw himself into sharecropper organizing. Stauffer recounts that Kester powerfully condemned sharecropping and wage labor by combining the republican conception of freedom as non-domination with socialist critiques of wage slavery.

Classic republican arguments for liberty presupposed colonies of enslaved and dominated persons. Kester was a labor republican, countering that sharecropping and the wage system were forms of slavery based on relations of mastery and subjection. He connected wage labor to wage slavery in organizing for the STFU, just as he bravely stumped for anti-lynching legislation that never passed in the US Congress. Kester's

---

[12] Dorrien, *Over from Union Road*, 265–67.

rhetoric of slavery and domination vividly described the conditions of the Black and White sharecroppers for whom he bravely labored in the STFU. He had come to STFU activism through his friendships with two divinity school classmates who became union organizers, Claude Williams and Ward Rogers. Stauffer accentuates that the STFU leaders relied on the religious faith they practiced, drawing on the ethos and hymnody of the Black church. Writing later in life while working for the Fellowship of Southern Churchmen, Howard Kester emphasizes the importance of organizing in the churches by saying that they must keep "hammering away in the church, at the church, with the church." In the fields, the newspapers, and the political system, Kester and his STFU allies faced down constant vilification and oppression, winning precious few victories. In the churches, they took heart that they stood on solid ground. The God of love was their basis for believing that a cooperative commonwealth was not only possible, but is already the law of the divine moral order, the commonwealth of God.

American political scientist James C. Scott, in his controversial book *Seeing Like a State: How Certain Schemes to Improve the Human Condition Have Failed* (1998), argued that modern states overconfidently assume their ability to pursue social engineering in accordance with scientific laws discovered by the social sciences. State governments, he said, force "legibility" on their subjects by eradicating local cultural traditions and knowledge, creating homogenized societies that generate economies of scale while submitting to state control. Social ethicist Joe Strife, a longtime antipoverty activist and scholar, offers a critique of liberal Protestant social activism that turns on Scott's distinction between two types of knowledge, *metis* and *techne*.[13]

Metis is the tactile, local, enmeshed, commonsense knowledge of everyday life. *Techne* is the abstract, generalized, spreadsheet knowledge of the social scientist and the technocrat. Strife recounts that the social gospel founders sought earnestly to align Christian teaching and practices with the emerging social sciences. Jane Addams, a quintessential social gospel activist and the founder of the Hull House social settlement in Chicago, was an astute exponent of the street-level knowledge she acquired at Hull House. She spoke the embodied democratic language of *metis,* defending the virtues of the working-class people with whom she worked, but she also shared the

---

[13] James C. Scott, *Seeing Like a State: How Certain Schemes to Improve the Human Condition Have Failed* (New Haven, CT: Yale University Press, 1998).

enthusiasm of the settlement movement for the technocratic purview of sociology, with occasional snorts of class superiority and White privilege. The social work movement earnestly sought social scientific validation on its way to becoming a profession with academic status. As Strife drolly puts it, the settlement movement traded its grounding in everyday *metis* for Master of Social Work degrees. The democratic language of embodied practices from below gave way to the authority of the technocratic view from above.

Strife notes that the casework method arose as an attempt to reconcile the differences between these orientations. It was another form of social mediation resting on the good intentions of a friendly visitor, but now armed with an impersonal method of information gathering and assessment that suited the managerial needs of hospitals, schools, and governments. Three generations of White Protestant social gospel activists, Strife recounts, sanctified the gospel of sociology. Instead of touting what made Christian communities peculiar, particular, democratic, and at least potentially countercultural, liberal Protestants baptized the technocratic ethos and machinery of the administrative state.

After World War II, Strife observes, a new breed of Protestant activists tried to renew the social witness of mainline Protestant churches. Countering the mainline flight to the suburbs, three graduates of Union Theological Seminary—Don Benedict, Archie Hargrave, and George Webber—founded the East Harlem Protestant Parish (EHPP) in 1948. It was an echo of the settlement movement conviction that apprenticeships in urban life might inspire young people to struggle for social change.

EHPP trained thousands of seminarians and clergy in community organizing, notably Letty Russell, William Stringfellow, George Todd, Mary Todd, and George Younger. The new Protestant activists were more political and much less churchy than their social gospel forerunners. They developed a national network of action training programs operating across twenty denominations, pioneered the "urban plunge" tactic of dropping gently-raised students into urban neighborhoods, and adopted the community organizing approach of Saul Alinsky, especially his concept of politics as a struggle for power among self-interested individuals and communities. Strife allows that the EHPP's embrace of the Alinsky model could be interpreted as the consummate capitulation of liberal Protestantism to secular liberalism. But he counters that Alinsky's deep commitment to the dignity and empowerment of ordinary people at least enabled liberal Protestants to retrieve the language of life-giving community that it lost to technocratic secularism. Strife holds little hope for the old mainline Protestant denominations that once assumed a moral guardianship role in society, but he can imagine a new age of the Spirit that disrupts all denominations.

Social ethicist Nicholas Hayes-Mota builds on the work of Catholic historians Paul Misner and John Coleman in arguing that the papal tradition of Catholic Social Teaching is only a partial and doctrinal strand of the Catholic social tradition, which is best called social Catholicism. The European tradition of social Catholicism, he observes, preceded by decades the pioneering work of John A. Ryan. This point marks a key difference between the Catholic and ecumenical Protestant traditions of social ethics. In *Social Ethics in the Making* (2009), I extensively analyzed the work of Catholic ethical thinkers Ryan, Dorothy Day, John Courtney Murray, Charles Curran, Michael Novak, Richard John Neuhaus, Dennis P. McCann, Lisa Sowle Cahill, Daniel C. Maguire, Ada María Isasi-Díaz, María Pilar Aquino, and David Hollenbach. There were also discussions of Rosemary Radford Ruether and the formerly Catholic Mary Daly. I took the same approach to organized Catholicism that I took to the organized ecumenical movement, digging the church tradition issue out of major thinkers who featured it in their writings and were players in ecclesiastical organizations. Ryan, Murray, Curran, Cahill, and Hollenbach were the foremost examples. All fixed on the ecclesiastical tradition of a single communion, the Roman Catholic Church, in a way that lacked any parallel among the leading social ethicists of the ecumenical Protestant traditions. Even the Anglican figures in this story—W. D. P. Bliss, Richard Ely, Vida Scudder, and Gibson Winter—came off as ecumenical Protestants on this issue, not as almost-Catholic. The Catholic tradition factor is as distinct as Hayes-Mota suggests.

Hayes-Mota shows that social Catholicism is a distinct tradition of modern politics and a sub-tradition within the Roman Catholic tradition. It began in the 1830s with Catholics who disliked the Enlightenment, were hostile to the French Revolution, and shuddered at socialists who saw themselves as the successors to both. Social Catholicism was politically conservative, except when it wasn't, as in the liberalism of Félicité de La Mennais and the socialism of Philippe Buchez.

Hayes-Mota stresses that *Rerum Novarum* established a doctrinal core for social Catholicism, taking positions on how to interpret Thomas

Aquinas, what to think about labor unions, and how to oppose socialism. It established that Catholic Social Teaching expounds two central values: personal human dignity and the primacy of the common good. Hayes-Mota draws upon Alasdair MacIntyre's contention that a tradition is a historically extended phenomenon with a socially embedded argument that includes an argument about the goods that constitute the tradition. Traditions are ongoing and internally pluralistic arguments. With the exception of Scandinavia and Britain, Hayes-Mota observes, it was the social Catholicism of the Christian Democratic parties that built Europe's welfare states. In the United States, social Catholicism never approached its European influence, but Murray made historic arguments for religious liberty that were vindicated at Vatican Council II, Day's Catholic Worker movement is nearly a century old, and the community organizing tradition founded by Alinsky in Chicago in 1940 has historically spoken the social Catholic language of personal dignity and the common good. Hayes-Mota contends that interfaith organizing cannot do better than to feature these two central values of social Catholicism.

The story of the National Welfare Rights Organization (NWRO) usually revolves around George Wiley, who took a leave in 1965 from his chemistry professorship at Syracuse University to serve as Associate National Director of the Congress on Racial Equality (CORE), resigned a year later from CORE, and founded in May 1966 the Poverty Rights Action Center, which morphed the following year into the NWRO. Wiley and NWRO president Johnnie Tillmon built a renowned advocacy organization demanding welfare reform and a guaranteed federally financed income. The NWRO quickly burgeoned into a national organization of 125,000 members led predominantly by poor Black women.

The story of the West Side, New York City chapter of NWRO that scholars customarily recount is the one that Columbia University social work professors Richard Cloward and Frances Fox Piven told in describing their experience of it. Cloward and Piven first proposed in a May 1966 article in *The Nation* to stoke a political crisis by increasing the number of welfare recipients. Overloading the existing welfare system, they reasoned, would force the governing Democratic Party to institute a minimum guaranteed income as an alternative to expanding the welfare rolls. Cloward and Piven went on to write important books about poor people's movements, welfare policy, and the disciplining of poor people. They wrote as activist participants in the movements they studied, which strengthened their personal authority as experts on their subjects, but they marginalized the charismatic leadership of Beulah Sanders in telling a story that revolved too much around themselves.[14]

Carolyn Baker, who carries on the revolutionary community center work of her father at the General Baker Institute in Detroit, and Colleen Wessel-McCoy, a social ethicist at Earlham School of Religion and a longtime antipoverty activist, restore Sanders in memory to the standing she earned in the welfare rights movement. Sanders grew up among ten siblings in North Carolina, moved to New York City in 1955, founded the West Side Welfare Recipients League ten years later, and became vice chair of NWRO in 1969. She was a champion of the view that antipoverty organizations must be led by poor people. The NWRO made the process of applying for welfare less onerous and expanded the number of welfare programs available to poor families.

In 1971, one year before Wiley resigned and Sanders began her two-year term as national chair, the organization peaked at 800 affiliated chapters. Wiley's resignation set off a financial meltdown that stripped the NWRO of its funding in the ecumenical movement and terminated the organization in 1975. Baker and Wessel-McCoy offer a close reading of Sanders's December 1972 speech to the General Assembly of the National Council of Churches in Houston, Texas. In a perilous moment for a reeling NWRO, Sanders told the church leaders that too many of them blamed the poor for their poverty. The church needed to be biblical-Christian, not White-American, in the ways it treated the poor. It had to push back, she said, against "legislation that oppresses poor people, Black people, Chicano people, Indian people, Puerto Rican people, and all other people." Baker and Wessel-McCoy present Sanders as a prophet of the call to struggle against poverty, the opposite of perpetuating the usual forms of punishing its victims.

For those of us who entered social justice organizing chiefly through the door of socialist movements, trade unionism, or industrial unionism, the very term "organizing" tends to register first as "labor organizing." The late labor organizer Jane McAlevey, who died in 2024, began her

---

[14] Richard Cloward and Frances Fox Piven, "The Weight of the Poor: A Strategy to End Poverty," *The Nation*, May 2, 1966; Piven and Cloward, *Poor People's Movements: Why They Succeed, How They Fail* (New York: Vintage Books, 1977).

extraordinary career as an Alinsky-style student organizer, environmental activist, and community organizer before moving in 1997 into union organizing in Stamford, Connecticut. There she developed her signature "whole worker" approach to organizing. McAlevey taught that unions must conceive workers as integral members of communities to build community power. The two dominant approaches to union organizing, she argued—advocacy and mobilization—rely too much on like-minded experts and unionists. The advocacy model features professional advocacy by experts, lawyers, and lobbyists. The mobilization model relies on the protest activism and electoral campaigning of committed union members. McAlevey contended that real organizing is harder, cuts deeper, and is more inclusive than the advocacy of professional experts and the "shallow organizing" of the mobilization approach. Real organizing persistently engages whole communities of workers and citizens, conducts one-on-one conversations with all members of enterprises and local communities, and cultivates organic leaders who possess the requisite personal credibility to influence holdouts and disbelievers. It builds grassroots mass organizations of workers, concentrating its resources on holdouts and disbelievers.[15]

K. B. Brower is a veteran labor organizer who worked with McAlevey and is a disciple of her approach, except Brower is a seminary graduate with a Christian basis who focuses on labor unions and faith communities working together. Brower argues that McAlevey's signature critique of the mobilization strategy applies very much to the organizing that occurs in faith communities. Christian nationalism, she observes, is rampant in the United States, which shows that much of the Church has lost entirely what it means to practice Christian discipleship. Brower tells a dismal story about a campaign she ran in DuBois, Pennsylvania, where 300 hospital nurses tried to form a union. The campaign had widespread support until the hospital management threatened to fire the campaign leaders, hired ten union busters, and flooded the town with anti-union propaganda. The campaign was crushed, and Brower wished she had begun by engaging local clergy. Later she worked with McAlevey in a campaign to unionize 1,000 nurses at a North Philadelphia hospital. This time, the campaign began by cultivating relationships with local congregations and church leaders,

---

[15] Jane McAlevey, *No Shortcuts: Organizing for Power in the New Gilded Age* (New York: Oxford University Press, 2016); McAlevey, *A Collective Bargain: Unions, Organizing, and the Fight for Democracy* (New York: HarperCollins, 2020).

succeeded at identifying organic leaders, and beat the anti-union tactics that had worked in DuBois. McAlevey learned a great deal from this campaign, Brower says, and so did Brower.

Capitalism has commodified everything and everyone, including the natural world. Brower writes that only two institutions in our hyper-commodified civilization have any chance of re-sanctifying the world—communities of faith and labor unions. When workers organize a union, they defy the message of their society that their lives do not matter, their work has no dignity, and nothing has sacred value.

Prominent social ethicist Cynthia Moe-Lobeda reports on her experience of teaching broad-based community organizing at Pacific Lutheran Theological Seminary in Berkeley, California. In 2017, she and Christian Testament scholar Ray Pickett launched a required course for M.Div. and M.A. students in faith-based community organizing. Moe-Lobeda knew from her many years of teaching social ethics at Christian seminaries that White supremacy and wealth-based supremacy permeate seminary education despite decades of teaching liberation theologies. She also knew that a great deal of intellectual energy is routinely wasted on theory that only academics care about. Much of what passes as social justice ministry gets no further than mere talk, plus acts of charitable service, with no comprehension of systemic injustices. Moe-Lobeda yearned for ways of cultivating whole-person spirituality for ministry before she discovered that teaching faith-based organizing is a valuable way to do it. The ecofeminist theology of communion that suffused her previous work, she now brought to teaching community organizing: The aim of theological education should be to cultivate the community that God wants, a spiritual work of love that combats the interlinked injustices of racial capitalism.

Failures occurred, and lessons were learned. Many students experienced the use of agitation in organizing as abusive. Some protested that they enrolled at seminary to become pastors, not organizers. Some felt threatened by the presence of ecclesiastical authorities and officers holding power over them. Moe-Lobeda and her teaching team responded by dropping the language of training, integrating theology and Scripture into the course, placing the course more explicitly into contexts of congregational ministry, and grounding the course in practices of relationality. Confrontation has its place in organizing, but the Alinsky model exaggerates it. Alinsky organizing has a history of thrusting aggressive White males into congregations, and its emphasis on interests militates against the very communion that church

Introduction   xxxi

members seek. Moe-Lobeda aptly stresses that community organizing is changing within and outside congregations. New organizing networks led by women, people of color, and queer people are emerging. Theory that refutes myths of superiority, she argues, is indispensable, but so is the last aspect of decolonial theory—*action* that negates the myths.

Vanderbilt Divinity School social ethicist C. Melissa Snarr is the author of a valuable book, *All You That Labor* (2011), that describes how faith-based community organizing identifies pertinent issues, builds collective will, develops leaders, attains power, and catalyzes social change. She welcomes the surge of interest in teaching community organizing that has occurred over the past decade, commending theological educators for recognizing the practical importance of organizing in congregational contexts. In her contribution to the present book, Snarr argues that social movement theory is an underdeveloped resource for scholars and activists interested in the intersections between social ethics and social justice movements. Social ethics, she observes, arose in tandem with the social sciences, but contemporary theological education pays little heed to sociology. Seminaries still teach psychology of religion in practical theology courses, but do not teach about new developments in sociology. Snarr contends that social ethicists could benefit from social movement theories that explain how movements emerge, individuals are moved to act, activists choose their tactics, and movement activists are formed by movements.[16]

Early forms of social movement theory sought to explain the rise of fascism in Europe, developing psycho-social accounts of alienation and irrationality. This tradition of analysis continues in numerous studies of alienated followers of Donald Trump's MAGA movement. Snarr writes about two newer traditions of social movement theory inspired by the civil rights movement, both of which contend that social movements are more rational than the theories that sought to explain fascism. Resource mobilization theory emphasizes that all movements have a material history, whereas political process theory stresses that movements engender collective values and emotions. According to resource theorists, grievances are persistent and ubiquitous, so movements do not arise from an escalation of grievances. Movements arise when aggrieved groups acquire the material and leadership resources to achieve lift-off. Snarr credits civil rights historian

---

[16] C. Melissa Snarr, *All You That Labor: Religion and Ethics in the Living Wage Movements* (New York: New York University Press, 2011).

Aldon Morris for originating the resource theory that people do not move spontaneously and irrationally into collective action. They move into action when they judge that they have the requisite resources to remedy a grievance. The political process school, meanwhile, focuses on how movements provide meaning for onlookers and movement participants, helping them to make sense of the world. Snarr commends the new social movement theories for turning aside overworked debates about why masses of people behave irrationally or selfishly. Studying the comparatively small number of people who join social movements, she argues, is more fruitful. For what we really need is to understand the "how" of ethical action.

Malinda Elizabeth Berry, during her years as a doctoral student in theology and social ethics at Union Theological Seminary, helped many people who did not know each other build community at Union through knowing her. This outward-reaching spirit pervades her contribution to this book, where she characteristically flips the focus from the organizer-leader to the experience of being organized as a student, trainee, faculty member, neighbor, and activist. As a Black, Mennonite, Womanist, senior professor of theology and social ethics at a Mennonite seminary, Malinda was already aware that the moral pride of earnest White Christians is often fragile and hair-trigger when their complicity in racist systems of domination is revealed. Then the Black Lives Matter protests of 2020 drove her to ask anew why her faculty colleagues demonstrated "gross lack of skill" in dealing with the racism of others and themselves. What is lacking in the customary antiracism workshops and courses?

Berry offers two answers to this question. One is that antiracism training usually avoids any reference to, or sense of, spirituality. Berry's spirituality is "luxocratic," a metaphysical, pedagogical, and social ethical "rule by Light" that instills an egalitarian and benevolent way of life. Her formulation of it is influenced by Baháʼí Womanist theorist Layli Phillips Maparyan, who conceives luxocratic spirituality as a broader name for the traditional Womanist emphasis on doing the work that one's soul requires and helping others discover the treasures within themselves. Womanist luxocracy, Maparyan says, is a critique of domination and oppression, rooted in everyday experience, and is explicitly non-ideological, communitarian, and spiritual. Berry reflects that antiracist training usually lacks this emphasis on spirituality, overemphasizes ideological definition, and does not provide maps that identify a group's location in relation to its goal or purpose. She draws on the work of British social geographer

Alastair Bonnett in fleshing out different answers to a question too seldom asked: "What do I believe is wrong about racism?" It helps, Berry argues, to become aware of one's often too-readily assumed answer to this question. One might assume that racism is bad primarily because it disrupts community, or it is malignantly alien, or it sustains the domination of a ruling class, or it hinders the progress of the group oppressed by racism, or it is bad science, or it distorts the psychological identities of individuals and groups, or it violates the right to equality. When trainees become aware of their assumed matrix of beliefs on this question, they are better able to appreciate why people in the group practice antiracism in different ways.

Christophe Ringer teaches Christian social ethics at Chicago Theological Seminary, an institution located on Chicago's South Side, in the Woodlawn community, bordering South Shore. On May 4, 2024, he attended a meeting at South Shore International College Preparatory School at which hundreds of community residents gathered to protest against the City of Chicago's announced plan to use a nearby former public school as a respite center for migrants awaiting placement in a shelter. Texas Governor Greg Abbott had dispatched, since August 2022, over 16,000 Venezuelans seeking asylum to Chicago. The school had been shut down in 2013 by a Democratic mayor, Rahm Emanuel. The city had designated it in 2020 as a police training center without consulting the neighborhood. Four years later, the neighborhood seethed at being treated again as a dumping ground, again without being consulted.

Ringer's neighbors decried that the city had abandoned them in every way excepting the heavy hand of police. Some made ugly demands to expel the foreigners and close the border, but Ringer did not write them off as nativists. He heard the pain of neighbors struggling in a poor and hurting community. One woman crystallized the despair in the room. "We want to be loving," she said, "but part of love is reciprocity." If the City of Chicago could use South Shore to provide for Venezuelans, why did it do nothing for the people of South Shore?

Ringer explores the meaning of reciprocity as explicated by Harvard political theorist Tommie Shelby and the late Black feminist theorist bell hooks. Shelby describes justice as the fair reciprocity of citizens to each other and of government to all citizens. On welfare policy, reciprocity might be conceived as the relationship between a government that provides a benefit and debtors that repay the debt by working. Or it might be conceived as a mutual benefit on the model of free trade theory. Or it might be conceived as a Rawlsian social contract geared to produce a fair result in which the government guarantees a full-employment economy. Shelby endorses the third type of reciprocity, which Ringer applies to the tensions between established residents and newcomers on Chicago's South Side. It is doubly unfair, he argues, to compel longtime downtrodden communities to bear the burden of housing and support for hurting newcomers. A government that cares about justice has to lift up the longtime poor while spreading the burden of caring for newcomers. Ringer adds, drawing on hooks, that Rawlsian-style social contract egalitarianism never gets far if love is torn apart from justice. Love is the will to extend oneself for the sake of the well-being of another or others. It is intentional and active beyond mere emotional feeling.

Stacey Floyd-Thomas is an eminent teacher, scholar, theorist, preacher, administrator, and organizer who explicates in this book her brilliantly full-orbed practice and pedagogy of Christian Social Liberation Ethics. As the E. Rhodes and Leona B. Carpenter Professor of Ethics and Society at Vanderbilt, she has significantly influenced the field of social ethics through her scholarship and teaching. Floyd-Thomas grew up in Corpus Christi, Texas, where she puzzled over a confounding question: "Why do Christians behave as though God doesn't exist?" Specifically, White Christians treated Black persons with contempt, and middle-class Black Christians spurned poor Blacks and the unchurched. This quandary propelled Floyd-Thomas into social ethics, studying with the founder of womanist ethics, Katie Cannon. Floyd-Thomas absorbed Alice Walker's historic definition of womanism and Cannon's historic Christian account of the moral wisdom of Black women. The first wave of womanist ethics was based on Walker's definition, Cannon's virtue ethic of dignity, grace, and courage, and Emilie Townes's explication of womanist spirituality. Floyd-Thomas launched the second wave with a pioneering book on womanist methods, *Mining the Motherlode* (2006), and a reader on womanist horizons, *Deeper Shades of Purple* (2006).[17]

Floyd-Thomas's *Mining the Motherlode* reformulated Walker's tenets as radical subjectivity, traditional communalism, redemptive self-love,

---

[17] Cannon, *Black Womanist Ethics*; Emilie Townes, *In a Blaze of Glory: Womanist Spirituality as Social Witness* (Nashville: Abingdon Press, 1995); Stacey M. Floyd-Thomas, *Mining the Motherlode: Methods in Womanist Ethics* (Cleveland: Pilgrim Press, 2006); Floyd-Thomas, ed., *Deeper Shades of Purple: Womanism in Religion and Society* (New York: New York University Press, 2006).

and critical engagement. It employed literary analysis, sociology, and historiography to elucidate the womanist virtues described by Cannon. And it made an argument about the relation of womanist ethics to White feminist ethics and androcentric forms of Black theology: Womanist wisdom, Floyd-Thomas said, is about right relationships and integral wholeness, not an oppositional discourse. Walker, Cannon, and Townes were eloquent on this point. Walker said the souls that Black women save may be their own; Cannon repeatedly urged her students to do the work that their souls required; Townes cautioned against living in the folds of old wounds. In *Deeper Shades of Purple,* Floyd-Thomas showed that womanists did not merely aspire to reach beyond their inherited Protestant and Catholic traditions. Womanism, she said, was already an interfaith, global, multicultural womanist reality radiating "deeper shades of purple." It began as Walker's definition, developed as an ethical and theological movement pioneered by Cannon, Townes, and Delores Williams, and bloomed as an epistemology that crosses disciplinary boundaries. Floyd-Thomas stressed that womanism is not only the name of a moral-cultural ethos or a theological school. It is a way of knowing that has become indispensable for how the academy studies liberation, enabling the academy to study liberation in multiple fields and interdisciplinary contexts.

That does not mean, she argues, that womanism is most important as a broadly useful way to teach liberation studies. Saving one's soul transcends academic study; moreover, as a form of Christian ethics, womanism makes normative claims that are steeped in the Hebrew prophets, the teaching of Jesus, and biblical faith more broadly. The normative religious questions that drove Floyd-Thomas into social ethics remain her ultimate concerns. Why do people act as though God doesn't exist? How should we interpret and follow Christian ethical teaching? Floyd-Thomas contends that womanist liberationism is a biblically-based ethic of justice that rises to the level of a normative ethical standard and enlists in sociopolitical struggles for justice: "To separate the ethical pursuit of justice from its scriptural moorings is to sever it from its deepest source of inspiration and prophetic power."

She proposes a shorthand name, "just ethics," for this ethic of justice, or shorter yet, "JUSTethics." The just ethics that we need, she writes, cannot be merely a system of deontological norms, or utilitarian rules, or dogmatic utterances. Just ethics is a way of seeing the world shaped by a womanist-liberationist way of knowing. It is critical, expansive, and relational, affirming with bell hooks that education either integrates students into the regnant system of domination or it is a practice of liberation that seeks to transform the system. It is expansive in drawing on biblical faith, interfaith scholarship, the history of theology, intersecting academic disciplines, the entire history of abolitionist and liberationist struggles, and the various movements that created and sustained Christian social ethics as a field. My five-stranded rope of theology, social ethics, philosophy, political theory, and intellectual history is one attempt to marshal a similar range of sources and commitments; Floyd-Thomas is characteristically astute and generous in assessing it.

We are the ones, she writes, whom the visionaries held in mind before they were cut down. Martin Luther King Jr., peering from his spiritual mountaintop, saw a better world coming, "in fact, a world house, a beloved community with all of us in it." Floyd-Thomas luminously urges her readers and students to summon their spiritual courage: "Let's foil the evil of our day by doing justice, loving mercy, and walking humbly with the God whose spirit gives us perspective and power." In her expanding corpus of scholarship and teaching, Floyd-Thomas contributes to liberationist ethics a strategic womanist discourse about being in right relationship, an argument about womanism as a new way of knowing that applies to interdisciplinary studies of liberation, and a normative Christian fusion of scriptural faith and praxis: "By integrating the wisdom of scripture with the demands of social justice, we can create a more just and compassionate world for all."

Aaron Stauffer brings this book to a close by reprising the argument he made in his groundbreaking book, *Listening to the Spirit: The Radical Social Gospel, Sacred Value, and Broad-based Community Organizing* (2024). In 2010, he was serving as an IAF (Industrial Areas Foundation) organizer in San Antonio, Texas, when legendary organizer Ernesto Cortés remarked to him that organizing is about values, not issues. Issues fade, Cortés explained, but values don't fade. Stauffer's book offers a rich synthesis of social ethics, theology, political history, philosophy, and social theory written in the spirit of Cortés's maxim and expanding theologically upon it, arguing that BBCO (broad-based community organizing) works best by embracing the sacred values it engenders and runs upon, not by marginalizing faith. In our closing chapter, Stauffer distills his argument, envisioning a better form of community organizing than the classic model pioneered by Alinsky and longtime IAF executive director Edward Chambers.[18]

---

[18] Aaron Stauffer, *Listening to the Spirit: The Radical Social Gospel, Sacred Value, and Broad-based Community Organizing* (New York: Oxford University Press, 2024).

Broad-Based-Community-Organizing-as-usual carefully selects winnable issues, focuses relentlessly on material interests and building power, avoids polarizing issues such as racial and sexual identity, abortion, and the death penalty, and usually revolves around White-male-cisgender individual organizers. Power is built, on this view, by winning winnable issues, while divisive religious values are best left at the door along with other identity claims and markers. Stauffer pushes back that good organizing builds relational power grounded in values that individuals and communities hold dear. Organizing on the basis of sacred values, he argues persuasively, is central to BBCO. At its best, BBCO develops practices that instill cooperative relationships and values; it is not merely a venue for organizing issue campaigns.

Like Anglican theologian Luke Bretherton, Stauffer makes a theological argument for the spiritual significance of organizing, conceives BBCO communities as alternative communities of interpretation, opposes assimilationist and accommodationist strategies that aim merely for a place at the table, and believes that BBCO organizing should aim to achieve a common life. Unlike Bretherton, Stauffer is not allergic to Marxist theory, does not claim that Christianity has its own social theory, does not oppose the counter-public concept of organizing, and is deeply rooted in the social gospel traditions that enlisted churches in struggles for social justice, created the ecumenical movement, and founded the field of social ethics. Bretherton conceives community organizing as middle-ground mediation between various groups pursuing a common life. Stauffer is closer to George Woodbey and Cornel West, arguing that the most important kind of organizing sides with dominated and exploited people in resisting oppression. Organizing, at its best, strives to be in solidarity with those suffering exploitation, expropriation, and domination. Stauffer compellingly describes the relational meetings and listening campaigns of BBCO as social practices—repertoires of activity grounded in ethical relationships that define institutions. As such they are religious practices that instill, and are guided by, sacred values of cooperation, relationality, solidarity, and normative principles of behavior.[19]

This section on Stauffer adapts material from Gary Dorrien, "The Radical Social Gospel as Broad-Based Community Organizing," *Interventions*, April 5, 2024.

[19] Luke Bretherton, *Resurrecting Democracy: Faith, Citizenship, and the Politics of a Common Life* (New York: Cambridge University Press, 2015); Bretherton, *Christ*

Stauffer draws on two camps of contemporary Hegel scholarship: the social theorizing of Pierre Bourdieu and the vast literature analyzing Bourdieu's analysis of social practices to undergird his theological case for conceiving BBCO as a spiritual practice. Mutual recognition, he argues, with help from Hegel and Bourdieu, is a social practice that is also a religious practice bearing sacred value. His genealogical undergirding is the radical social gospel that produced theologies of Christian socialism. Four historical traditions have fed community organizing even in its non-theorized iterations: the Protestant social gospel, Catholic social teaching, Black liberation theology, and Latin American liberation theology. The Spirit calls us to practice the golden rule in a spirit of love and community to build a cooperative commonwealth. But if that is true, Stauffer says, we need a BBCO that disrupts White supremacism and actualizes radical democracy, overcoming the assimilationist legacy of customary-BBCO.

---

and the Common Life: Political Theology and the Case for Democracy (Grand Rapids: Eerdmans, 2019).

PART I

PART I

1

The Problems and Promise of Radical Social Gospel in Organizing Movements

Aaron Stauffer

"The status of tenancy demands complete dependence."[1] So opens a liturgy of the Southern Tenant Farmers Union (STFU), written by social gospeller Howard Kester in January of 1937. "Ceremony of the Land" is a call and response litany that draws equally from the Christian scriptures as it does from Christian socialist visions of justice. Organizing in some of the harshest conditions of the early twentieth century, the STFU used rituals and secret codes in order to protect their members' lives and property and to build trust and solidarity in the union. This ceremony was used as the climax of the union's annual convention in 1937.[2] Kester's ceremony brings forward the degree to which STFU's political and economic concepts of freedom and liberation were connected to labor republicanism and Christian conceptions of the cooperative commonwealth. In this sense, sharecropping and farm tenancy—and the sort of dependence and domination they require—are deeply connected to conceptions of slavery, while the alternatives proposed find their roots in a political and economic vision of freedom that is enacted through anti-capitalist, cooperative economic congregational experiments.

Kester goes on in the ceremony to illustrate the degree of planter domination over sharecroppers. The ceremony makes clear that this sort of domination is near total, from production, distribution, to consumption of the crop, to paying sharecroppers in "scrips" that force them to purchase all

---

[1] Nan Elizabeth Woodruff, *American Congo: The African American Freedom Struggle in the Delta* (Cambridge, MA: Harvard University Press, 2003), 166.

[2] "Ceremony of the Land," Folder 214 in the Howard Kester Papers #3834, Southern Historical Collection, Wilson Special Collections Library, University of North Carolina at Chapel Hill.

their daily necessities at the plantation's shop, to determining sharecropper's state of housing, and how their children would be educated. The planter's will is nearly absolute. As Kester says in another place, "Their [planters'] will was, practically speaking, a sovereign will."[3]

> The landlord assumes the prerogative of direction in the choice of crop, the method by which it shall be cultivated, and how and when and where it shall be sold. He keeps the records and determines the earnings. Through the commissary or credit merchant, even the choice of diet is determined. The landlord can determine the kind and amount of schooling for the children, the extent to which they may share benefits intended for all the people. He may even determine the relief they receive in the extremity of their distress. He controls the courts, the agencies of law enforcement, and can effectively thwart any efforts at organization to protect their meager rights.... Since the civil war, whether white or colored, the sharecropper has been the equivalent of slave labor.... It is quite clear that the planters want to keep the sharecroppers in a state of slavery.[4]

For Kester and others organizing in the STFU, what was at stake was not merely the transformation of a system of farming that exploited its workers, but capitalism's institutionalized social order that dominated sharecroppers as slaves, and they said so.[5] "Wage slavery" was one of the most common descriptors of sharecropping in the 1930s, and many of those making such claims grew up with family who were enslaved through chattel slavery. This was not hyperbole, but a claim about the situation of domination that characterized plantation sharecropping. As Clyde Woods, a scholar of Black Studies, notes, the forms of domination of "slavery, sharecropping, mechanization, and prison, wage and migratory labor are just a few of the permutations possible within a plantation complex."[6] Those who called out the evil

---

[3] Howard Kester, *Revolt among the Sharecroppers* (New York: Covici, Friede, 1936), 72.

[4] "Ceremony of the Land," Folder 214 in the Howard Kester Papers #3834, Southern Historical Collection, Wilson Special Collections Library, University of North Carolina at Chapel Hill.

[5] The phrase "institutionalized social order" comes from Nancy Fraser, "Behind Marx's Hidden Abode," *New Left Review*, no. 86 (April 1, 2014): 55–72.

[6] Clyde Adrian Woods, *Development Arrested: The Blues and Plantation Power in the Mississippi Delta* (London: Verso, 2017), 6.

domination of sharecropping as wage slavery drew from experience—if not their own, their community's—that recognized new forms of old evils.

This chapter makes the case that the STFU's discourse about the specific condition of domination in sharecropping in the Arkansas and Missouri Delta region depended on conceptions of slavery drawn from the labor republican tradition, and their dreams of freedom draw from Christian democratic socialism. Such an argument is not so simply made, as labor republican understandings of domination and slavery present their own paradoxes, and so cooperative economic visions of freedom as characterized in the "cooperative commonwealth" are meant to resolve specific problems posed by labor republicanism.

Kester's work for the STFU was multipronged, but it was to the point of building a more powerful organizing network of STFU and its allies. Kester understood that power is relational and therefore collective. In order for STFU to win its campaigns, it needed to build a stronger organization. This meant the pragmatic work of recruiting supporters and funders, but it also meant the ideological work of organizing sharecroppers and tenant farmers. This was not a purity politics, but a pragmatic effort of workers mobilizing other workers, communal education on their conditions, and collective discernment of the appropriate actions in their current economic and political conditions. Kester's activist organizing was grounded in the radical social gospel and meant to build a stronger STFU structure.[7]

In the first section of the chapter, I make the case that "wage slavery" can be seen as a rhetorical and conceptual device connected to the labor republican tradition, which depends on a particular critique of wage slavery as domination. I then outline the complications that arise from this analysis. The paradox of slavery for labor republicans, as political historian Alex Gourevitch has shown, is that the republican version of freedom depends on the domination of someone else. The free are free in a free community because a separate, other community is dominated and enslaved, most often as a colony. What is more, labor republicans' argument of wage slavery as conceptually connected to chattel slavery lacks a conception of how race domination and class exploitation are related and mutually supporting in racial capitalism. And yet Black nationalists in the Mississippi Delta region who joined up with STFU endorsed these claims of sharecropping as a

---

[7] For more on the importance of structure in organizing, see Marshall Ganz, *People, Power, Change: Organizing for Democratic Renewal* (New York: Oxford University Press, 2024), 147–75.

form of slavery. The point for organizers in the STFU was not reduction of race-based chattel slavery—or a dismissal of the role of race in capitalism—but instead the mutation of racial capitalism's domination and exploitation of labor from chattel slavery to sharecropping.

Republican freedom seems to require the enslavement of a colony. But for labor republicans, their version of freedom was enhanced by democratic socialism and, often, Christian socialist versions of freedom as articulated in terms of the cooperative commonwealth. In the second section, I illustrate how Christian socialist conceptions of the church inspired this vision of freedom that does not require domination of an other. Indeed, throughout the 1930s and 1940s, churches were crucial agents in radical movements for social change. I do not mean that *all* churches were—in fact, *many* churches were supporters of white supremacy and racial capitalism and actively sought to enshrine white plantation capitalism through the local, state, and federal governments. But many other churches, often Black and Christian socialist, sought to liberate everyone from wage slavery and its evils. Nor do I mean that all churches played the same role in the cooperative commonwealth. Congregations and para-church organizations played a differentiated role in these radical political and economic fights. The second section explores the organization and conceptual contribution that churches and the ecumenical movement broadly contributed to cross-racial class-based organizing efforts like the STFU.

In the conclusion of the chapter, I extrapolate some lessons for those of us today who appreciate the complicated and yet valuable role that social gospel organizing can play in supporting people's movements.

Labor Republicans, Howard Kester, and the Southern Tenant Farmers Union

Civic republicans imagine freedom principally in terms of nondomination.[8] It is often contrasted with alternative definitions of negative or positive freedom. Negative freedom posits an arena of personal freedom that is free from interference. Coercion, then, involves an infringement

---

[8] Cf. Isaiah Berlin, *Liberty: Incorporating Four Essays on Liberty*, ed. Henry Hardy (Oxford: Oxford University Press, 2002); Philip Pettit, *Republicanism: A Theory of Freedom and Government* (Oxford: Oxford University Press, 1997). See also Melvin L. Rogers, *The Undiscovered Dewey: Religion, Morality, and the Ethos of Democracy* (New York: Columbia University Press, 2009), esp. chap. 5.

on an individual's arena of agency. Negative freedom is most often found in "freedom from" discourse. Positive freedom, by contrast, is most often found in "freedom to" discourse and is conceived primarily as self-development, as autonomy, as being one's own master in terms of the self's goals. Positive and negative versions of freedom imagine the unfree individual as bound and gagged. In both of these versions of freedom, it is possible to conceive a free person as having a benevolent master. By contrast, the civic republican versions of freedom emphasize nondomination. Domination exists when someone is in the position to arbitrarily exercise their own will over someone else. The dominated individual is prototypically imagined as the slave. Free people do not have masters, even benevolent ones.

The issue is, as Gourevitch has illustrated, republican arguments for liberty "emerged with and presupposed slavery."[9] Gourevitch's argument draws principally from ancient republican sources, from ancient Rome and Greece, but one could easily make similar points about additional sources of republican freedom, like Machiavelli, whose own defensive account of republican freedom for a city-state required colonies that were enslaved and dominated.[10]

Labor republicans are those who see a fundamental conflict between republican versions of freedom as nondomination and the system of wage labor.[11] "Wage labor was considered a form of dependent labor, different from chattel slavery, but still based on relations of mastery and subjection."[12] One of the most notable examples of labor republican organizing was the Knights of Labor, which was the "largest and most powerful labor organization of late-nineteenth century North America."[13] In some senses, the Knights of Labor were ahead of their time—and perhaps because of that doomed from the start—as they sought to build "a national union with a communal socialist agenda and no exclusions based on race, gender, or trade skill."[14] The Knights organized for the end

---

[9] Alexander Gourevitch, *From Slavery to the Cooperative Commonwealth: Labor and Republican Liberty in the Nineteenth Century* (New York: Cambridge University Press, 2015), 30.

[10] Gourevitch, *From Slavery*, 136–37.

[11] Gourevitch, *From Slavery*, 6.

[12] Gourevitch, *From Slavery*, 6.

[13] Robert E. Weir, *Beyond Labor's Veil: The Culture of the Knights of Labor* (University Park: Pennsylvania State University Press, 1996), xiii.

[14] Gary Dorrien, *American Democratic Socialism: History, Politics, Religion, and Theory* (New Haven, CT: Yale University Press, 2021), 56.

of an exploitative and dominating wage system and sought to replace it with the cooperative commonwealth. Labor republicans like the Knights of Labor left a political and economic program that conceptually connected wage-labor to wage-slavery, motivated by the social, political, and economic freedom promised in the cooperative commonwealth.

Writing about "political slavery" or "wage slavery" is not without complications and challenges.[15] Post-emancipation, sharecroppers, and STFU organizers had to demonstrate that their metaphorical and analogical usage of "slavery" was not *merely* discursive. Wage slavery is not chattel slavery. And yet "wage slavery" was a term that was often used by Black and white sharecroppers to characterize sharecropping. Owen Whitfield, a Black pastor and STFU organizer, put it starkly, stating that the STFU was fighting to "free themselves and their wives and children from wage slavery and get some of the things that God prepared for us from the foundation of the world, and that is Land for the Landless, Food for the Hungry, Freedom for the Wage Slave."[16] As historian Nan Woodruff argues, "Planters and their supporters shaped the law in order to dominate black people socially, politically, and economically."[17] "We are just slaves here," one sharecropper remarks as he writes to the National Association for the Advancement of Colored People (NAACP) to communicate the conditions in the South; and another wrote, "The truth is the colored people have never been free since they were said to be emancipated."[18] The hard challenge for STFU and its allies was to make the case that the social, political, economic, legal, and personal conditions of sharecropping constituted domination—the sharecropper was effectively under the arbitrary power of the planter class.

This is what Howard Kester aims to do in *Revolt Among the Sharecroppers*, namely by "portray[ing] the life of the Arkansas sharecropper and the struggles of the Southern Tenant Farmers' Union against the domina-

---

[15] Mary Nyquist, *Arbitrary Rule: Slavery, Tyranny, and the Power of Life and Death* (Chicago: University of Chicago Press, 2013). Vincent Lloyd also recently raised a similar point in acknowledging that civic republicans need to more deeply consider the role of race in their accounts of freedom. See Vincent W. Lloyd, *Black Dignity: The Struggle against Domination* (New Haven, CT: Yale University Press, 2022), 166n14.

[16] Jarod Roll, *Spirit of Rebellion: Labor and Religion in the New Cotton South* (Urbana: University of Illinois Press, 2010), 1.

[17] Woodruff, *American Congo*, 128.

[18] Woodruff, *American Congo*, 122–23.

tion of the plantation overlords."[19] Born in Virginia in 1904, Kester spent the majority of his childhood in Martinsville, Virginia, when his father, William, transitioned from being a salesman to a tailor.[20] The Kester family was deeply shaped by Victorian values and soon moved to the outskirts of Martinsville, where they would remain until William Kester's tailoring business collapsed, and the family lost everything but their house. Howard quickly became responsible for his share of the family's income and took a job with a local road construction crew in Martinsville. William started a second tailoring business in nearby Beckley, West Virginia, a booming coal town. Beckley was a local industrial center and grew steadily during Kester's time there—and so did the local Black population, which raised racial tensions. Kester's father soon joined the local Ku Klux Klan, and, as one of Kester's biographers put it, William "shared its white, Protestant, middle-class bias and probably equated membership with good citizenship."[21] William, however, found the violence abhorrent and soon withdrew his membership. Howard's mother, Nannie, was deeply religious, being raised in Southern Presbyterianism, and she more than anyone else impressed upon him the importance of religion and education.[22]

Kester attended Lynchburg College, where he was active in the ministerial association and the Young Men's and Young Women's Christian Association (YMCA and YWCA), the World Student Christian Federation, and the Student Volunteer Movement. He served as a student pastor for two local Presbyterian rural congregations, including one in Thurmond, West Virginia, where miners were actively striking. Kester soon joined them, causing local elders to investigate and reprimand him for his unorthodox behavior.[23]

Kester originally enrolled in Princeton Theological Seminary in the fall of 1925 but left that next spring after finding the sort of education he was receiving there could not help him minister to or preach to his own

---

[19] Kester, *Revolt among the Sharecroppers*, 37. Parts of the following paragraphs on Kester are adapted from Aaron Stauffer, "Power in the Social Gospel: Howard Kester, Claude Williams, and the Southern Tenant Farmers Union," *Religions* 15, no. 9 (September 1, 2024): 1091.

[20] Robert Martin, *Howard Kester and the Struggle for Social Justice in the South, 1904-1977* (Charlottesville: University Press of Virginia, 1991), 6.

[21] Martin, *Howard Kester*, 15.

[22] Martin, *Howard Kester*, 9.

[23] Martin, *Howard Kester*, 17–40.

Southern congregation. Kester was deeply involved in the YMCA, taking leadership roles and working to integrate YMCA summer camps. His time with the YMCA was deeply powerful, throwing him deeper into racial and economic justice fights, as Kester joined others seeking to integrate student gatherings. He met Benjamin Mays and George Washington Carver, with whom he formed a deep friendship.[24]

In 1926, he enrolled at Vanderbilt School of Religion, where Alva Taylor was teaching social gospel social ethics. Taylor attracted students like Kester: Claude Williams, Ward Rodgers, and Don West, all of whom would become highly active in economic and racial justice fights in the South in the 1930s and 1940s. In Nashville, Kester became increasingly involved in racial justice fights, joining the local Interracial Committee, leading local student protests in Vanderbilt, and becoming especially active with striking miners in Wilder, Tennessee. Kester and his wife, Alice, helped form the Wilder Emergency Relief Committee.[25]

The history of mining in Tennessee is a fraught one that involves deep exploitation of workers and their families in incredibly unsafe working conditions. Miners' bodies and those of their families were worn down, blown off, tired out, or slowly beaten down by disease or malnutrition. When strikes happened, and they often did, the state sent in the militia to protect private companies and their property. Famously, at the turn of the century, the state followed the advice of the companies and replaced striking miners with prison laborers.[26]

During the strike in Wilder, Tennessee, Taylor and his Vanderbilt students Kester, Ward Rogers, and Don West were often present, looping in the larger ecumenical and social justice world and connecting figures like socialist party leader Norman Thomas and Union Theological Seminary professor of social ethics Reinhold Niebuhr with the action on the ground.

---

[24] Martin, *Howard Kester*, 26–27.

[25] Martin, *Howard Kester*, 47. See also Anthony P. Dunbar, *Against the Grain: Southern Radicals and Prophets, 1929–1959* (Charlottesville: University Press of Virginia, 1981); Donald H. Grubbs, *Cry from the Cotton: The Southern Tenant Farmers' Union and the New Deal* (Chapel Hill: University of North Carolina Press, 1971).

[26] For an excellent history of mining and prison labor in Tennessee at the turn of the twentieth century, see Karin A. Shapiro, *A New South Rebellion: The Battle against Convict Labor in the Tennessee Coalfields, 1871–1896* (Chapel Hill: University of North Carolina Press, 1998).

Kester, Thomas, and Niebuhr, along with others, helped start relief organizations based in Kester's living room.[27] These organizations worked hand in hand with the striking miners and their union representation, the United Mine Workers of America—at that time one of the more radical industrial unions fighting for radical political and economic democracy for all workers, not just the skilled craft workers of the American Federation of Labor.[28] The local leader in Wilder was Barney Graham, but Graham was shot dead one evening before he had to the chance to cause too much damage. Howard and Alice stayed at the Graham home through the night of Graham's murder, comforting Graham's widow and their three children. Kester would later write,

> There was not a crumb of food in the house except for the groceries we had brought. Furniture was scarce and no beds were available so we spent the night in two straight back chairs. The only light available came from a cotton string wick inserted in a Coca Cola bottle partially filled with kerosene. It was an awesome and terrible night as sobs of grief came from Mrs. Graham and the children.[29]

After Vanderbilt, Kester's commitments to racial and economic justice led him to work with the Fellowship of Reconciliation and the Fellowship Youth for Peace, to his own deep engagement with Christian Socialism, to his work with the Highlander Folk School (now Highlander Research and Education Center), and eventually to his work with the NAACP as a lynching reporter. Traveling secretly to Southern towns, Kester wrote reports on major lynchings that would help unveil the psychosocial, economic, and political roots of white supremacy and racial capitalism in the US South. The relationships formed at Vanderbilt in the fights for economic and racial justice would introduce Kester to the Southern Tenant Farmers Union and lead to his writing *Revolt Among the Sharecroppers*. Kester's pamphlet on the STFU carries forward much of what he learned at Vanderbilt in Taylor's classes.[30]

---

[27] Dunbar, *Against the Grain*, 6–7.
[28] See Dorrien, *American Democratic Socialism*.
[29] Kester in Dunbar, *Against the Grain*, 9.
[30] For more on Kester's life and work see Martin, *Howard Kester*; Dunbar, *Against the Grain*; and Woodruff, *American Congo*.

Kester begins *Revolt* with the story of John Alden, a sharecropper who has been organizing with the STFU and whose planters are running him off the plantation due to that organizing. Giving him twenty minutes before they chase after him with guns and dogs, Alden flees, trudging through deep marsh and woods. He makes it out, but only barely, leaving his family behind, struggling to evade the planters. He eventually crosses the Harahan Bridge connecting Arkansas with Tennessee. Several days later his wife joins him in Memphis. Kester ends this story with Alden's voice as he first embraces his wife, "You and I have got to stand by the union, wife; it's our children's hope and ours."[31]

Alden's story illustrates why Kester wrote *Revolt*. It dramatically illustrates the political, economic, social, and personal conditions of sharecropping in the Arkansas Delta that the STFU was hoping to transform.[32] In no uncertain terms, Kester explains,

> Of all the agricultural workers in America none are more exploited, brutalized, and degraded than the cottonfield workers of the South. For all our talk about democracy and the high standards of living of American workmen, virtually millions of our fellow-citizens are living in practical slavery. To call these workers in the cotton fields "slaves" is not to indulge in wild or fancied statements.... The men and women who toil in the fields care nothing for our fine reasoning and the traveler among them today will find them referring to themselves as "slaves" pure and simple.[33]

Again and again, Kester characterizes the form of domination in sharecropping as "slavery." As a conceptual tool and historical example, it forcefully lays out the state of the economic, political, social, and personal relations that constitute sharecropping.

Kester begins with Alden's story but quickly moves to consider the historic and current conditions of sharecropping and its plantation form of capitalism. The plantation is the origin of Southern society, Kester writes,

---

[31] Kester, *Revolt among the Sharecroppers*, 16.
[32] Kester, *Revolt among the Sharecroppers*, 37: "The object of this study is to portray the life of the Arkansas sharecropper and the struggles of the Southern Tenant Farmers' Union against the domination of the plantation overlords."
[33] Kester, *Revolt among the Sharecroppers*, 36

informing the "psychology of the people, the habits, manners, traditions, etc., which the plantation created and which now shadows the whole of southern life."[34] What the plantation set up has outlasted its original form; plantation capitalism pervades the "mills, mines and factories" that have come with increasing industrialization in the South.[35] Beginning in the colonial period, where white and Black people were indentured slaves, plantation capitalism reached its zenith in chattel slavery and King Cotton. For Kester, the point is that the Civil War never ended. "Free" labor—Black and white—now exists to only accept or reject what the planters offer sharecroppers for their labor. In plantation capitalism, white laborers quickly found themselves provided with racial reasoning to explain their domination. The "divide and rule" strategy of pitting poor white people against poor Black people was to the benefit of the planters.[36]

That strategy still rules as Kester is writing his pamphlet—even in the policies of the New Deal.[37] Kester notes that nearly 70 percent of farms in the South are farmed by tenant farmers.[38] The Arkansas Delta was not always land well-groomed for cotton and sharecropping.[39] At the turn of the century, the land was dramatically reshaped by the forestry industry, and new technologies were used to redirect tributaries and floodplains of the Mississippi. As Nan Woodruff and Jarod Roll have brilliantly unveiled, before the clearing of forests was mechanized and industrialized, trees were downed by hand, logs dragged across great lengths and floated to

---

[34] Kester, *Revolt among the Sharecroppers*, 18.

[35] Kester, *Revolt among the Sharecroppers*, 18.

[36] Kester, *Revolt among the Sharecroppers*, 18–19.

[37] This and the following paragraph expand on material in Stauffer, "Power in the Social Gospel," 6–7.

[38] Kester notes that he does not distinguish between tenant farmers and sharecroppers, saying, "We make no attempt to draw any sharp distinction between tenant farmers and sharecroppers, for in our opinion the difference between them is negligible, and of little significance, if any at all" (Kester, *Revolt among the Sharecroppers*, 37).

[39] Kester's numbers on the rate of sharecropping may be inflated. Donald Grubbs notes that, "After about 1910 the entire Delta was brought under cultivation, and by the 1930's tenancy dominated the area more completely than ever. Six out of ten Arkansas farms were tenant-operated in 1935, but the tenancy rate in the Delta was 80 percent" (Grubbs, *Cry from the Cotton*, 7–8).

mills.⁴⁰ Malaria, pellagra, and typhoid reigned, as families lived in tents in the woods. This labor led to vast wealth for companies, and the land that was cleared made possible the continuation of this exploitation of labor through sharecropping. Times were already hard in the Delta when the Great Depression hit, and times only got harder. President Hoover's "conservative response" for rural Southern workers did little to help, and President Roosevelt's New Deal policies, especially the Agricultural Adjustment Act (AAA), only continued the hard times, just under the guise of the New Deal.⁴¹

The AAA was the result of political pressure starting in the 1920s from federations of farmers and corporations, such as the American Farm Bureau Federation. Cotton prices in the early twentieth century were volatile and unpredictable due to increased global and domestic production rates, along with rapid industrialization and alternative products to cotton.⁴² Cotton prices fell after the Great War, and the 1920s had a few good years but were mostly bad or worse. As Alison Collis Greene writes, "The past decade had brought plummeting cotton prices, a flood that burst through the Mississippi River levees and filled the Delta like a bathtub, and a rash of deadly tornadoes that ripped through the buildings the flood left standing. The year 1930, hoped many desperate Delta farmers, just had to bring better luck than the 1920s."⁴³ At first, the AAA promised relief for sharecroppers.

---

⁴⁰ Roll, *Spirit of Rebellion;* Woodruff, *American Congo.*

⁴¹ "In January 1932, the Hoover administration established the Reconstruction Finance Corporation (RFC), which Congress authorized to provide emergency loans to banks and corporations. Hoover's first attempt to use the power of the government rather than the power of moral persuasion to address the Great Depression represented a departure in federal policy, but it still did little for the hungry and unemployed" (Alison Collis Greene, *No Depression in Heaven, The Great Depression, the New Deal, and the Transformation of Religion in the Delta* [New York: Oxford University Press, 2016], 98).

⁴² Woodruff, *American Congo*: "Mechanization of cotton occurred first in the Arkansas and Mississippi delta, in part because large plantations had more capital to expend on technology. But because mechanization occurred in stages, beginning first in the 1920s with tractors used for cultivation, and expanding in the 1950s to include the actual picking and weeding of cotton, the social consequences of the process were spread across three decades. Full mechanization did not occur until the 1960s," 159.

⁴³ Greene, *No Depression in Heaven*, 9.

There was a glimmer of hope as progressive and conservative administrators shared the implementation of the AAA, but the liberals were quickly ousted.[44] The key to the failure of the AAA was that it vested local control and accountability only in the planters and landowners, who often controlled the judiciary.[45] The hallmark of the AAA that affected sharecroppers most were its "plow up" and reduction programs that paid subsidies to planters for plowing up portions of their cotton crop or simply not planting on a certain amount of land.[46] Planters were supposed to dispense a proportion of this subsidy to their tenants and sharecroppers. Few did. Plenty more planters forcibly removed their tenants and sharecroppers, kicking them out of their homes, separating them from their only source of food and income. The AAA laid bare the degree of domination planters had over sharecroppers. Domination, as civic republicans have defined it, is about arbitrary power over someone. Planters controlled the social, economic, political, and judicial life of sharecroppers. They were the law, as many judges and justices were planters themselves and the political representatives who appointed the judges were planters themselves.

The example of Paul D. Peacher is a case in point. As Nan Woodruff relates the story, Peacher was a previous deputy sheriff who led a mob to break up a STFU meeting. The mob shot and wounded several STFU members, murdered one who refused to sign a falsified affidavit exonerating Peacher and his posse, and beat another STFU member, Mrs. Eliza Nolden, who later died from the beating. Social gospeller Sherwood Eddy later investigated Peacher's plantation and wrote a report that reached a national audience and led to Peacher's conviction on federal peonage charges. As

---

[44] See Grubbs, *Cry from the Cotton*, chap. 3.

[45] Kester, *Revolt among the Sharecroppers*, 32: "The cotton control program was written in behalf of the landlords and planters and is correctly known as the 'landlord's code.' In the Commodity Information Series the question is asked, 'Where does the responsibility for the administration of the cotton program rest? Answer. The administration is primarily local, resting upon the community and county committees chosen by the cotton producers.' Since the control of the program was lodged in the hands of the landlords, it is rather obvious that whatever the tenants and sharecroppers got out of the program depended upon their relationship to the landlord. The record shows that the relationship was a poor one for the majority of tenants and sharecroppers."

[46] Kester, *Revolt among the Sharecroppers*, 28; Woodruff, *American Congo*, 157–60.

Woodruff states, "Thus laws, even vagrancy laws, not only served economic ends, but also buttressed white supremacy, reasserting planter authority through law and terror.... Peacher's trial revealed the interconnectedness of Delta society. A former town sheriff, town marshal, and plantation owner, Peacher secured hearings and convictions based simply on his word."[47]

Kester's aim in illustrating all of these conditions is then to highlight the power and threat the STFU poses to the dominant power structure. As an "indigenous movement," the STFU arose from the "very soil which bore the sharecroppers' bitter grievances."[48] Those who organized with the STFU understood their condition in this way—as one of wage slavery and its domination over their economic, political, social, and personal lives. The STFU was "interested in organizing the sharecroppers to abolish the planters' organized system of semi-slavery."[49] "Now the sharecroppers were no longer willing to be slaves," Kester says earlier. "Now that the white and black slaves had stopped fighting one another and had joined together to struggle against their common enemy, the planter could no longer use the white man to beat down the black man or the black man to beat down the wages and living conditions of the white man."[50] The promise of the STFU was that it was a class-based, cross-racial organizing strategy that understood the power of religion.

The STFU organizing strategy drew heavily from the political and organization culture of Black churches. Union locals often met in Black churches, and STFU organizers were often preachers.[51] Indeed, as Roll and Woodruff have illustrated, the political culture of Black Nationalism, especially through the United Negro Improvement Association and the NAACP, helped lay the groundwork for the success of STFU locals in certain Arkansas counties where the majority of sharecroppers were Black.[52] But the STFU and those who supported it drew heavily from white and Black Christian socialist visions of justice, as Kester himself found his way to the STFU through his colleagues Claude Williams and Ward Rogers at Vanderbilt who were now union organizers. This

---

[47] Woodruff, *American Congo*, 174–75.

[48] Kester, *Revolt among the Sharecroppers*, 54.

[49] Kester, *Revolt among the Sharecroppers*, 58.

[50] Kester, *Revolt among the Sharecroppers*,15.

[51] Woodruff, *American Congo*, 165; Parts of this paragraph expand work done in Stauffer, "Power in the Social Gospel," 7.

[52] Woodruff, *American Congo*, 165; Roll, *Spirit of Rebellion*, 95–102.

Christian political imagination and social ethics concretized their visions of freedom, providing them with examples to point to where glimpses of God's kingdom were possible. It was most often conceptualized as the "cooperative commonwealth," but, even aside from that term, the "spiritual urgency" that fed the STFU was tangible to outsiders. As Roll relates a comment from a white sharecropper, "When they first started talking about the union I thought it was a new church."[53] The connection between STFU organizing strategy and the Christian socialist vision of freedom is not without consequence for the paradox of slavery found in labor republican discourse on wage slavery. Indeed, STFU organizers and others found sharecroppers in a position of domination, and they had a vision of freedom that didn't require the enslavement of others but pointed to a cooperative culture that applied the ethics of Jesus.

Churches, Organizations, and the Cooperative Commonwealth

Kester's work with the STFU coincides with a transformation in his understanding of the role of churches in radical social transformation. In the 1920s, he was "indifferent" to the role of churches.[54] Now, he saw congregations—as groups that can join in solidarity with the STFU's cause—and the Church broadly conceived as a theological concept, as crucial tools. Writing later while working for the Fellowship of Southern Churchmen, he wrote, "We will keep hammering away in the church, at the church, with the church in the knowledge that we stand on solid ground and with the ages and not on the sand which already slips away as the rains descend and the winds of a new day blow with might."[55] For Kester, the promise of the congregations in radical social justice movements outweighs the problems.[56]

This may not be all that surprising giving the degree to which Kester was an institutionalist.[57] His own biography includes a long list of ecumenical

---

[53] Roll, *Spirit of Rebellion*, 97.
[54] Martin, *Howard Kester*, 147.
[55] Martin, *Howard Kester*, 147–148.
[56] Stauffer, "Power in the Social Gospel," 8.
[57] Jarod Roll makes this characterization of Howard Kester in Aaron Stauffer, "Sacred Roots: Exploring the Social Gospel in the Southern United States (Grant Series)." Religion and Justice. Accessed June 5, 2024. https://open.spotify.com/show/0ejqgxSgGGfCdPc20wGBoZ. Wilson Dickinson makes a similar point

social justice organizations that mobilized and organized new folk into the racial and economic justice efforts. Yet a point that Jarod Roll makes about the role of religion in STFU is relevant here: "Religious-style enthusiasm alone, however, did not make a political movement."[58] Indeed, recent historians have made claims that Christian social gospellers were at the least ineffective in their support of radical social transformation, and at the most they openly stifled the movement, actively and intentionally engaging against it.[59] What is more, even if Christian social gospellers like Kester did in fact throw in with radical racial and economic justice fights like the STFU, this still doesn't resolve the paradox raised by civic republican conceptions of freedom as depending on the enslavement of another.

Kester's life provides a view into the unique strength and breadth of the deep and wide network of ecumenical organizations that fostered and incubated racial and economic justice fights from the birth of the twentieth century on. Through figures like Sherwood Eddy and Kirby Paige, especially in the YMCA, the ecumenical movement and liberal politics were woven tightly together at a global level.[60] But the domestic terrain is equally impressive.[61] As Kester's own role illustrates, these organizations did not replace grassroots organizing and organization development. Instead, they often played crucial supportive, amplifying, philanthropic, and educational roles. These institutions were important instruments in building and adding structure to the cooperative commonwealth.

---

in Gabriella Lisi and George Schmidt, "Counter Memory with Wilson Dickinson," Religion and Justice. Accessed June 5, 2024. https://www.buzzsprout.com/2237315/14373019-counter-memory-with-wilson-dickinson-grant-series.

[58] Roll, *Spirit of Rebellion*, 98.

[59] See Janine Giordano Drake, *The Gospel of Church: How Mainline Protestants Vilified Christian Socialism and Fractured the Labor Movement* (New York: Oxford University Press, 2024); David Burns, *The Life and Death of the Radical Historical Jesus* (New York: Oxford University Press, 2013).

[60] For its impact on the Black Freedom movement see Sarah Azaransky, *This Worldwide Struggle: Religion and the International Roots of the Civil Rights Movement* (New York: Oxford University Press, 2017); Quinton Hosford Dixie and Peter R. Eisenstadt, *Visions of a Better World: Howard Thurman's Pilgrimage to India and the Origins of African American Nonviolence* (Boston: Beacon Press, 2011).

[61] Michael G. Thompson, *For God and Globe: Christian Internationalism in the United States between the Great War and the Cold War* (Ithaca, NY: Cornell University Press, 2015); Curtis J. Evans, *A Theology of Brotherhood: The Federal Council of Churches and the Problem of Race* (New York: New York University Press, 2024).

The cooperative commonwealth was a common adage among labor republicans, social gospellers, and Christian socialists in the late nineteenth and early twentieth centuries. Fueled in part by Christian eschatological hope in the coming socialist society, the cooperative commonwealth imagined organizing production, distribution, and consumption cooperatively, establishing freedom and equality to members of society, and establishing democracy in the economy, in politics, and in people's private lives.[62] Far from being free of gendered, heterosexist, nationalist, or racial biases, the cooperative commonwealth eschatologically held the already and the not yet that characterized the economic and political imagination of labor republicans. While accenting their constructive contribution to resolving Gourevitch's paradox of slavery, connecting the STFU and social gospellers like Howard Kester to the lineage of labor republicanism begins to unearth often overlooked connections between radical social gospellers and grassroots organizing movements that built real economic and political power.

Consider the financial role that these organizations and figures played in actualizing the cooperative commonwealth in cooperative ventures in the South, especially in the specific examples of Delta and Providence Farms. In 1936, hundreds of sharecroppers were evicted from their land. Many were STFU members. Kester, Claude Williams, and others had long been interested in starting a cooperative farm. They proposed the idea to social gospeller Sherwood Eddy when he was visiting STFU locals, and, three days later, he personally put down a deposit to hold farmland in Mississippi. Eddy soon found the rest of the funds to purchase what would be the experiment in Christian socialism and cooperative farming first named Rochdale Farms (after the cooperative experiment in England), but later named Delta Cooperative Farm.[63] Indeed, many of the cooperative

---

[62] The complications and imperfections of this vision are obvious throughout Gary Dorrien's magisterial account in *American Democratic Socialism*.

[63] Rick Nutt, *The Whole Gospel for the Whole World: Sherwood Eddy and the American Protestant Mission* (Macon, GA: Mercer University Press, 1997), 273–77; Robert Hunt Ferguson, *Remaking the Rural South: Interracialism, Christian Socialism, and Cooperative Farming in Jim Crow Mississippi* (Athens: University of Georgia Press, 2018). Kester's hope for a project like this is hinted at in *Revolt among the Sharecroppers*, as he says, "My experience with sharecroppers and tenant farmers in Arkansas and elsewhere leads me to believe that co-operative farming on a large scale would be most acceptable. There are certain invaluable things which may be achieved in co-operative farming which cannot be achieved among widely separated individual farm homes.

ventures in the South, especially Commonwealth College, which Claude Williams later directed as he organized directly with the STFU, were largely supported by the American Fund for Public Service.[64] Or recall the UMWA strike in Wilder and the role that Kester, Taylor, Niebuhr and others played in raising awareness and funds for striking miners.

The relationship between local grassroots democratic organizing movements for racial and economic justice and the "grass tops" organizations that play supportive, educational, and amplifying roles is richly complex, yielding multiple sides to stories about the best lessons to learn in response to questioning the role of institutions and structure in organizing movements. The complexity of these movements reveals a rich institutional ecology that is needed to support organizing movements. For Kester and others, churches play a crucial—and *differentiated*—role in radical social movements. Indeed, this is reflective of his own position in STFU. Kester at times played the role of pastor, author, speaker, organizer, and educator.

Organizing movements need structure to win. Power organizations are grounded in relationships that can withstand change and the tumultuous challenges that come with fights for political and economic democracy. The organizations that cannot change are the weak ones: They are brittle and will crumble when forced to adjust to the shifting sands of political life. Kester's work in the STFU demonstrates what that tumult can look like. Organizational structure, however, comes with tensions inherent in group life.[65] Building structure requires different roles—not everyone can play the same role as democratic group life is at least in part about authority, responsibility, and accountability. If groups are to be truly democratic, the importance of working for stronger organizational structure that does not dominate working people, whom the organization is supposed to fight for in the first place, is preeminent. Congregations have typically played feeder roles for organizations—they mobilize the people who will then engage in the life of organizing that includes educating working people about their collective conditions and taking action for liberation.

Such a plan means, for example, that the farm workers would live on a large plantation or farm. The farmers would be entitled to the land as long as they occupied and used it, and it could not be taken away from them on any account as long as they fulfilled their obligations to the community or to the state" (92).

[64] William H. Cobb, *Radical Education in the Rural South: Commonwealth College, 1922–1940* (Detroit: Wayne State University Press, 2000).

[65] Ganz, *People, Power, Change*, 150–67.

STFU organized to end the domination of wage-slavery from the planters and landholders. They envisioned freedom in the cooperative commonwealth, and Christian socialists and radical social gospellers like Kester enacted that political and economic vision through their work with congregations. They found their vision of freedom as theologically grounded in the applied ethics of Jesus and embodied in the cooperative commonwealth, which they actively sought to build through cooperative economic ventures and organizing efforts like the STFU.

2

Making Ministers or Training Technocrats?
Religious Education for Social Transformation and the Problems of Professionalized Democracy

Joseph Strife

In the years after the Civil War, Mainline Protestant leaders struggled to respond to a country being remade by immigration, urbanization, and industrial capitalism. The self-assured position of middle-class Protestantism had been deeply shaken, its paternal hand thrown aside by an increasingly militant, independent, and Catholic working class. Cities were the geographic expression of the wreckage of the traditional moral and social order, and seminaries seemed ill-equipped to produce the leadership capable of answering the urban "social question."[1] How could Protestants remain relevant to a secularizing world that showed little interest in coughing up premium prices for pew seats? What emerged was a transformation in seminary education, where ministers supplemented instruction in biblical Greek with an apprenticeship in city life and a sustained engagement with the emerging discipline of sociology. Immersed in the practical realities of industrial capitalism and inspired by social gospel leaders like Josiah Strong and Walter Rauschenbusch, these clergy would go on to drive progressive change in areas like temperance, government corruption, hygiene, and labor rights.

---

[1] Francis Peabody, *Jesus Christ and the Social Question* (New York: Macmillan, 1900), 2. As Harvard professor Francis Peabody framed it, "Behind all the extraordinary achievements of modern civilization, its transformations of business methods, its miracles of scientific discovery, its mighty combinations of political forces, there lies at the heart of the present time a burdening sense of social mal-adjustment which creates what we call the social question."

In 1948, Don Benedict, Archie Hargraves, and George Webber founded the East Harlem Protestant Parish (EHPP) in hopes of renewing the church's mission to the city. After World War II, white Protestants had decamped to the suburbs by the millions, leaving urban neighborhoods without their resources or witness. Benedict, Hargraves, and Webber moved into East Harlem, beginning an apprenticeship in urban life that would inspire a generation of seminarians. EHPP alumni would go on to develop urban training centers across the country, training thousands of clergy in urban realities and community organizing techniques. In 1967, Harvey Cox would describe this generation as a "new breed" of Protestant leaders who were spreading the gospel in picket lines and town halls rather than traditional congregational forms.[2]

In this chapter, I explore the traditions of urban ministry and organizing that connect Progressive-era reformers like Graham Taylor with the "new breed" activist clergy like Benedict, Hargraves, and Webber. Taylor was important in establishing Christian social ethics as a discipline, fieldwork as a seminary practice, and social work as a profession. But his students' efforts at Christianizing the social order were largely circumscribed and disciplined by the bureaucratized expertise of the emerging order of social welfare professionals. New breed activists rebelled against the conservatism of social work but did so from the same position of educated and trained professionals working for social change in neighborhoods that were not their own. This history reveals persistent contradictions between the ends of participatory democracy and professional training—demonstrated in this volume in the conflict between the bottom-up leadership of the National Welfare Rights Organization (NWRO) and the credentialed leadership of the National Council of Churches (NCC). Community organizing traditions sit uneasily within this tension between grassroots and technocratic leadership, often relying on trained professionals employing organizing techniques for (ideally) democratic ends. This chapter examines the ways Mainline Protestants equipped themselves for social engagement, navigating between training for technocratic authority and formation for democratic life.

---

[2] Harvey Cox, "The 'New Breed' in American Churches: Sources of Social Activism in Religion," *Daedalus* 96, no. 1 (1967): 135.

Graham Taylor, Chicago Theological Seminary, and the Birth of Social Work

The struggle to be relevant to an industrialized, urbanized world was in no sense abstract to Graham Taylor. As a young pastor, he was called from preaching total depravity to farmers in upstate New York to the Fourth Congregational Church in inner-city Hartford, Connecticut. Taylor arrived to find a congregation of 40-some souls awkwardly filling a sanctuary built for 1,200. Outside the church, immigrant factory workers contended with difficult working conditions, family breakdown, and substance abuse with few institutions willing and able to help. Taylor felt his seminary training had done little to prepare him for the realities of leading a congregation in an industrial neighborhood.[3] His response was to set his eyes and heart outside the sanctuary, leading worship in parks and baseball fields, doing face-to-face evangelism in the police stations, jails, and door-to-doors.[4] Taylor's engaged response to the "social question" landed him a job teaching at Hartford Seminary, where he made a practice of sending seminarians into the city to gain practical experience in mission.

Taylor was not a theological liberal, and his approach to ministry was stubbornly rooted in the stories and social vision he found in Scripture. But his experience in Hartford was a key text through which he interpreted the scripture, seeing the ways social conditions shaped individual souls. Finding resonance between Hartford and the writings of social gospel pioneers like Washington Gladden, he embraced a social gospel hope in the redemption of both soul and society: "The evangelization of industrial and social conditions is necessary to the evangelization of the soul, still more of the world."[5] For Taylor, "religion" was the gift of the church to the world, leading to a social salvation expressed in secular terms—growth, health, reconciliation, and order. He prayed for the redemption of the world, but the shape of that redemption was often expressed in the categories of sociology:

> Heredity and environment are newly appreciated but prime factors in the problems of personal and social salvation. Without them, neither the cause nor the cure of pauperism, intemperance and

---

[3] Graham Taylor, *Pioneering on Social Frontiers* (Chicago: University of Chicago Press, 1930), 347–48.
[4] Taylor, *Pioneering on Social Frontiers*, 363.
[5] Taylor, *Pioneering on Social Frontiers*, 110.

crime can be appreciated. Sanitary, social and spiritual conditions are the moulds of personal and public character. To the imperative mandate "Ye must be born again" is added the church's obligation to improve the hereditary and environing conditions of birth and life in this world.[6]

"Pauperism, intemperance, and crime" were the watchwords of an older generation of Protestant reformers, Victorians who attempted to challenge the ways capitalism and urbanization had corroded individual character, family life, and the social order. Thomas Chalmers, a disciple of Thomas Malthus, pioneered the model for what would become known as "scientific charity": efficient administration, surveillance, an emphasis on the character of the poor, a strong aversion to giving direct assistance, and professional distance between administration and those in poverty.[7]

In the late nineteenth century the Charity Organization Society (COS) would bring scientific charity to cities across the North Atlantic, enlisting an army of "friendly visitors" to carry the values and wisdom of the upper classes into the homes of the impoverished. Despite their commitment to data and evidence, the "just-so stories" driving the work of the COS said much more about the social anxieties and fantasies of the Victorian elite than the actual lives of those in poverty, and little headway was made restoring class harmony.[8] Taylor was part of a new generation that was influenced by the development of sociology beyond social Darwinism and viewed the social problem as an environmental issue more than one of individual character. The settlement house movement was the most prominent vehicle of this new sensibility, and Taylor became deeply taken with its approach.

If the city had become the wilderness, there were plenty willing to settle it. The settlement house movement began in 1884, when Rev. Samuel Barnett and his wife moved into London's notorious East End, establishing a house where rich and poor could learn from one another and share a common life. This was Toynbee Hall, the first settlement house. Barnett aimed to "bridge the gulf that industrialism had created between rich and

---

[6] Taylor, *Pioneering on Social Frontiers*, 387.

[7] Stewart Brown, *Thomas Chalmers and the Godly Commonwealth in Scotland* (Oxford: Oxford University Press, 1983).

[8] Michael Katz, *In the Shadow of the Poorhouse* (New York: Basic Books, 1996), 68–87.

poor, to reduce the mutual suspicion and ignorance of one class for the other, and to do something more than give charity."⁹ Barnett looked to the Christian socialism of John Ruskin and William Morris rather than Malthus and Spencer. Young educated men and women flocked to Toynbee Hall and started their own settlement house experiments in cities across England and the United States. There was more in common between the COS friendly visitors and settlement house workers than either would like to admit—both shared a vision of healing class divisions, and both implicitly assumed those in poverty would profit from the salutary influence of the higher classes. However, over and over again, settlement workers experienced a transformation of consciousness that led them to think very differently about urban problems than COS leaders. Educated in the systems of exploitation that structured the slums, they looked to environmental solutions, including better working conditions, education, and public parks.¹⁰

Jane Addams would become the most prominent leader of the settlement house movement. Addams had education, means, a sharp mind, and a passion for justice. After a stay at Toynbee Hall, she renovated an abandoned manor in the Chicago slums and moved in with her partner Ellen Gates Starr, establishing Hull House in 1889. It soon grew to house over two dozen residents, serving thousands of visitors from the neighborhood on a weekly basis. Hull House provided tutoring, childcare, English classes, art exhibitions, art classes, continuing adult education, and public meeting space.

In 1902, Addams published her first book, *Democracy and Social Ethics*, articulating her social democratic vision. Democracy, for Addams, was more than a political system, it was a way of life, centered in everyday practices of fellowship across lines of difference.¹¹ But *Democracy and Social Ethics* was not a winsome appeal to open one's eyes to other perspectives. It was a sharp, prophetic word from eyes that had been opened. In six areas—charity, family, domestic labor, industrial labor, education, and politics—

---

⁹ Allen Davis, *Spearheads for Reform: The Social Settlements and the Progressive Movement, 1890–1914* (New York: Oxford University Press, 1967), 3–12.

¹⁰ Don Kirschner, *The Paradox of Professionalism: Reform and Public Service in Urban America, 1900–1940* (New York: Greenwood Press, 1986).

¹¹ Jane Addams, *Democracy and Social Ethics* (Urbana: University of Illinois Press, 2002).

Addams offered finely grained critiques of how dominant practices, policies, models, and assumptions failed to appreciate how they functioned at the level of everyday life. Nowhere was this sharper than her critique of scientific charity and friendly visiting. Addams offers an inversion—the visitor who investigates for evidence of idleness or other immorality knows little of the determination, savvy, creativity, and sacrifice needed to simply survive. Where those in poverty routinely share with one another, even sacrificially, the visitor comes with more than enough coats, shoes, coal, and houses, but would never think to share them, having substituted a "theory of social conduct for the natural promptings of the heart."[12] She knows that only those at their utmost need are likely to endure the humiliation and risk entailed with asking for help from these lady bountifuls, weathering the indignity of performing the script of the deserving poor (grateful, submissive, earnest, etc.) to get a pittance of actual help.[13]

Addams does not romanticize the working class. She recognizes that the demands of life at the margins require hard choices that can wound the soul.[14] But over and over again, the easy assumptions of the COS wither before the complexity of everyday life:

> The visitor is continually surprised to find that the safest platitude may be challenged. She refers quite naturally to the "horrors of the saloon," and discovers that the head of her visited family does not connect them with "horrors" at all. He remembers all the kindnesses he has received there, the free lunch and treating which goes on, even when a man is out of work and not able to pay up; the loan of five dollars he got there when the charity visitor was miles away and he was threatened with eviction. He may listen politely to her reference to "horrors," but considers it only "temperance talk."[15]

James C. Scott, in *Seeing Like a State* (1998), identifies two types of knowledge—*metis* and *techne*. *Techne* is knowledge that is principled, generalized, abstract. *Metis* is knowledge at the level of everyday life, knowledge

---

[12] Addams, *Democracy and Social Ethics*, 16.
[13] Addams, *Democracy and Social Ethics*, 16–17.
[14] Addams, *Democracy and Social Ethics*, 23–24.
[15] Addams, *Democracy and Social Ethics*, 18–19.

that is woolly and complex, knowledge that cannot be reduced to the cell of a spreadsheet without violence. *Techne* is the language of policy, the view from above, the map of the technocrat; *metis* is the language of practice, the view from below, the territory of the democrat.[16] Addams's *Democracy and Social Ethics* is a torrent of *metis* and a defense of its virtues, a call to embodied democratic life.

Addams's inductive method was not limited to the kind of street-level knowledge represented in *Democracy and Social Action*; she was as passionate about data as any COS leader. In 1895 *Hull House Maps and Papers* was published, presenting an archive of years of empirical research. Building on the statistical surveys and geographic models of charity reformer Charles Booth, *Maps and Papers* gave a detailed pictured of wages, working conditions, ethnic diversity, and housing in Chicago's neighborhoods surrounding Hull House.[17] It was a landmark text in empirical sociology. The project of mapping and quantifying society would continue to develop, bolstered by W. E. B. Du Bois's work in Philadelphia, into forms like the social survey movement and urban sociology, driven by the technocratic hope that better data would lead to better policy. Michael Katz notes, "In [American settlement house publications] ... are the theoretical, methodological, even personal origins of the Chicago school of urban sociology, which dominated American urban research for decades."[18]

How might we reconcile the democratic faith of *Democracy and Tradition* with Addams's enchantment with the promise of the social sciences? They were held together in the lives of the Hull House residents. They were educated men and women (mostly women) who had immersed themselves in democratic life and were forever changed by this baptism. Hull House alumni would go on to astonishing accomplishment: Julia Lathrop, Edith Abbot, Florence Kelley, John Dewey, Francis Perkins, and Harry Hopkins would all lead major social welfare institutions, private and public, in the coming decades.[19] But the tension was also held in the interval between the residents and their neighbors.

When the story of the settlement house movement is told, it is the story of women and men whose lives were changed by their baptism into

---

[16] James C. Scott, *Seeing Like a State: How Certain Schemes to Improve the Human Condition Have Failed* (New Haven, CT: Yale University Press, 1998).

[17] *Hull House Maps and Papers* (New York: Crowell, 1895).

[18] Katz, *In the Shadow of the Poorhouse*, 164.

[19] Katz, *In The Shadow of the Poorhouse*, 167.

working-class life—not the story of neighbors and neighborhoods who were transformed. These educated, proto-professional advocates maintained a mediating position between neighborhood and government, between labor and capital. They supported labor issues but not as members of unions. They interpreted the needs and condition of those in poverty to broader society. They were "for not of" the neighborhood, however much their sojourn in the settlement house might have blurred that line.

As for the neighbors, they did not necessarily appreciate being spoken for. "'They're like the rest,' one immigrant community leader noted, 'a bunch of people planning for us and deciding what is good for us without consulting us or taking us into their confidence.'"[20] In his history of community organizing, Robert Fisher notes that, when the settlements actually took on the local machine, they generally got trounced.[21] Residents mostly relied on the same social networks they had built before the settlement arrived:

> Instead of turning to a settlement organized and run by outsiders, working-class people relied on themselves, their families, and their own self-help ethnic and religious institutions. Reformers were wrong, not to mention ethnocentric, in assuming that urban slums were "disorganized" and that neighborhood residents needed externally initiated efforts to organize their community. Neither industrialization, immigration, or slum life destroyed people's need for or ability to create supportive community networks.[22]

Settlement house workers took real risks and made real sacrifices to share the lives of the poor, but they failed to build genuine democratic power.

Liberal Protestantism as a whole attempted to hold this place of mediation—Graham Taylor was proud to be called upon to arbitrate labor disputes, respected by both sides. Theirs was an enlightened and compassionate paternalism, developing expertise disciplined by both social science and democratic experience. Michael Katz argues that the

---

[20] Robert Fisher, *Let the People Decide: Neighborhood Organizing in America* (New York: Twayne, 1994), 11.

[21] Fisher, *Let the People Decide*, 9. The exception, Fisher notes, was with the support of upper-middle-class residents in numbers that could counter immigrant support for the machine (9).

[22] Fisher, *Let the People Decide*, 11.

settlement house movement prefigured the professionalization of social work, public health, urban planning, and other disciplines that would fill the bureaucracies of twentieth-century welfare states.[23] But the professional ideal entailed a cultivated and dispassionate distance from social problems, losing the *metis* gained through proximity. Addams wrote unfortunate pieces on prostitution and lynching and, in 1901, was taken to task by Ida B. Wells for uncritically accepting the narrative that lynching victims had committed crimes—a lie those with first-person experience knew too well. Wells led her own settlement house, as did Reverdy Ransom, but it was an exception to the movement's abysmal record on integration. By the 1940s, settlement house workers had traded MSW degrees for the experience of living in the neighborhoods they served.[24]

Seminaries, churches, and mission organizations struggled to navigate these tensions between formation for democratic relationship and professionalization in their own projects of education and reform, and again this played out in the life of Graham Taylor. Taylor found that the baptism in democratic life modeled by the settlement house movement resonated with his own experience in Hartford. He had achieved some notoriety at Hartford Seminary, giving his students hands-on experience in urban missions. Chicago Theological Seminary (CTS) lured him to Chicago, offering him the chance to shape the first department of Christian sociology. Taylor was a good fit for CTS, which was dedicated to updating the professional training of ministers by incorporating the kind of practical training found in the legal and medical professions.[25] Taylor accepted, with the condition that he would require a proper laboratory for hands-on learning and social experimentation. He had in mind the kind of immersive education offered by settlement houses, and, with guidance from Addams, he established his own settlement house, the Chicago Commons. "Chicago Commons was moved to adventure its own development by the motive of these pioneer settlements' democratic faith, neighborly educational methods, and fundamentally religious relationships and hope."[26] Taylor

---

[23] Katz, *In the Shadow of the Poorhouse*, 174–75.

[24] Judith Ann Trolander, *Professionalism and Social Change: From the Settlement House Movement to Neighborhood Centers, 1886 to the Present* (New York: Columbia University Press, 1987), 2–3.

[25] Arthur Cushman McGiffert, *No Ivory Tower: The Story of the Chicago Theological Seminary* (Chicago: Chicago Theological Seminary, 1965), 236.

[26] Graham Taylor, *Chicago Commons through Forty Years* (Chicago: Chicago Commons Association, 1936), 6.

lamented the lack of proper textbooks in Christian sociology, but insisted "the street, the shop, the school, the mission are the first text book."[27] CTS students experienced a broad spectrum of urban life, including YMCAs, social settlements, the Salvation Army, temperance societies, citizens' associations, labor organizations, jails, and so on.[28] Other Protestant seminaries, including Union, Yale, and Harvard, found the answer to the "social question" in this kind of practical education, immersing their students in the life of the streets.[29] But Taylor was also convinced of the need to cultivate professional expertise in those tasked with the increasingly secular work of urban mission. He partnered with the University of Chicago to form the Chicago Institute of Social Science, which would become the first graduate school of social work.

By the beginning of the twentieth century, the conflict between the COS and the settlement house movement had cooled, unifying the nascent profession of social work—the moralism of the COS had been disciplined by decades of experience (particularly the depression of 1893), and both were being drawn forward by the same developments in social science. In 1905, this détente was made official. The main journals of the two movements merged into one, *The Charities and the Commons* (later *The Survey*), and Jane Addams was elected president of the National Conference on Charity and Corrections (NCCC). But social work's status as a profession was still in doubt. In 1915, Abraham Flexner, who was influential in professionalizing medicine, addressed the NCCC to argue that social work was *not* a proper profession. This shook the conference, and social work stood at a crossroads. What would it take to be legitimated as a profession? And what would be the cost? Was this a choice between *metis* and *techne*? The dilemma echoed in the seminaries—how much authority should be given (or ceded) to social science?[30]

This question continues to haunt social welfare and Christian social ethics. Social work stands, at times uneasily, between private charity and public welfare, between the voluntary work of citizens and the

---

[27] McGiffert, *No Ivory Tower*, 102.

[28] McGiffert, *No Ivory Tower*, 98–99.

[29] Aaron Abell, *The Urban Impact on American Protestantism 1865–1900* (Cambridge, MA: Harvard University Press, 1943), 230–44.

[30] Kirschner, *The Paradox of Professionalism*, 54–57. For a further discussion of the professionalization of Protestant seminaries, see Ted Smith, *The End of Theological Education* (Grand Rapids: Eerdmans, 2023).

technical skill of trained professionals. A professional claims expertise and authority by virtue of specialized knowledge and training. Could social work claim authority over territory once occupied by concerned citizens, political leaders, and the church? This is the problem of technocracy—professionalization reduces, or obscures, the space of politics. Professionalization is, in some basic sense, antidemocratic, transforming the citizen into client and democratic cooperation into service delivery. Professionals render a community legible, translating the diverse and complex life of a person or neighborhood into bounded qualities and categories, units that could be plugged into the algorithms of proper service—or provide data to improve those algorithms. Professionals, John McKnight argued, end up defining people and communities in terms of needs they are uniquely authorized to meet.[31] The more social work claimed the mantle of professionalism, the greater the distance from the democratic life once preached by Addams.

In social work, the charms of professionalism won decisively. In 1917, Mary Richmond published *Social Diagnosis,* giving social work the distinctive methodology—casework—it needed to be recognized as a profession. But casework is meant to help people adjust to their environment, not transform it, and many of the radical and democratic possibilities found in the settlement house movement were foreclosed. Social welfare historian Michael Katz reads this as a story of decline: "As social workers rejected urban mediation and abandoned social reform, they became second-class therapists, inferior in standing, if not in competence, to psychologists and psychiatrists.... With some irony, social workers did not in fact become either therapists or professionals. Instead, they became badly paid servants of bureaucracies and the state."[32]

In *Christian Critics*, Eugene McCarraher argues that Protestants followed a parallel path away from democratic possibilities, effacing Christian particularity in the process.[33] Social gospel leaders saw the

---

[31] John McKnight, "Professionalized Service and Disabling Help," in *The Disabling Professions,* ed. Ivan Illich (London: Marion Boyars, 1977), 69–91. McKnight established one of the primary streams of contemporary community development, Asset-Based Community Development (ABCD) as a protest against the clientalization of vulnerable communities.

[32] Katz, *In the Shadow of the Poorhouse,* 172.

[33] Eugene McCarraher, *Christian Critics: Religion and the Impasse in Modern American Social Thought* (Ithaca, NY: Cornell University Press, 2000).

Kingdom of God being realized in the progress of the Progressive era; Graham Taylor preached, "The gospel of the Kingdom is sociology with God left in it, with the Messianic spirit as the bond of unity, with the new birth of the individual for the regeneration of society, and the dynamic spirit of religion as the only power adequate to fulfil its social ideals."[34] Progressive leader Richard T. Ely proclaimed that the love commandment, "when elaborated, becomes social science or sociology."[35] However, this universalizing, and ultimately secularizing, language did more to baptize the social sciences than evangelize the forces remaking society. Christianizing the social order became enfolded with the descriptions, diagnoses, and prescriptions offered by the social sciences.

> Preaching what David Hollinger has dubbed an "intellectual gospel" that ascribed salvific significance to scientific labor and professional knowledge, liberals sanctioned a cognitive and social bifurcation of "ideals" and "facts" in which the former were assigned (with decreasing warrant) to theologians and ministers, while the latter became the bailiwick of the growing postbellum academic and professional intelligentsia.[36]

As the scale and complexity of industry and government grew, a new stratum of secular professionals emerged to wield credentialed authority over social problems. "Trained and employed in seminaries, colleges, universities and church bureaucracies, liberal Protestant intellectuals—and social gospelers in particular—constituted a clerical arm of this professional-managerial-class."[37] We should note that these were not the only Protestant voices, nor were Mainline Protestant elites the only religious forces shaping the era—movements for labor rights and racial justice succeeded in drawing together racially and economically diverse, faith-filled constituencies in ways that escaped Progressive-era reformers.[38] In any case, it wouldn't be

---

[34] Graham Taylor, *Religion in Social Action* (New York: Dodd, Mead, 1913), 104.

[35] Richard Ely, *The Social Aspects of Christianity* (London: Thomas Y. Crowell, 1889), 16.

[36] McCarraher, *Christian Critics*, 10.

[37] McCarraher, *Christian Critics*, 11.

[38] For example, see Dorothy Brown and Elizabeth McKeown, *The Poor Belong to Us: Catholic Charities and American Welfare* (Cambridge, MA: Harvard University Press, 2000); Heath Carter, *Union Made: Working People and the Rise of Social*

long before Mainline Protestantism's comfortable relationship with social and technical power would be challenged by a revival of radical and democratic possibilities.

Suburbanization and the New Breed

At the end of World War II, facing down the godless Soviets, the place of Mainline Protestantism was secure. Church attendance was at an all-time high, the seminaries were overflowing, and the denominations were flush with resources. But cities were struggling. White Protestants had decamped to the suburbs by the millions, along with their resources. Between the Great Migration and suburbanization, cities increasingly became structured in racialized—and racist—terms. In this same period, industry began its own migration to the suburbs, to the South, and abroad. Factories were the heart of industrial neighborhoods, ordering and sustaining families and institutions. It would take decades before these wounds would have even a chance to heal. Urban renewal often struck the final blow, as professional urban planners and architects marked vulnerable neighborhoods as "blighted" and sentenced them to destruction. A new generation of Protestant leaders committed to a theology of social change would once more attempt to make Protestant witness relevant to the secular city.

Don Benedict, Archie Hargraves, and George Webber were seminarians at Union Theological Seminary in New York. Following the lead of European urban innovators like the Iona community and the French worker-priest movement, they spent their final year at Union designing a new style of urban mission in East Harlem. East Harlem was a devastated community of Puerto Ricans, Italians, and African Americans served by Catholic and storefront Pentecostal churches, struggling to hold together broken pieces of family, community, and spirit. Like the settlement house workers of the Gilded Age, Benedict and company chose to move into the

---

Christianity in Chicago (New York: Oxford University Press, 2015); Gary Dorrien, *The New Abolition: W. E. B. Du Bois and the Black Social Gospel* (New Haven, CT: Yale University Press, 2015); Kenneth Heineman, *A Catholic New Deal: Religion and Reform in Depression Pittsburgh* (University Park: Pennsylvania State University Press, 1999); Evelyn Higginbotham, *Righteous Discontent: The Women's Movement in the Black Baptist Church, 1880–1920* (Cambridge, MA: Harvard University Press, 1993); and Aaron Stauffer's chapter in this volume (Chapter 1).

neighborhood, sharing life with the families of East Harlem. Together, the Group Ministry formed a "rule of life," like earlier monastics, governing their rhythms of worship, play, and social action. The ministry grew to several storefront churches, Bible studies, social action committees, and other neighborhood involvements.[39]

The East Harlem Protestant Parish (EHPP) caught the imagination of a generation of seminarians and denominational leaders. Like the settlement house workers, the EHPP group ministry members were transformed by their encounter with the severity of the situation, the complexity of its causes, and the strength of neighbors who daily made a way out of no way. Like the settlement house workers, the men and women baptized into urban life at EHPP (including hundreds of seminarians) would go on to national leadership in religious life and social reform, including William Stringfellow, George Younger, George and Mary Todd, and Letty Russell. Mainline church bodies formed or revived departments of urban mission.[40] Rev. David Barry, executive director of the New York City Mission Society, proclaimed "that the 'inner city' was the 'most crucial evangelical frontier' for American Protestantism."[41] "Inner city" acquired its current connotation—a geography defined by poverty, race, and cultural pathology—from white Protestants streaming into the city as a mission field.[42]

Don Benedict, George Webber, and Archie Hargraves would all go on to develop important educational and training institutions for urban ministry. The foremost of these was the Urban Training Center (UTC) in Chicago, launched by Benedict in 1963. Gibson Winter, who prophetically denounced *The Suburban Captivity of the Churches*, assisted from the University of Chicago Divinity School.[43] UTC partnered with twenty denominations, with significant support from private foundations.[44] A national network of

---

[39] George Todd and Trey Hammond, *Exposure and Risk: The Great Coming Church* (CreateSpace Independent Publishing Platform, 2016), 17–36.

[40] George Younger, *From New Creation to Urban Crisis: A History of Action Training Ministries, 1962–1975* (Chicago: CSSR, 1987), 31.

[41] Bench Ansfield, "Unsettling 'Inner City': Liberal Protestantism and the Postwar Origins of a Keyword in Urban Studies," *Antipode* 50, no. 5 (2018): 1166.

[42] Ansfield, "Unsettling 'Inner City.'"

[43] Gibson Winter, *The Suburban Captivity of the Churches: An Analysis of Protestant Responsibility in the Expanding Metropolis* (Garden City, NY: Doubleday, 1961).

[44] Richard Henry Luecke, "Protestant Clergy: New Forms of Ministry, New

"action training" institutions and programs developed, providing "training for social change"—or, more precisely, training "to develop the power of those who are participating in the liberation of society."[45] The signature program was the "urban plunge," during which participants were dropped into urban neighborhoods and left to their own devices for several days, providing "intense personal exposure" to problems like unemployment, crime, and so on. Once again, Protestants had discovered the transformative power of immersion—a secular baptism—in urban life. Beyond the "plunge," participants were educated in concepts, tools, and techniques derived from community organizing—assessing a community to identify "interests," gathering data, planning for action, the rhythm of "action and reflection," and so on. Community organizing tools were supplemented by education in the politics of cities, backed by masses of data filling file cabinets in institute offices.[46] Education in the facts of urban politics, and the "plunge" in particular, was predicated on an interval of identity, a position of vision and belonging from *outside* the inner city. But this missionary generation was being radicalized through their experiences working for social reform, either in the inner city or the civil rights movement, and increasingly sought a radical democratic politics "with, not for" the inner city. Harvey Cox named this generation the "new breed":

> This group has accepted the "political" rather than the social service definition of the crisis of urban poverty. Its leaders sharply criticize the traditional programs of churches and mission societies. They advocate the utilization of church resources to help mobilize the poor in various types of community organizations. They speak unapologetically of the struggle for power in the city and the churches' responsibility to enter into the struggle on the side of the exploited and powerless. In Rochester, Buffalo, Chicago, and other cities they have used church funds to support Saul Alinsky or other organizers in setting up energetic programs for organizing the poor.[47]

Forms of Training," *Annals of the American Academy of Political and Social Science* 387 (1970): 90.

[45] Younger, *From New Creation to Urban Crisis*, 14, 19.

[46] Younger, *From New Creation to Urban Crisis*, 28.

[47] Harvey Cox, "The 'New Breed' in American Churches: Sources of Social Activism in Religion," *Daedalus* 96, no. 1 (1967): 138.

Saul Alinsky was a prophet of democratic life, critical of educated projects of social engineering, including the settlement houses.[48] He called out how projects of social reform were seldom genuinely democratic—"it is a rare phenomenon today to discover a community organization in which the indigenous interests and actions of groups of the community not only participate but also play a fundamental role in the organization."[49] Alinsky's radical democratic vision came to dominate American community organizing, and so, when EHPP alumni began their own programs of training in urban ministry, Alinsky's principles of power, interest, and organization formed the grammar.

As much as he critiqued the settlement house movement, Alinsky's method built on the legacy of Addams and Taylor, passed on through the University of Chicago school of sociology. Since the 1920s, Robert Park and Ernst Burgess had developed a distinctive approach to sociology, an "ecological" approach that was strongly grounded in empirical research. This research provided evidence for Burgess's environmental claims—that social disorganization, not individual pathology, was the root cause of problems like juvenile delinquency.[50] Burgess was critical of the settlement houses, rejecting enlightened technocracy in favor of grassroots organization around self-defined neighborhood interests.[51] But in the tradition of *Hull House Maps and Papers,* Park and Burgess sent students across the city to collect quantitative and qualitative data on questions like housing patterns, family structures, race relations, and criminality. Alinsky was one of these students, beginning with surveys of juvenile delinquency in Chicago; he was soon hired by the Chicago Area Project to organize neighborhoods to combat delinquency. Using the neighborhood as a unit, the project sought to build local leadership around locally defined goals. After a year of research and relationship building, Alinsky launched the Back of the

---

[48] Mark Santow, *Saul Alinsky and the Dilemmas of Race* (Chicago: University of Chicago Press, 2023), 130–33. The liberal *Christian Century* was among Alinsky's fiercest early critics, wary of his outreach to pro-segregation urban Catholics. There is a clear parallel with Progressive-era anti-corruption campaigns targeting Catholic urban machines.

[49] Saul Alinsky, "Community Analysis and Organization," *American Journal of Sociology* 46, no. 6 (1941): 800.

[50] Lawrence Engel, "Saul Alinsky and the Chicago School," *Journal of Speculative Philosophy*, new series, 16, no. 1 (2002): 50–61.

[51] Trolander, *Professionalism and Social Change*, 144.

Yards Organizing Council (BYOC); the council brought together churches and labor to take on the meatpacking industry.[52] This was far beyond the project's brief and Alinsky was fired, but he was just getting started. While organizing the BYOC, he met John L. Lewis, and the Alinsky organizing method emerged from Chicago school sociology, the union organizing of Lewis, and Alinsky's own outsized personality.[53]

In his article "The 'New Breed' in American Churches," Harvey Cox articulated a theological logic behind their radical democratic commitments.[54] The new breed were found "organizing welfare unions, tenants' councils, rent strikes and school boycotts," pressing the Church to "identify itself much more radically with the interests of the poor, the 'losers,' the outcasts and the alienated."[55] In this work, Cox argued, the new breed had rediscovered the holiness of the poor and the radical egalitarianism that distinguished the early Christians but had been thoroughly vitiated since the Protestant Reformation.[56] These together, a repudiation of Victorian contempt for the poor and the "equalitarian vision of blessed community" pressed the new breed beyond charity to radical democracy.[57]

Again, the community organizing precepts of Saul Alinsky captured the imagination of the New Breed as the practical expression of this democratic vision. Alinsky was an agnostic Jew with a pugilistic spirit. He described politics in modern, secular terms, as a contest between formations of power guided by self-interested individuals. This could be seen as the final capitulation of liberal Protestantism to secularism, the purging of the residual millenarian hopes of the social gospel. But Alinsky's dogged devotion to the dignity, empowerment, and life of ordinary people deeply resonated with the retrieval of Christianity's commitment to community and abundant life among the outcasts of Empire.

Like the settlement house movement, the new breed proclaimed a commitment to working "with, not for" those on the margins. Protestant leaders received training in the principles of community organizing,

---

[52] Engel, *Saul Alinsky and the Chicago School*, 60.

[53] Fisher, *Let the People Decide*, 50.

[54] Cox, "The 'New Breed' in American Churches."

[55] The word "pressing" in Cox, "The 'New Breed' in American Churches," 136; the phrase "identify itself" in Eugene Carson Blake, "The Church in the Next Decade," *Christianity and Crisis* 26, no. 2 (1966): 17.

[56] Cox, "The 'New Breed' in American Churches," 142–45.

[57] Cox, "The 'New Breed' in American Churches," 145.

but most did not transcend the interval—expressed in racial, economic, cultural, linguistic and geographic terms—between them and the communities they sought to empower. The trained organizer, in some sense, occupied that same space of social mediation held by social work, the application of professional techniques to communities considered insufficiently empowered.

Was this a reprise of the technocratic evasion of politics—for democratic ends? The New Breed did not ultimately transcend its position in the professional-managerial class. They moved in the spaces of policymakers, foundations, and nonprofits. They had influence beyond their numbers in seminaries, denominations, and mission boards. Cox argued that the New Breed's radicalization was actually *fueled by* its insulation from local churches and lay accountability:

> Despite explicit doctrines of congregational autonomy and grassroots authority, something like a "managerial revolution" has taken place in the church. Many church leaders form and lead rather than merely reflect and represent the opinions of their constituencies. The coming of the managerial revolution to Protestantism means that the wrangle between the New Breed and its opponents is in no sense a battle for the freedom of laymen against a dominating clergy. It is often the reverse.[58]

The New Breed championed democratic empowerment but did so from the position of educated privilege, resources, and social capital. Here, again, was an enlightened paternalism, deployed to facilitate democratic empowerment.

This tension rankled in several directions. EHPP leaders like Norman Eddy had listened to criticism and attempted to genuinely support indigenous leadership, but, by the late 1960s, tolerance for white leadership from outside Black and Brown communities was wearing thin, to say the least.[59] "In 1967, an outgoing minister from the East Harlem Protestant Parish delivered a bitter final sermon denouncing the program ... as the 'East Harlem Protestant Plantation.'"[60] Benjamin Alicea's dissertation

---

[58] Cox, "The 'New Breed' in American Churches," 141.

[59] Mark Wild, "Liberal Protestants and Urban Renewal," *Religion and American Culture: A Journal of Interpretation* 25, no. 1 (2015): 128.

[60] Wild, "Liberal Protestants and Urban Renewal," 128.

on the EHPP was titled "Christian Urban Colonizers."[61] Conflicts over race, leadership, and resources ran through nearly every liberal Protestant institution. The New Breed fared no better on the other side; insulated from parish life, they failed to bring the denomination along with them. This came to a head in the Chicago Freedom Movement, in which fractures within religious support for Civil Rights erupted into violence.[62] By the 1980s, most of the institutional force of the New Breed had dissipated.

However we understand the relationship between secularism, the retrenchment of the 1970s, and the decline of Mainline Protestantism, today churches are struggling to reconstruct faith-filled community in a time of profound disconnection. Community organizing efforts are likewise fighting to create democratic spaces in a time of technocratic, managed, and marketized politics. In a time when institutions are struggling, what is the place of education—professional or otherwise—in supporting a democratic faith?

Throughout the history given here, the temptation of technocracy was entangled with the interval between religious leaders and the communities they helped, hurt, or otherwise experimented upon. There is a danger of reducing this interval to a flattened notion of identity that avoids the messiness of democratic life. What, for example, does it mean to come from a neighborhood when so many people are in constant motion? Who is given the authority to represent a given community? In organizing, this can lead to a politics of brokerage, where individuals claim an identity to position themselves as gatekeepers for information and resources. These brokers may or may not be leaders in Alinsky's sense (i.e., recognized as leaders by members of that community), and some wield the authority for dubious ends (e.g., personal gain). Most of us belong to multiple communities, and most communities are internally diverse. If we are serious about indigenous leadership, we need to hold all the complexity of indigeneity.

The question of indigenous leadership is further complicated by the position of the minister, who wields spiritual authority that cannot be reduced to technical expertise (although some Protestants have traveled a great distance in this direction). There is an important history of ministerial

---

[61] Benjamin Alicea, "Christian Urban Colonizers: A History of the East Harlem Protestant Parish in New York City, 1948–1968," PhD diss., Union Theological Seminary, 1989.

[62] Casey Bohlen, "The Politics of Conscience: Religious Activism and Social Change in Postwar America," PhD diss., Harvard University, 2016.

leadership, and a complex relationship between social status, education, professionalization, ministerial competence, and spiritual anointing. We can recognize the important place of clergy leadership just as we can recognize that clergy participation is not a substitute for broad democratic engagement.

Graham Taylor was dazzled by Chicago's aptly named "White City," the exhibition at the Chicago Columbian Exhibition of 1893 that showcased the possibility of a city made and remade by the power of technocracy. In *Azusa Reimagined*, Keri Day reads the democratic logics at work in the Pentecostal revival at Azusa Street as an inversion of the White City.[63] Azusa was unseemly, improper, and illegible to the Babylonian order represented by White City. In Taylor's bedazzlement we see the failure of white Progressive-era reformers to sustain attention to the vital Spirit at work in the lives of people of faith without racial power or credentialed authority. Neither could the EHPP see the Pentecostal storefronts covering East Harlem as anything other than otherworldly—though such churches were more successful at cultivating indigenous leadership, and even Archie Hargraves admitted to being outpreached.[64] Day makes an important connection between the unruly speech of Pentecostalism and the untidy practices of democratic life that resist being reduced to a spreadsheet cell. Whatever form theological education takes in the next era, it needs to develop sustained attention to the Spirit alive in the lives of God's people.

A Church marked by a Spirit that tends to be most manifest in those with the least social power should be suspicious of the promises of professional authority and expertise. But it is also true that our struggles are important sources of lifelong learning, and our common life deserves nothing less than our best efforts to listen, learn, and grow. The welfare rights slogan "the struggle is a school" points to something lost in an Alinsky-esque reduction of politics to interest and power, but present in the early evangelism of Graham Taylor: The Spirit does not leave us as we are. Democratic life and the Christian journey are both processes of transformation, transfiguring our identities and interests into something larger and deeper. We are asked to be "born again" in a way that troubles the algorithms that circumscribe our lives. We need formation, whether in the seminary classroom or on the protest line, not just information.

---

[63] Keri Day, *Azusa Reimagined: A Radical Vision of Religious and Democratic Belonging* (Stanford, CA: Stanford University Press, 2022).

[64] Wild, "Liberal Protestants and Urban Renewal," 122.

3

Traditions in Organizing:

A Social Catholic Perspective

Nicholas Hayes-Mota

Organizing and Tradition

Organizing is a practice with many traditions. There are diverse traditions *of* organizing: the organizing tradition descended from Saul Alinsky, for example, or the independent Black tradition exemplified by Ella Baker.[1] There are also diverse traditions *in* organizing: the larger intellectual, ethical, religious, and political traditions that invariably inform organizing traditions, such as the Social Gospel and democratic socialist traditions discussed elsewhere in this volume.[2] Traditions like these are important because they typically furnish the moral ideals and ethical frameworks that give broader vision and values to organizing. Reciprocally, traditions of organizing make these larger traditions politically effective in history by embodying them in specific practices, institutions, and, ultimately, communities of people.

The Catholic social tradition—or what I alternately call "social Catholicism"—is among the larger traditions that have informed and inspired organizing in many parts of the world, including the United States.[3] In the US context, however, this tradition remains either generally

---

[1] On these two traditions, see, respectively, Aaron Schutz and Mike Miller, eds., *People Power: The Community Organizing Tradition of Saul Alinsky* (Nashville: Vanderbilt University Press, 2015); Charles M. Payne, *I've Got the Light of Freedom: The Organizing Tradition and the Mississippi Freedom Struggle* (Berkeley: University of California Press, 2007).

[2] Many of the contributors, including myself, are students of Gary Dorrien, who is a historian of traditions (these and others) par excellence.

[3] In adopting this nomenclature, I follow, among others, Paul Misner, *Social*

unfamiliar or poorly understood, not least among Catholics and organizers themselves. This is unfortunate for at least two reasons. First, although more prominent in other organizing contexts, social Catholicism *has* played a significant role in the history of US organizing, in particular, that of the Alinsky tradition. Second, social Catholicism, in addition to being a distinctive strand within the Catholic religious tradition, is equally a distinct tradition of social ethics and politics. Much like "liberalism" and "socialism," with which it has often competed historically, social Catholicism advances a particular moral vision of society, which the tradition's members have developed and promoted through both their theorizing and their institutional practice. A greater familiarity with the Catholic social tradition can thus offer fresh insight into the forms of organizing it has influenced historically—in particular, into the moral vision and values that animate them. Simultaneously, I maintain, social Catholicism has both much to contribute to, and much to learn from, contemporary debates about the future of organizing. For it to have a voice in such debates, however, some grasp of the tradition and its history is first necessary, on the part of its own representatives as much as its interlocutors.

My primary aim in this chapter is to introduce social Catholicism as a distinct tradition in organizing and to identify some of its contributions to organizing in the United States. I begin, in the next section, by clarifying how I understand "tradition," drawing on the work of Alasdair MacIntyre.[4] In the following section I turn to social Catholicism to better define it as a tradition and to specify some of its distinct characteristics. Then I show how social Catholicism has played a critical and insufficiently appreciated role in organizing tradition descended from Saul Alinsky, tracing back to Alinsky himself. Finally, in the conclusion I consider some of the larger insights this history offers into the role of "tradition" in organizing.

Catholicism in Europe: From the Onset of Industrialization to the First World War (London: Darton, Longman, and Todd, 1991); and John A. Coleman, "The Future of Catholic Social Thought," in *Modern Catholic Social Teaching: Commentaries and Interpretations*, ed. Kenneth R. Himes (Washington, DC: Georgetown University Press, 2005), 522–44. In my assessment, Misner and Coleman are, respectively, the preeminent historical and theological US interpreters of social Catholicism.

[4] Although I adopt this particular element of MacIntyre's thought, I should not be understood as endorsing his entire theoretical and political project. As will become clear in my conclusion, even on the question of tradition, I diverge from MacIntyre in fundamental respects.

Thinking through Tradition: A MacIntyrean Approach

In *After Virtue* (1981), still his most widely read work, the Scottish moral philosopher Alasdair MacIntyre influentially defined a tradition as "an historically extended, socially embodied argument, and an argument precisely in part about the goods which constitute the tradition."[5] By defining tradition this way, MacIntyre immediately marked his opposition to an alternative and more commonplace conception of it, most famously represented by Edmund Burke (1729–1797). As MacIntyre critically observed, for Burke and other "conservative political theorists" who have put the category to "ideological uses," a tradition is an unquestioned and pre-reflective social consensus, preserved from generation to generation and essentially insulated from rational criticism; as such, it is defined by stability and continuity, and opposed to change and contestation.[6] Against this position, MacIntyre argues that traditions are better seen as "continuities of conflict," characterized by dynamic evolution as well as ongoing debate. In fact, MacIntyre suggests, it is the debate within a tradition that keeps it alive, by enabling it to adapt to continually changing circumstances and the new theoretical and practical problems they occasion. By contrast, "When a tradition becomes Burkean, it is always dying or dead."[7]

Beyond this most fundamental feature of traditions—that they are dynamic "arguments"—MacIntyre's definition succinctly identifies three further features of them; all, however, require further exposition to be properly understood. First, traditions are arguments about *goods:* ends of real human desire, which persons actively strive to achieve.[8] That traditions revolve around objects of desire is essential to understanding how they are characterized by both continuity and conflict across time. On one hand, the shared desire of a tradition's adherents for certain ends is part of what binds it together, uniting otherwise heterogeneous groups of people across diverse times and places. On the other hand, the conflicts within the

---

[5] Alasdair MacIntyre, *After Virtue: A Study in Moral Theory* (Notre Dame, IN: University of Notre Dame Press, 1984), 222.

[6] MacIntyre, *After Virtue*, 221.

[7] MacIntyre, *After Virtue*, 222.

[8] For MacIntyre's most developed exposition of his theory of "goods," which is broadly Aristotelian, see Alasdair MacIntyre, *Ethics in the Conflicts of Modernity: An Essay on Desire, Practical Reasoning, and Narrative* (Cambridge: Cambridge University Press, 2016), 1–69.

tradition are likewise fueled by disagreements over the goods that define it. These disagreements take many forms: Some may concern how best to achieve the goods in question, others how best to prioritize them when they appear to conflict, and still others—arguably the deepest disagreements—how to understand these goods themselves, or even what they consist in. By framing traditions as arguments about goods, MacIntyre thus also highlights how both reason and desire drive their development over time. Against conservative partisans and rationalist critics who juxtapose "tradition" to "reason," MacIntyre argues that every tradition has an immanent rationality: Its members not only disagree with each other, but pursue their disagreements through rational argument, relying on premises and standards internal to the tradition itself.[9] At the same time, traditions are not *only* creatures of reason. Only insofar as they engage the desires, imagination, and passions of their adherents will the latter become invested in the argument at all, much less remain involved in it.

Second, traditions are *historically extended* arguments. By this, MacIntyre means that their history is not accidental but essential to them, defining their identity and conditioning their possible future *as* the particular traditions they are: "Living traditions, just because they continue a not-yet-completed narrative, confront a future whose determinate and determinable character, so far as it possesses any, derives from the past."[10] Consequently, one can only learn what a particular tradition is by learning how it has come to be what it is, through the process of its historical development. Likewise, those who seek to enter into the argument of a tradition must first familiarize themselves with how that argument has gone "thus far." This is a precondition for being able to contribute constructively to it, whether by affirmation or critique.[11]

Third, traditions are *socially embodied* arguments. According to MacIntyre, even traditions that appear primarily theoretical or intellectual in nature are invariably "embodied with greater or lesser degrees of imperfection in social and political institutions which also draw their life from other sources."[12] The "Aristotelian tradition" of philosophy, for

---

[9] On the "rationality of traditions," see Alasdair MacIntyre, *Whose Justice? Which Rationality?* (Notre Dame, IN: University of Notre Dame Press, 1988), 349–69.

[10] MacIntyre, *After Virtue*, 223.

[11] On this point, see, e.g., MacIntyre, *Whose Justice? Which Rationality?* 1–11.

[12] MacIntyre, *Whose Justice? Which Rationality?* 349.

example, emerged "from the rhetorical and reflective life of the [Greek] *polis* and the dialectical teaching of the Academy and the Lyceum," whereas the "Augustinian tradition" of theology "flourished in the houses of religious orders and in the secular communities which provided the environment for such houses."[13] Far from being disembodied currents of ideas, in other words, intellectual traditions are the products of collective thinking by real communities of people. And these communities, in turn, rely on certain kinds of institutions, through which successive generations within a tradition are first introduced to its ideas; trained to understand, appreciate, and engage with them; and provided with the resources needed to preserve, develop, and promote them.

More radically, MacIntyre insists that the ideas specific to a tradition are not merely sustained but shaped by and embodied in the particular practices and institutions associated with it. "Philosophical theories give organized expression to concepts and theories already embodied in forms of practice and types of community," MacIntyre summarizes; reciprocally, "Forms of social institution, organization, and practice are always to greater or lesser degree socially embodied theories and, as such, more or less rational according to the standards of that type of rationality which is presupposed by tradition-constituted inquiry."[14] "Theory" and "practice," for MacIntyre, are thus not opposed categories, but complementary ones. They name analytically distinct but reciprocally interdependent features of social reality, such that practices "embody" implicit concepts and theories whereas explicit theories "express" or "articulate" the ideas already inherent in practices, while thereby making them susceptible of further analysis, critique, and development. This holistic understanding of theory and practice founds MacIntyre's further claim that there are "traditions" not only of theory but also of practice. In fact, for MacIntyre, every true practice has its own tradition, which exemplifies all of the general features of a tradition I have just described. Such traditions of practice may be understood as the historically extended and socially embodied arguments through which the goods at which a practice aims—and the "standards of excellence" associated with those goods—are clarified, debated, and, over time, both refined and reinvented.[15]

---

[13] MacIntyre, *Whose Justice? Which Rationality?* 349.
[14] MacIntyre, *Whose Justice? Which Rationality?* 390.
[15] MacIntyre, *After Virtue,* 193–94.

Summarized in these terms, MacIntyre's general account of traditions may accordingly be applied to organizing. As I have argued elsewhere, organizing is very much a form of "practice," in MacIntyre's sense, and as such, possessed of a tradition.[16] More precisely, the term "organizing" can be understood to refer to a broad family of practices that meaningfully resemble each other yet that have developed through a variety of historically and institutionally distinct, if often intersecting, traditions.[17] Furthermore, these traditions themselves often contain multiple branches, which may in turn be treated as traditions (as MacIntyre conceives them) in their own right.[18] The Alinsky tradition of organizing that I consider below, for example, arguably encompasses both the "faith-based" or "broad-based" organizing tradition that grew out of Alinsky's Industrial Areas Foundation (IAF) in the 1970s, as well as the related-yet-distinct tradition of farmworker organizing that emerged and branched off from the IAF earlier, in the 1960s.[19] Both of these sub-traditions within the Alinsky tradition trace back historically to Alinsky himself, yet each developed a distinct conception of organizing, as well as a distinct set of practices and institutions to embody and promote it.

If MacIntyre's general theory of traditions is thus applicable to organizing, it also provides an illuminating lens through which to reflect on it, for several reasons. First, seeing organizing as a broad family of practices that have developed in and through multiple traditions acknowledges the rich pluralism, as well as the historical variability, that has always been characteristic of organizing as a field of practice. Second, it foregrounds the pervasive presence of contention, both *within* individual traditions

---

[16] Nicholas Hayes-Mota, "Principle in Practice: A MacIntyrean Analysis of Community Organizing and the Catholic Social Tradition," *Journal of Catholic Social Thought* 21, no. 2 (2024): 207–28.

[17] In its most general sense, I understand "organizing" to refer to forms of practice that build relationships and develop social agency among individuals to form a constituency capable of strategic collective action, and that in turn mobilize that constituency to achieve collectively determined ends.

[18] This characteristic is not unique to traditions of organizing: the concept of "tradition" itself, as MacIntyre theorizes it, is susceptible of multiple levels of application, just as the concept of "practice" is.

[19] Both are discussed, as branches of the Alinsky tradition, in Schutz and Miller, *People Power*, 87–123, 195–244.

of organizing and *across* the diverse traditions of organizing.[20] Third, MacIntyre's framework clarifies that the arguments among organizing traditions are always simultaneously about both "theory" and "practice"; these two dimensions are reciprocally interdependent and mutually informing. Fourth, MacIntyre also helps us understand why debates in organizing can be so sharp, as they frequently are. Ultimately, these conflicts are about goods, things human beings want and for which they strive; even disputes about apparently technical matters of practice (tactical questions, say) or abstract points of theory may therefore have at their base more fundamental disagreements over the goods at which organizing's practitioners aim. And often, in organizing, these goods are weighty ones indeed.

This is in part because individual traditions of organizing are typically themselves informed by what MacIntyre (in *After Virtue*) calls "larger social traditions," from which "the traditions through which particular practices are transmitted and reshaped never exist in isolation."[21] Such larger social traditions, exemplified by religious and philosophical traditions, furnish the overarching conceptions of "the good"—the more or less coherent visions of a good human life, a good society, and the moral order of the world—that gives collective identity and ethical orientation to entire societies, including the whole complex of practices and institutions that subsist within them.[22]

Although all practices depend on these larger traditions, organizing is especially dependent on them. Most forms of organizing are explicitly directed toward bringing about significant changes in the social order. To this extent, they presuppose some orienting conception of the good (or the better) society they seek to bring about. These conceptions, of course, may be more or less theoretically articulate, explicit, and coherent, as well as more or less conscious on the part of practitioners. Just because they are often implicit and relatively unconscious, however, does not mean they are not present in the practice itself.

An important task of theoretical reflection on organizing, it follows, is to make these larger visions of the good and their associated ethical frameworks explicit, so that they become available for more intentional

---

[20] MacIntyre theorizes both kinds of contention in *Whose Justice? Which Rationality?* esp. 349–403.

[21] MacIntyre, *After Virtue*, 221.

[22] Alasdair MacIntyre, "Politics, Philosophy, and the Common Good," in *The MacIntyre Reader*, ed. Kelvin Knight (Oxford: Polity Press, 1998), 235–54, esp. 239–43.

rational examination, debate, and development (or, possibly, rejection). One way to accomplish this is by bringing to the foreground the larger social traditions that have influenced particular traditions of organizing and showing how they have done so. Such is what I now propose to do, turning to the Catholic social tradition.

Social Catholicism as a Tradition: History, Vision, and Institutions

What is the Catholic social tradition, or "social Catholicism," as I shall alternately call it here? Let me begin by distinguishing it from what it is not. Most important, social Catholicism is neither the same as, nor coextensive with, the Catholic tradition as a whole. To the contrary, it is a specific and distinctly modern sub-tradition *within* Catholicism, which originated only two centuries ago and which has only ever counted a comparative minority of Catholics among its actively engaged members.[23] Moreover, social Catholicism, though related to doctrinal "Catholic Social Teaching" and "Catholic social thought," is not reducible to either.[24] "Catholic Social Teaching" refers to the Catholic hierarchy's formal body of doctrinal teaching on social and political questions and is typically traced back to Pope Leo XIII's landmark 1891 encyclical, *Rerum Novarum*. "Catholic social thought," meanwhile, refers to the broader current ideas from which Social Teaching arose, and through which it has been further developed. "Social Catholicism," by comparison, is a broader category, naming the larger tradition that produced both Catholic Social Teaching (the tradition's doctrinal expression) and Catholic social thought (the tradition's intellectual expression). As a socially embodied tradition in MacIntyre's sense, social Catholicism is not only a tradition of theories or ideas but also of practices and institutions.[25] It is also an explicitly *political* tradition, which

---

[23] Misner, *Social Catholicism in Europe*, 40.

[24] In distinguishing these three terms, I follow Coleman, "The Future of Catholic Social Thought," 522–25.

[25] Here I diverge from Johan Verstraeten, who has previously interpreted the Catholic social tradition on MacIntyrean lines. Verstraeten concentrates almost exclusively on Catholic social *thought*, to the neglect of the tradition's social embodiment. See Johan Verstraeten, "Re-Thinking Catholic Social Thought as Tradition," in *Catholic Social Thought: Twilight or Renaissance?* ed. J. S. Boswell, F. P. McHugh, and J. Verstraeten (Leuven, Belgium: Leuven University Press, 2000), 59–78.

has served as the mobilizing ideology for millions of people. As such, it may be fruitfully compared with the analogous traditions of liberalism and socialism, against which social Catholics have frequently defined themselves since the tradition's formative decades.[26]

Like all traditions, social Catholicism cannot be understood in abstraction from its history. It originated during the 1820s and 1830s in Western Europe, when Catholic thinkers across the continent—then the church's intellectual and institutional center—began to grapple with "the social question." As Paul Misner explains, the "social question" at the time referred to the whole constellation of new problems occasioned by the rise of industrial capitalism, such as the breakdown of traditional social institutions (including church institutions); rural dislocation and chaotic urbanization; growing economic inequality; the immiseration of the urban working class; and escalating class conflict.[27] Within this context, what distinguished social Catholics from both earlier Catholic thinkers and most of their Catholic contemporaries was their specific preoccupation with the social question and their conviction that addressing the problems associated with it would require serious social reform, not merely traditional charity. On both counts, social Catholics resembled their counterparts in the socialist tradition, which arose in roughly the same time and context to address the same concerns. Unlike most socialists, however, social Catholics believed that the Catholic Church itself had a (perhaps *the*) central role to play in saving society from the evils of modern capitalism and "modernity" writ large. Indeed, many ascribed these evils to modern "individualism," whose roots they traced back to Enlightenment liberalism and its own pernicious parent, the Protestant Reformation.[28]

To early social Catholics, in other words, addressing the social question could not be separated from re-Catholicizing society, in one way or another. This feature of the tradition, which has endured throughout its history, has often given it a conservative tendency, which for most of the nineteenth century was the dominant one.[29] Nevertheless, even then, as John Coleman notes, the tradition was characterized by plurality and contention—in

---

[26] John A. Coleman, "Neither Liberal nor Socialist: The Originality of Catholic Social Teaching," in *One Hundred Years of Catholic Social Thought: Celebration and Challenge*, ed. John A. Coleman (Maryknoll, NY: Orbis Books, 1991), 25–42.

[27] Misner, *Social Catholicism in Europe*, 39–40.

[28] Misner, *Social Catholicism in Europe*, 42–43.

[29] Misner, *Social Catholicism in Europe*, 42.

short, by argument. In France, for example, long one of social Catholicism's major centers, Coleman identifies no fewer than five competing political expressions of the tradition: "reactionary, traditionalist authoritarianism," "paternalist reformist aristocrats," "liberal Catholicism," "Christian Democrats and meliorists," and "Christian socialists."[30] All of these strands of the tradition, Coleman continues, shared certain common characteristics, including an anti-capitalist bias, a privileging of "the social" over "the political," a pluralistic (rather than state-centric) view of authority, and a bias toward social and economic rights (as distinct from, and sometimes in opposition to, civil and political liberties).[31] Beyond these commonalities, however, they diverged sharply in the larger social visions they endorsed, as well as the concrete political agendas they sought to advance.

When Pope Leo XIII promulgated *Rerum Novarum* ("Of New Things")—the first papal encyclical on "the social question"—in 1891, he effectively constituted a doctrinal center of gravity for the tradition, one that has continued to endure to this day.[32] In MacIntyrean terms, Leo's encyclical established new standards for doctrinally legitimate argument within the tradition, both by identifying certain premises and principles as especially fundamental to it, and by identifying the boundaries beyond which it could not go (for example, the total abolition of private property, which Leo explicitly rejected). Subsequent documents of doctrinal Social Teaching, beginning with Pius XI's *Quadragesimo Anno* (1931) and continuing up to the present with Pope Francis's social encyclicals (such as *Laudato Si'* [2015] and *Fratelli Tutti* [2020]), have continued to exercise this regulative function, while further elaborating the doctrinal core that has ever since defined the tradition's mainstream.[33]

At the same time, it is important to recognize that all these documents, starting with *Rerum Novarum* itself, are as much *products* of the Catholic social tradition as authoritative statements of it: Both the theoretical frameworks they employ and the specific practical and institutional proposals they advance derive from the wider tradition

---

[30] Coleman, "Neither Liberal nor Socialist," 28–32.

[31] Coleman, "Neither Liberal nor Socialist," 32–35.

[32] On the historical context and reception of this encyclical, see Misner, *Social Catholicism in Europe*, 213–26.

[33] The core documents of Catholic Social Teaching, up to 2015 and in English translation, are compiled in David J. O'Brien and Thomas A. Shannon, eds., *Catholic Social Thought: Encyclicals and Documents from Pope Leo XIII to Pope Francis*, 3rd rev. ed. (Maryknoll, NY: Orbis Books, 2016).

they subsequently function to regulate. In *Rerum Novarum*'s case, for example, the well-developed ethical framework the encyclical used to analyze the social question derived from the neo-Thomistic "social philosophy" first pioneered by Luigi Taparelli D'Azeglio (1793–1862), the former Jesuit mentor of Leo himself.[34] Likewise, the encyclical's various practical proposals, from its support for labor regulations to its explicit defense of labor unions, all reflected prior ideas—and responded to prior arguments—within the wider tradition.[35]

Through this dynamic interplay between the ongoing argument within social Catholicism, on one hand, and the consolidating influence of Catholic Social Teaching, on the other, the Catholic social tradition has increasingly come to revolve around certain "core principles." Collectively, these principles have given further definition to the larger vision of the goods shared across the tradition's various strands, even as the precise number, order, and formulation of them remains subject to debate.[36] In my view, however, two such principles stand out as especially fundamental to the tradition as it has developed thus far. The first is the *dignity of the human person;* the second is the *primacy of the common good*.[37]

As now understood within social Catholicism, the dignity of the person refers to the sacred, unique, and transcendent value possessed by each human being simply by virtue of her creation in the image of God and

---

[34] On Taparelli, see Thomas C. Behr, *Social Justice and Subsidiarity: Luigi Taparelli and the Origins of Modern Catholic Social Thought* (Washington, DC: Catholic University of America Press, 2019).

[35] For more on the intellectual and political context of *Rerum Novarum*, see Thomas A. Shannon, "Commentary on *Rerum Novarum* (The Condition of Labor)," in *Modern Catholic Social Teaching: Commentaries and Interpretations*, ed. Kenneth R. Himes et al. (Washington, DC: Georgetown University Press, 2005), 127–50.

[36] In 2004, under Pope John Paul II, the Pontifical Council for Justice and Peace issued a *Compendium of the Social Doctrine of the Church*, which articulated a number of such core principles. Both its enumeration and its exposition of these principles, however, have been subject to debate. The *Compendium* is available online at https://www.vatican.va/roman_curia/pontifical_councils/justpeace/documents/rc_pc_justpeace_doc_20060526_compendio-dott-soc_en.html.

[37] I follow Todd Whitmore, among others, in seeing these two principles as equally fundamental. See Todd David Whitmore, "Catholic Social Teaching: Starting with the Common Good," in *Living the Catholic Social Tradition: Cases and Commentary*, ed. Kathleen Maas Weigert and Alexia K. Kelley (Lanham, MD: Rowman & Littlefield, 2005), 59–85.

her vocation to final communion with God. On account of this dignity, all human beings are equal in value, regardless of natural ability or social status; conversely, no human being can be rightly subordinated as an instrumental means to any other individual or societal end, such as the maximization of wealth or the pursuit of national power and glory. To the contrary, society itself exists for the sake of the persons who constitute it, such that it is obligated to promote their integral (bodily, social, moral, and spiritual) flourishing above all.[38] Doctrinal Catholic Social Teaching further insists that an expansive array of human rights follow by rational necessity from human dignity, including both the civil and political rights historically emphasized by classical liberal traditions and the social and economic rights (to healthcare, education, employment, a just wage, and so on) emphasized by socialist traditions.[39]

Meanwhile, doctrinal Catholic Social Teaching formally defines the common good itself as "the sum of those conditions of social life which allow social groups and their individual members relatively thorough and ready access to their own fulfillment."[40] Both the sheer existence of the common good (the fact that human beings really do share such a thing) and its essential characteristics as such are understood to derive from the constitutively social nature of the human person. Because human beings are made by God for relationship with others, our flourishing as individuals is dependent in manifold ways on the "social conditions" we share with others. Furthermore, we can only attain flourishing as individuals and actualize our own dignity as persons by actively contributing to the common good we all share.[41] Reciprocally, however, because the common good is itself nothing other than the complex of social conditions that promote persons'

---

[38] For the authoritative doctrinal exposition of these aspects of human dignity, see Pope Paul VI, *Gaudium et Spes*, 1965, 12–17, 23–25; available online at https://www.vatican.va/archive/hist_councils/ii_vatican_council/documents/vat-ii_const_19651207_gaudium-et-spes_en.html. For a fuller philosophical and theological elaboration, see Anna Rowlands, *Towards a Politics of Communion: Catholic Social Teaching in Dark Times* (London: T&T Clark, 2022), 46–72.

[39] See Pope John XXIII, *Pacem in Terris*, 1963, para. 8–27, available online at https://www.vatican.va/content/john-xxiii/en/encyclicals/documents/hf_j-xxiii_enc_11041963_pacem.html.

[40] *Gaudium et Spes*, para. 26. See para. 27–32 for further development.

[41] For further reflection on the theological foundations of the common good, as it is understood in Catholic thought, see Rowlands, *Towards a Politics of Communion*, 125–75.

flourishing, it cannot be defined in opposition to individual rights or well-being. Indeed, doctrinal Catholic Social Teaching affirms that the first and most fundamental requirement of the common good is establishing a juridical order that fully recognizes, and institutionalizes, the rights of the person, while also specifying each person's corresponding obligations to serve the common good by exercising those rights responsibly.[42]

Other core principles of the Catholic social tradition further flesh out this basic conception of the common good. What is now termed the *principle of solidarity*, for instance, specifies that a society truly promotive of the common good must foster a strong sense of community and mutual responsibility among all of society's members: Their *feeling* that they share a common good, and are obligated to pursue it together, is a critical element of the common good itself.[43] Correlatively, the *principle of subsidiarity* specifies that a social order reflective of the common good must sustain a flourishing civil society of "intermediary institutions" (that is, institutions that stand between the individual and the state), such as families, religious congregations, fraternal associations, cooperative societies, labor unions, and civic organizations. Only through such institutions, the principle holds, can individuals form the relationships, develop the practical skills and moral dispositions, and share in the structured collective agency required to fully contribute to the common good. For this reason, intermediary institutions—and specifically those closest to the level of the individual person—must be given as much freedom, agency, and social responsibility as possible.[44]

This emphasis on intermediary institutions as the essential vehicles for promoting the common good, succinctly encapsulated in the principle of subsidiarity, has been a consistent feature of social Catholicism from its

---

[42] *Pacem in Terris*, para. 60.

[43] On solidarity, see, e.g., Gerald J. Beyer, "The Meaning of Solidarity in Catholic Social Teaching," *Political Theology* 15, no. 1 (2014): 7–25. Cf. Pope John Paul II, *Sollicitudo Rei Socialis*, 1987, para. 35–40, available online at https://www.vatican.va/content/john-paul-ii/en/encyclicals/documents/hf_jp-ii_enc_30121987_sollicitudo-rei-socialis.html.

[44] On subsidiarity, see Rowlands, *Towards a Politics of Communion*, 215–37. Cf. Pope Pius XI, *Quadragesimo Anno*, 1931, 78–80, https://www.vatican.va/content/pius-xi/en/encyclicals/documents/hf_p-xi_enc_19310515_quadragesimo-anno.html; *Pacem in Terris*, para. 23–24; Pope Francis, *Laudato Si'*, 2015, 156–57, https://www.vatican.va/content/francesco/en/encyclicals/documents/papa-francesco_20150524_enciclica-laudato-si.html.

origins to the present. By centering such institutions, and the broader sphere of civil society, social Catholics have sought to steer a course between atomistic "individualism" and state-driven "collectivism," which the tradition's polemicists have respectively (and often unfairly) equated with liberalism and socialism.[45] Neither is social Catholicism's stress on intermediary institutions confined only to its theory and normative vision of society. It is just as much reflected in the tradition's own practice, socially embodied in a long history of organizing and institution building.

That history, too, traces back to the mid-nineteenth century, when social Catholic institution-builders first began to create new kinds of organizations as a first line of response to the problems associated with the social question. As the century progressed, they cultivated a rich ecosystem of social Catholic institutions throughout Europe, ranging from cooperative societies to experimental economic enterprises to popular education associations. Most of these, while explicitly Catholic in identity, ideology, and constituency, were not directly incorporated into the formal hierarchical structure of the church.[46] Toward the end of the nineteenth century, social Catholics also began to develop more directly political forms of association, such as confessionally Catholic labor unions and, later, Catholic political parties. Collectively, these "carrier institutions" created both a mass base and a leadership class for the tradition, enabling it to directly compete with other major political blocs (liberals, socialists, Protestants, and secular conservatives) in the arenas of organized labor and parliamentary politics.[47]

Subsequently, during the first half of the twentieth century, social Catholicism grew into a truly transatlantic mass movement, spanning Western Europe, Latin America, and to a lesser extent the United States. Under Pius XI (1922–1939), leaders operating under the banner of "Catholic Action" (and with the pope's blessing) built out a vast international network of lay-led organizations, drawing in millions of

---

[45] This is a central theme of Coleman, "Neither Liberal nor Socialist."

[46] For an overview of these efforts across Western Europe, see Misner, *Social Catholicism in Europe,* 56–212.

[47] I take the concept of "carrier institutions" from John Coleman. See, e.g., Coleman, "The Future of Catholic Social Thought," 526–59. For more on Catholic unions and parties, see Misner, *Social Catholicism in Europe,* 227–318, as well as its sequel: Paul Misner, *Catholic Labor Movements in Europe: Social Thought and Action, 1914–1965* (Washington, DC: Catholic University of America Press, 2015).

Catholics from both the elite and popular classes and forming them in the ideas and ideals of social Catholicism.[48] Although some strands of Catholic Action notoriously collaborated with fascist and authoritarian regimes, as did many officials in the church hierarchy, other branches served as critical centers of non-cooperation or resistance. After World War II, Catholic Action in turn provided the primary base, as well as the intellectual and political leadership, for the new Christian Democratic parties that rapidly rose to power across Western Europe and, somewhat later, in parts of Latin America. Ideologically founded on Catholic Social Teaching, but broad-based and ecumenical in membership, these Christian Democratic parties created many of Western Europe's now decades-old welfare states, with the notable exception of those in Britain and Scandinavia, where, for want of a large enough Catholic constituency, they never attained a meaningful presence.[49] In Latin America, most of Catholic liberation theology's founding generation likewise emerged from the organizations of Catholic Action and Christian Democracy, before their experiences in the late 1960s led them to turn toward a more radical form of theology and politics.[50] Though they initially defined themselves against social Catholicism's midcentury mainstream, and aroused strong opposition from its defenders, these liberationists developed new ideas (such as the preferential option for the poor) and institutional forms (such as ecclesial base communities) that were eventually recognized as vital contributions to the tradition by doctrinal Catholic Social Teaching itself.[51]

In the United States, by contrast, social Catholicism never established an institutional, intellectual, or political foothold comparable to that which

---

[48] Misner, *Catholic Labor Movements in Europe*, 121–42, 184–211.

[49] For an overview of Christian Democracy across the transatlantic, see Carlo Invernizzi Accetti, *What Is Christian Democracy? Politics, Religion and Ideology* (Cambridge: Cambridge University Press, 2019). On its role in postwar Europe, see James Chappel, *Catholic Modern: The Challenge of Totalitarianism and the Making of the Church* (Cambridge, MA: Harvard University Press, 2018), 144–226. On the movement in Latin America, see Scott Mainwaring and Timothy Scully, eds., *Christian Democracy in Latin America* (Stanford, CA: Stanford University Press, 2003).

[50] On the roots and genesis of Latin American liberation theology, see Christian Smith, *The Emergence of Liberation Theology: Radical Religion and Social Movement Theory* (Chicago: University of Chicago Press, 1991), 71–149.

[51] On the long and contentious relationship between liberation theology and doctrinal Catholic Social Teaching, see Donal Dorr, *Option for the Poor and for the Earth: From Leo XIII to Pope Francis*, rev. ed. (Maryknoll, NY: Orbis Books, 2016).

it achieved in Europe and Latin America. One reason for this may be the United States' distinctive character as a country historically dominated (demographically and culturally) by Protestantism yet constitutionally committed to freedom of religion. As a result, US Catholics have had at once less to gain, and more to lose, by mobilizing politically around their Catholic identity than they have elsewhere. Another reason may be the largely immigrant composition and ethnic diversity of the Catholic Church in the United States, which have made it more difficult to foster a sense of shared Catholic identity. Consequently, though Catholics in the United States did construct a vast network of intermediary institutions (parochial schools, hospitals, and so on) to serve the needs of their communities, they tended to eschew the more politically oriented institutions—confessionally Catholic labor unions, politicized Catholic Action organizations, Christian Democratic parties—that created the constituency for social Catholicism in other countries. Hence the relative unfamiliarity of most US Catholics today with even doctrinal Catholic Social Teaching, to say nothing of the larger Catholic social tradition.[52]

That being said, there are important exceptions. At the intellectual level, the United States has produced some truly outstanding, and widely influential, social Catholic thinkers, such as John Ryan and John Courtney Murray.[53] At the institutional level, social Catholicism within the United States has borne fruit in various forms of labor organizing: most famously, perhaps, the Catholic Worker movement, which Dorothy Day and Peter Maurin founded in New York in 1933.[54] Another, much less-recognized expression of social Catholicism, however, is the tradition of community organizing descended from Saul Alinsky.[55] I now proceed to justify that claim.

---

[52] My assessment of social Catholicism in the United States here draws principally on Coleman, "The Future of Catholic Social Thought"; John A. Coleman, *An American Strategic Theology* (New York: Paulist Press, 1982); and José Casanova, *Public Religions in the Modern World* (Chicago: University of Chicago Press, 1994), 167–207.

[53] Both Ryan and Murray are profiled, respectively, in Gary Dorrien, *Social Ethics in the Making: Interpreting an American Tradition* (Malden, MA: Wiley-Blackwell, 2009), 185–215 and 334–61.

[54] The Catholic Worker is also profiled in Dorrien, *Social Ethics in the Making*, 361–77.

[55] This claim was made earlier by John Coleman in "The Future of Catholic Social Thought," 536–37.

Traditions Intertwined:
Social Catholicism and the Alinsky Tradition

The suggestion that the Alinsky organizing tradition represents an expression of social Catholicism may seem, at first, quite implausible. For one, Saul Alinsky himself was certainly not Catholic. Jewish in heritage and agnostic for most of his adult life, he was also notoriously irreverent toward organized religion, including the Catholic Church.[56] Neither did Alinsky nor the organizers he trained ever seek to create explicitly or exclusively Catholic organizations, as social Catholics often did elsewhere. Indeed, though Alinsky and his Industrial Areas Foundation (IAF) built local "people's organizations" that counted Catholic churches among their members, these organizations included many other kinds of institutions (labor unions, block clubs, fraternal associations) as well. Furthermore, the people's organizations Alinsky built in the later part of his career (1958 to 1972) were intentionally ecumenical in orientation, uniting white Protestants, Black Protestants, and Catholics at a time when collaboration among these groups was still rare.[57] In this regard, the major faith-based organizing networks descended from Alinsky—the post-Alinsky IAF, Faith in Action (formerly Pacific Institute for Community Organization—PICO), Gamaliel, and DART (Direct Action Research and Training)—have only extended his legacy, embracing an overtly "interfaith" identity that is increasingly reflected in their mission, leadership, and membership.[58] Nevertheless, a closer examination of the Alinsky tradition's history reveals a long-standing, profound, and distinct connection to the Catholic social tradition, one that traces back all the way to the project that launched Alinsky's own career as an organizer.

The site of that project was Chicago's Back of the Yards neighborhood, where Alinsky began organizing in 1938. Made nationally notorious decades prior by Upton Sinclair's *The Jungle* (1906), Back of the Yards was

---

[56] For Alinsky's biography, see Sanford D. Horwitt, *Let Them Call Me Rebel: Saul Alinsky—His Life and Legacy* (New York: Vintage, 1989).

[57] As discussed in P. David Finks, *The Radical Vision of Saul Alinsky* (New York: Paulist Press, 1984), 109–228.

[58] On this interfaith turn, see Brad Fulton and Richard L. Wood, "Interfaith Community Organizing: Emerging Theological and Organizational Challenges," in *Yours the Power: Faith-Based Organizing in the USA*, ed. Katie Day, Esther McIntosh, and William Storrar (Leiden: Brill, 2013), 17–40.

a squalid, working-class neighborhood adjacent to the city's meatpacking stockyards. It was also over 90 percent Catholic, yet sharply divided along ethnic lines. The Polish, Irish, Lithuanian, Slovak, German, and Mexican immigrant Catholics who lived in the neighborhood all worshipped in their own national parishes, presided over by conservative old-world priests who wielded great authority and were quick to denounce anything that smacked of "socialism."[59] On account of the mutual hostility and cultural conservatism of the neighborhood's ethnic groups, all prior attempts to organize a labor union in Back of the Yards had failed. Alinsky won fame for himself by succeeding.

Within two years of his arrival, he had organized the neighborhood's parishes and other membership institutions into a single federation, the "Back of the Yards Neighborhood Council" (BYNC), and galvanized the new organization to throw its collective support behind a union drive, winning a contract shortly thereafter.[60] In significant part, Alinsky's triumph owed to the innovative organizing methodology he developed along the way, which set the basic template he would continue to employ, with ongoing revisions, throughout his career. Yet Alinsky's success was also dependent on the strong relationships he established with key Catholic leaders, and two in particular: Joseph Meegan and Bernard Sheil. Meegan, an Irish Catholic layman, was Alinsky's primary partner in organizing the BYNC, which he went on to lead for many years thereafter.[61] Sheil, to whom Meegan introduced Alinsky, was auxiliary bishop of Chicago and the figure who first made the connection between Alinsky and the wider tradition of social Catholicism.

When Alinsky met Sheil, the bishop already had a national profile. Steeped in the Catholic social tradition, he was the head of the national Catholic Youth Organization (CYO) and an outspoken advocate for organized labor.[62] Upon learning of Alinsky's project in Back of the Yards, the bishop was immediately struck by its alignment with the core values of social Catholicism. Though not a Catholic himself, Alinsky was bringing

---

[59] Horwitt, *Let Them Call Me Rebel*, 56–62; Finks, *Radical Vision of Saul Alinsky*, 16.

[60] Horwitt, *Let Them Call Me Rebel*, 67–76.

[61] On Meegan, see Horwitt, *Let Them Call Me Rebel*, 63–76, 83–85; Finks, *Radical Vision of Saul Alinsky*, 16–17.

[62] See Horwitt, *Let Them Call Me Rebel*, 69–76; Finks, *Radical Vision of Saul Alinsky*, 17–18.

working-class Catholics together across their ethnic divisions to advance their rights and pursue the common good, in solidarity with each other. In the process, he was also helping to foster a sense of shared Catholic identity, which was a priority of the Chicago archdiocese (a center of social Catholicism) at the time.[63] Furthermore, in accord with the principle of subsidiarity, Alinsky's organizing strategy was directly focused on intermediary institutions, whose collective agency it sought to enhance by uniting them under a new kind of intermediary institution, namely, the "people's organization." For all of these reasons, Sheil not only championed Alinsky's work in Back of the Yards, but also agitated the organizer to see its broader potential. After helping Alinsky get the BYNC off the ground by actively promoting it to neighborhood priests (Sheil was even the featured guest at its founding convention),[64] the bishop worked closely with him to create an institution that could develop analogous organizations around the country. That institution, of course, was the Industrial Areas Foundation (IAF), which Sheil co-founded with Alinsky and Marshall Field III (a progressive Protestant philanthropist, and a connection of Sheil's) in 1940. Beyond persuading Alinsky to create the IAF in the first place, Sheil also co-wrote its mission statement, recruited its board, and raised its initial operating funds.[65]

Through Sheil and his extensive Catholic connections, Alinsky in turn came into relationship with a number of other prominent social Catholics. One of these was Jacques Maritain, an internationally renowned neo-Thomist philosopher whose ideas exercised a pivotal influence on both the transatlantic movement for Christian Democracy and, eventually, the Second Vatican Council.[66] Like Sheil, Maritain was drawn to Alinsky because he saw his organizing as a uniquely promising vehicle for putting social Catholicism's vision into practice. Upon reading Alinsky's first book,

---

[63] See Horwitt, *Let Them Call Me Rebel*, 69–70; Luke Bretherton, *Resurrecting Democracy: Faith, Citizenship, and the Politics of a Common Life* (Cambridge: Cambridge University Press, 2015), 35–36.

[64] Horwitt, *Let Them Call Me Rebel*, 73.

[65] Horwitt, *Let Them Call Me Rebel*, 84–87; Finks, *Radical Vision of Saul Alinsky*, 23–24.

[66] For further background on Maritain and his relationship to Alinsky, see Nicholas Hayes-Mota, "Partners in Forming the People: Jacques Maritain, Saul Alinsky, and the Project of Personalist Democracy," *Journal of Moral Theology* 13, special issue, no. 1 (2024): 121–45.

Reveille for Radicals (1946), the philosopher pronounced that it revealed "a new way for *real* democracy, the only way in which man's thirst for social communion can develop and be satisfied, through freedom and not through totalitarianism in our disintegrated times."[67] Through the BYNC and the incipient IAF, Alinsky had developed a practice that could awaken people to their own dignity and their collective responsibility for the common good—of their own community, of their country, and perhaps even the wider world—simultaneously and created a plausible institutional vehicle for promoting both.[68] Because of the deep ethical, political, and spiritual affinity he felt with Alinsky, Maritain sustained a personal friendship with the organizer until the latter's death in 1972. He also passionately promoted his work, even arranging a meeting with the future Pope Paul VI in the hopes that that the Vatican might support Alinsky-style organizing projects across Europe, as a more grassroots—and, Maritain believed, superior—alternative to formal Christian Democratic political parties.[69]

If social Catholics like Sheil and Maritain saw Alinsky's organizing as an expression of their own tradition, to what extent did Alinsky himself see it this way? On one hand, by the time Alinsky formed relationships with his Catholic collaborators, he had already for the most part developed his basic methodology for organizing. Although multiple larger traditions informed his thinking (American pragmatism, Chicago sociology, radical democracy, populism, and perhaps his ancestral Judaism, among others), social Catholicism was not initially one of them.[70] The alignment Sheil and Maritain perceived was thus, at first, fortuitous.[71] On the other hand,

---

[67] Bernard Doering, ed., *The Philosopher and the Provocateur: The Correspondence of Jacques Maritain and Saul Alinsky* (Notre Dame, IN: University of Notre Dame Press, 1994), 11.

[68] See Maritain's original review of *Reveille*, reprinted in Doering, *The Philosopher and the Provocateur*, 18–20.

[69] Finks, *Radical Vision of Saul Alinsky*, 114–19.

[70] On the various traditions that influenced Alinsky, see, e.g., Bretherton, *Resurrecting Democracy*, 21–40; Lawrence J. Engel, "Saul D. Alinsky and the Chicago School," *Journal of Speculative Philosophy*, new series, 16, no. 1 (2002): 50–66.

[71] It could be argued that it was not *entirely* fortuitous, since some of the sources that influenced Alinsky—Alexis de Tocqueville (a liberal social Catholic), Aristotelianism (mediated through Deweyan pragmatism), Judaism—would have established a substantive common ground with his social Catholic counterparts. Further pursuing this argument, however, would take me beyond the bounds of this essay.

through his relationships with these and other social Catholics, Alinsky evidently came to recognize the alignment himself and actively further developed it. In private correspondence, for instance, Alinsky called Maritain "a man who has had more influence on me than anyone else I know and who is infinitely precious to me"; he likewise credited him as the catalyst and inspiration for *Reveille*.[72] Meanwhile, in his public writings, from *Reveille* to *Rules for Radicals* (1971), Alinsky explicitly anchored his larger vision of democracy in the dignity of the person and the primacy of the common good, while affirming that democracy rested on "Judeo-Christian" foundations.[73] Luke Bretherton is thus correct to conclude that in "the emerging expression of Christian Democracy and Roman Catholic social teaching, most notably through his relationships with Bishop Sheil and Jacques Maritain ... Alinsky found a political vision to complement and help him articulate his own."[74]

Alinsky's alignment with social Catholicism at the level of vision and ideas led to an abiding institutional relationship as well. For most of Alinsky's career after Back of the Yards, the Catholic Church was his primary institutional base, thanks especially to Monsignor John O'Grady, the powerful and well-connected director of Catholic Charities. A social Catholic like Sheil, O'Grady was Alinsky's foremost collaborator at the national level, both initiating and funding the bulk of his local organizing projects through the late 1950s; even Alinsky's first serious attempts at organizing white and Black Protestant churches in the late 1950s grew out of a multineighborhood organizing initiative the Chicago archdiocese sponsored at O'Grady's urging.[75] Most of Alinsky's organizing protégés at the IAF were likewise Catholics formed in the church's social tradition: Fr. Jack Egan (Chicago's famous "organizer priest"), Nick von Hoffman, and Tom Gaudette all had connections to Catholic Action, whereas Ed Chambers, who later succeeded Alinsky as IAF Director, was a former Benedictine seminarian and Catholic Worker.[76] Meanwhile, several Mexican American

---

[72] Doering, *The Philosopher and the Provocateur*, 92; Horwitt, *Let Them Call Me Rebel*, 164–65.

[73] I discuss these aspects of Alinsky's vision at length in Hayes-Mota, "Partners in Forming the People."

[74] Bretherton, *Resurrecting Democracy*, 36.

[75] On O'Grady and the numerous projects he supported, see Finks, *Radical Vision of Saul Alinsky*, 72–82, 110–13.

[76] On the Catholic connections of these organizers, see Horwitt, *Let Them Call*

Catholics became IAF organizers in California, under the mentorship of Fred Ross, Alinsky's quasi-independent IAF associate there. In the 1960s, three of them—Cesar Chavez, Dolores Huerta, and Gilbert Padilla—would break off to found the United Farm Workers, which, unlike Alinsky's IAF, explicitly incorporated the symbols, rituals, and Social Teaching of the Catholic church into its organizing practice.[77]

For all of these reasons, by the time Alinsky died in 1972, his organizing legacy was already closely tied to the Catholic social tradition, personally and institutionally as much as ethically and intellectually. After his death, some of the Catholic organizers who inherited his legacy would cultivate the link further. Particularly important, in this regard, was Ernie Cortés, one of several Catholics (alongside Ed Chambers and Mike Gecan) who assumed a leadership role in the post-Alinsky IAF. Organizing in his native San Antonio, Cortés pioneered the approach to "faith-based organizing" or "congregation-based" organizing that soon became dominant among the next generation of Alinsky's students.[78] Initially, Cortés focused his efforts almost exclusively on Catholic parishes because they seemed to be the only viable institutions for building a strong local organization on the city's Latino west side. With support from the San Antonio archdiocese and other Catholic institutions, some of which (like Cortés himself) had connections to the farmworkers, he accordingly developed COPS ("Communities Organized for Public Service") around a core nucleus of Latino Catholic parishes.[79] As he proceeded, however, Cortés found that organizing effectively in this context required him to revise Alinsky's

---

me Rebel, 269–72, 326; Schutz and Miller, *People Power,* 127–29. Schutz and Miller offer fuller profiles of von Hoffman (49–57), Gaudette (124–42), and Chambers (195–214). On Egan's life, including his role as a chaplain to Catholic Action, see Margery Frisbie, *An Alley in Chicago: The Life and Legacy of Monsignor John Egan* (Franklin, WI: Sheed & Ward, 2002).

[77] On Chavez, Huerta, and Padilla, see Finks, *Radical Vision of Saul Alinsky,* 61–72; Schutz and Miller, *People Power,* 101–23. On the role of Catholicism in the UFW, under Chavez's leadership, see, e.g., Frederick John Dalton, *The Moral Vision of César Chavez* (Maryknoll, NY: Orbis Books, 2003).

[78] On the multiple terms used to refer to this form of organizing, see Richard L. Wood and Brad R. Fulton, *A Shared Future: Faith-Based Organizing for Ethical Democracy* (Chicago: University of Chicago Press, 2015), 15–16.

[79] Mark R. Warren, *Dry Bones Rattling: Community Building to Revitalize American Democracy* (Princeton, NJ: Princeton University Press, 2001), 46–49.

methods significantly. Prioritizing deeper relationship-building and leadership training *within* individual congregations, he also began to anchor his organizing more explicitly in the core values, beliefs, and practices of Catholicism than Alinsky ever had, formulating what sociologist Mark Warren calls a "theology of organizing."[80]

This intentional integration of organizing and Catholicism entered a new chapter after COPS's launch in 1974, when Cortés found and trained a core group of Catholic women religious. Led by Sr. Christine Stephens, Congregation of the Divine Providence (CDP), they quickly emerged as his primary collaborators in building out a wider "Southwest IAF" network of local organizations based on the COPS model. Even as they expanded their organizing to include white mainline and Black Protestants, Cortés and the sisters continued to anchor the networks' training curriculum and institutional culture in Scripture, Catholic Social Teaching, and the theology of Vatican II.[81] Meanwhile, Cortés persuaded Chambers and his IAF colleagues to integrate theology more fully into their work.[82]

Within a decade, the striking successes of COPS and the Southwest IAF would move the IAF as a whole, as well as several other Alinsky-descended organizations, to adopt the new "faith-based" organizing approach.[83] By the 1990s, three of these other organizations, PICO, Gamaliel, and DART, had grown sufficiently to rival the IAF in scope, becoming regional or national networks of local faith-based organizing federations. Of these three, both PICO and Gamaliel had deep roots in social Catholicism.

PICO was founded in 1972 by John Baumann, a Jesuit priest mentored by Tom Gaudette, whereas Gamaliel was founded in 1968 by Greg Galluzzo, a former Jesuit and fellow Gaudette mentee. Both networks similarly turned to faith-based organizing in the 1980s under Catholic leadership: Beyond their respective founders, Scott Read and José Carrasco (who had trained for a time under Cortés) were the primary architects of PICO's turn, while Mary Gonzales worked closely alongside Greg Galluzzo to lead Gamaliel's.[84] Only DART, by comparison, did not have Catholic

---

[80] Warren, *Dry Bones Rattling*, 40–42, 50–52.

[81] Warren, *Dry Bones Rattling*, 57–65; Mary Beth Rogers, *Cold Anger: A Story of Faith and Power Politics* (Denton: University of North Texas Press, 1990), 127–42.

[82] Rogers, *Cold Anger*, 93–101.

[83] Wood and Fulton, *A Shared Future*, 23–24.

[84] On Baumann and Galluzzo, see Schutz and Miller, *People Power*, 124–25,

roots, growing out of an initiative initially sponsored by the United Church of Christ.[85] All four networks, however, had a substantial (in many cases, disproportionate) Catholic constituency, though it has declined in recent years.[86] For decades, their single largest funder was likewise the Catholic Campaign for Human Development (CCHD), an initiative the national Catholic bishops' conference had established in 1969 to support Alinsky-style organizing projects across the United States.[87]

It should, therefore, be no surprise that, as post-Alinsky faith-based organizing grew into a fully ecumenical and, eventually, interfaith field, it nonetheless bore a distinctively Catholic stamp. Sociologist Stephen Hart noted this characteristic in 1999, observing that, of the various religious traditions represented in faith-based organizing, it was Catholicism, and specifically Catholic Social Teaching, that had most influenced its "religious and political perspective," as well as its underlying conceptual framework.[88] In this regard, it is probably not coincidental that many of faith-based organizing's principal innovations on Alinsky's theory and practice *also* represent fuller applications of social Catholicism's core principles. Most fundamentally, faith-based organizing's greater emphasis on forming leaders, by teaching ordinary people how to identify and act on their core values as well as their self-interest (which are understood to be complements), has effectively centered the practice more fully on promoting the dignity of the person.[89] Similarly, faith-based organizing's focus on cultivating long-term public relationships based on shared values and interests has enhanced the practice's capacity to build solidarity for the common good; so, too, has its

---

170–73. On PICO and its turn to faith-based organizing, see Richard L. Wood, *Faith in Action: Religion, Race, and Democratic Organizing in America* (Chicago: University of Chicago Press, 2002), 291–97. On Gamaliel, see Wood and Fulton, *A Shared Future*, 23–24.

[85] On DART, see Wood and Fulton, *A Shared Future*, 23–24; cf. https://thedartcenter.org/about/.

[86] On Catholic participation in the field from the 1990s to the early 2010s, see Fulton and Wood, "Interfaith Community Organizing."

[87] On the CCHD, see Lawrence J. Engel, "The Influence of Saul Alinsky on the Campaign for Human Development," *Theological Studies* 59, no. 4 (1998): 636–61.

[88] Stephen Hart, *Cultural Dilemmas of Progressive Politics: Styles of Engagement across Grassroots Activists* (Chicago: University of Chicago Press, 2001), 49.

[89] On this shift, see, e.g., Warren, *Dry Bones Rattling*, 57–61, Hart, *Cultural Dilemmas of Progressive Politics,* 75–79.

intentional cultivation of "broad-based organizations" that span multiple kinds of diversity—race, class, religion, and political ideology—and address a wide range of issues.[90] Finally, while retaining Alinsky's original focus on intermediary institutions, faith-based organizers have also dedicated greater attention to strengthening the individual member institutions (principally but not exclusively congregations) that belong to local organizing federations, thereby better promoting subsidiarity.[91] In all of these ways, among others, faith-based organizing has come to more fully *embody* the vision and values of social Catholicism than Alinsky's original approach did: in its theory, practice, institutions, and, ultimately, its people.[92]

In sum, what began as a fortuitous affinity between Alinsky and social Catholicism, first perceived by Catholics like Sheil and Maritain, has grown over the course of eight decades into a more complete and intentional integration of the Catholic social tradition with the Alinsky organizing tradition—specifically, the tradition of faith-based organizing that grew out of the IAF after Alinsky's death. To this degree, the latter tradition may justly be regarded as an expression of social Catholicism, in all of the ways just described. At the same time, it is not *only* an expression of social Catholicism. The Alinsky tradition, after all, was not founded by a Catholic. And though Catholics have played a distinctly important role in it, they have hardly been its only proponents: Apart from Alinsky himself, myriad Protestant, Jewish, Muslim, and secular organizers have made significant contributions to this tradition of organizing, as have the diverse communities and institutions they represent. What ought one to make of this fact?

Conclusion:
Traditions in Conversation

In this chapter, I have argued that organizing is best understood as a practice of many traditions: both the diverse traditions of organizing themselves and the larger moral, religious, and political traditions that inform them.

---

[90] On the turn toward relationship-building and "broad-based" organizations, see Warren, *Dry Bones Rattling,* 61–67.

[91] On the new priority given to institutional development, see Warren, *Dry Bones Rattling,* 61–65.

[92] I develop this argument at far greater length in Nicholas Hayes-Mota, "Practicing the Common Good: Catholic Tradition, Community Organizing, and the Virtues of Democratic Politics" (PhD diss., Boston College, 2023), chap. 3.

I have also examined the relationship between a tradition of each kind, respectively, the Catholic social tradition and the Alinsky tradition. Along the way, I hope to have shed some new light on each, as well as to have demonstrated social Catholicism's relevance and historical importance to the field of organizing as a whole. More broadly, I hope to have illustrated the value of reflecting on organizing through the lens of "tradition." Yet beyond these more general points, what specific insights does the relationship between these two particular traditions offer into the role of traditions in organizing?

First, the relationship between social Catholicism and the Alinsky tradition reveals that traditions are not self-enclosed totalities, only capable of engaging each other through conflict.[93] Like the human persons who bear them, they are open and porous to relationship and able to sustain a variety of relationships through time. Indeed, individual traditions grow and develop themselves often through relationships to the other. Such is precisely what took place when Alinsky and his social Catholic collaborators first encountered each other. Through their relationship with Alinsky, social Catholics like Sheil, Maritain, and O'Grady discovered a new—and, they believed, a better—way of practicing their own tradition and began to re-form it accordingly. Reciprocally, through his relationship to them, Alinsky found a new way to articulate his own vision and a new community of people with whom to practice, institutionalize, and embody it.

Second, traditions are not mutually exclusive, or at least not necessarily so. That the Alinsky tradition of organizing has embodied the Catholic social tradition in a distinctive and integral way does not imply that it has *exclusively* embodied that tradition, any more than it exclusively embodies the other traditions that have participated in it (including Alinsky's own). Multiple traditions can inform practices and institutions, as well as the persons who create and sustain them. This is not to say that such coexistence is easy or harmonious. Insofar as traditions conflict, it may be quite the opposite. Nevertheless, the history of organizing is rife with examples of traditions that, through the work of their practitioners, have not only learned to coexist but mutually enriched and even transformed each other. Such is certainly the case with the Alinsky tradition, through

---

[93] Here I depart from MacIntyre, who, I believe, often (though not always) conceives tradition in this way. For a critique of MacIntyre along these lines, see Luke Bretherton, *Hospitality as Holiness: Christian Witness amid Moral Diversity* (Burlington, VT: Ashgate, 2006).

which people and institutions representing a wide variety of traditions have built solidarity and collectively contributed their own insights to the practice, while enriching their own traditions in turn.[94] Neither should this be surprising, at least from a social Catholic perspective. A cardinal premise of Catholic Social Teaching is that there *is* a common good to be found through dialogue and relationship, even across our manifold diversity.[95]

At the same time, and third, that common good can only be discerned by first attending carefully, and responsibly, to particularity. Hence another reason why reflecting on organizing through the lens of tradition is important. The social Catholic tradition, as I have shown, is a distinct tradition in organizing, one that has been formed through a particular process of historical development, in a particular set of communities and institutions, and around a particular vision of the good. It is also a tradition that has been closely intertwined with (at least) one particular tradition of organizing within the United States, which consequently embodies social Catholicism's vision and values. Even within the Alinsky tradition, however, representatives of other traditions may not see the practice, its history, or its values in quite the same way. And other traditions of organizing advance alternative approaches to the practice that differ not only in matters of tactics or technique, but also in the larger moral and political vision they embody. By attending more closely to the particular traditions of and in organizing, as well as the specific historical relationships between them, we lay the groundwork for a deeper conversation among them—one that may take the form of debate, as well as dialogue.

I cannot further pursue that conversation here. My intention in this chapter is to have carried it one step further along, making the voice of my own tradition—that of social Catholicism—more fully present within it. One of the most important contributions social Catholicism can make, perhaps, is to highlight the role of *tradition* itself. After all, thinking in terms of traditions is a peculiarly (though not exclusively) Catholic mode of reflection. Yet as the history of the Alinsky tradition attests, organizers from many other traditions have just as much to teach the Catholic social tradition as it has to teach them: about itself, each other, and the common good we share.

---

[94] For a thoughtful account of how this process has played out in the IAF, see Bretherton, *Resurrecting Democracy*, 76–110.

[95] For a fuller development of this point, see David Hollenbach, *The Common Good and Christian Ethics* (Cambridge: Cambridge University Press, 2002),137–70.

4

National Welfare Rights Organization's Beulah Sanders at the 1972 National Council of Churches Convention

Carolyn Baker and Colleen Wessel-McCoy

"If We Fail in Our Struggle, Christianity Will Have Failed"

In February 1968, Martin Luther King Jr. approached the National Welfare Rights Organization (NWRO) to ask for their help in organizing the Poor People's Campaign. At first, he tried to send his staff to meet with them, an offer they refused. So King came to Chicago to sit down with their leadership: poor Black and white women from across the country, each representing an entire chapter of the organization. NWRO had been organizing around a national poor people's platform since their founding in 1967, and their local welfare rights organizing work had been going on even longer. Their president, Johnnie Tillmon, recounted how the welfare mothers out-organized the leadership team from Southern Christian Leadership Conference, arranging the room to isolate King and framing the conversation around NWRO's priorities.[1] They asked King questions about the details of recent anti-welfare legislation. When he couldn't answer, they pushed him to admit it and acknowledge their leadership on these issues.

A few days later, King was interviewed on the *Tonight Show* while Harry Belafonte was the guest host. Belafonte said he heard King was organizing a million mothers, adding, "You're organizing everyone." King was quick to correct him and clarify that the march was being organized by NWRO. King was assassinated less than two months later. The Mother's Day March

---

[1] Paula Giddings, *When and Where I Enter: The Impact of Black Women on Race and Sex in America* (New York: Morrow, 1984), 312–13.

became the first action of the Poor People's Campaign. Coretta Scott King and Beulah Sanders were on the front line.

In 1965, Sanders founded the West Side Welfare Recipients League in New York, one of the first welfare rights groups in her area. By 1969, she was the vice chair of NWRO and eventually president. Born in New Bern, North Carolina, in 1935 and one of eleven children, she moved to New York City in 1955 and was a public housing resident on the Upper West Side. She and her children first received welfare in 1959.[2] The formation of the West Side Welfare Recipients League shares a common story with the welfare organizations across the country that came together to become NWRO. It began as a group of recipients discussing problems with their welfare benefits and supporting each other to contest benefit shutoffs and denials. As their work expanded to more neighborhoods, they created the Citywide Coordinating Committee of Welfare Rights Organizations, launched with a protest at the welfare department and a conference at Judson Memorial Church.[3]

Although she is most well known for her work with welfare rights, Sanders's organizing spanned education, housing, and antiwar issues. She was vice president of the school parents association (PS 84), was part of a 1968 peace mission to Paris to meet with North Vietnamese leaders, worked for a Head Start program, and ran for state senate as part of the Freedom and Peace Party ticket.[4] Historians and social theorists have written about her without saying her name, sometimes going out of their way to make her words anonymous. Social ethicists missed her totally. We join King in correcting those mistakes and being ready to learn what we don't know.

This chapter is an examination of Sanders's December 1972 speech at the National Council of Churches (NCC) 9th General Assembly in Houston. We show how, in this speech, Sanders names the social ethical vocation of the Church using the Cain and Abel story, saying the Church is "my brother's keeper" (Genesis 4:9). She rejected a charity interpretation of that injunction, emphasizing interrelatedness and mutual dependence as kinship relationships. We explore her method of Christian ethics, starting with a historical-materialist reframing of the question of who is poor, why

---

[2] Welfare Fighter, *The Welfare Fighter*, 3, no. 5 (June 1972), microform, Columbia University.

[3] Viki Morris, "The Woman from Welfare Rights," *World Magazine*, n.d., Beulah Sanders family collection.

[4] Welfare Fighter, *The Welfare Fighter*.

they are poor, and how the poor are interrelated to both the economy and the Church. Her approach is made possible by her practice as an organizer, as a Christian, and as a poor mom. She is a scholar of her own movement out of the necessity to sharpen it, situated in the unity of being both a "thinker and a fighter."[5] With the bold claim: "If we fail in our struggle, Christianity will have failed," Sanders invites churches to join the welfare rights movement.

National Welfare Rights Organization

NWRO was the nation's largest national organization of poor people. It operated from 1966 to 1975. Sanders was among its leaders from the start and served as its chairwoman from 1972 to 1974. NWRO reshaped the food stamp program, made the welfare application process more accountable to recipients, and expanded programs available to poor families.[6] At its height in 1971 NWRO was composed of 800 affiliated welfare rights groups in all fifty states.[7] They fought against the shift to workfare legislation that required poor mothers to work to receive cash assistance. They defied the malicious portrayal of the poor as living in poverty because of their own failures or incompetencies by organizing welfare recipients into a national network and by recipients holding all of the leadership roles in the organization.

Membership was limited to poor people, with rules prohibiting more than 10 percent of the membership being people living above the poverty threshold. Voting rights were extended only to recipients of welfare or social security. The membership was 85 percent Black, although its leadership insisted that their base was all poor people, noting that the majority of poor people in the United States were white. They were intentional about describing themselves as a "human rights movement" rather than a "civil rights movement." Within the organization, they referred to themselves as "welfare mothers" and proclaimed that they were building "motherpower."[8]

---

[5] Gen. Gordon Baker, untitled talk, US Social Forum, Detroit, 2010. General Baker Institute.

[6] Guida West, *The National Welfare Rights Movement: The Social Protest of Poor Women* (New York: Praeger, 1981), 6.

[7] West, *National Welfare Rights Movement*, 51–52.

[8] West, *National Welfare Rights Movement*, 44.

As a national network of local chapters, some of which had been organizing for years before NWRO formalized, Sanders argued that, if the "system were to be effectively changed, a strong, cohesive organization would have to be formed to link together the activities and purposes of the many neighborhood welfare rights groups."[9] The NWRO logo, resembling a chain link or infinity symbol, along with one of its slogans, "linking up the struggles," emphasized this relationship between local and national organizing.

National Council of Churches and NWRO

The National Council of Churches (NCC), the largest ecumenical organization in the United States, was founded in 1950 with a charter to be a community of Christian communion that comes together in "common mission, serving in all creation to the glory of God."[10] NCC grew out of the Federal Council of Churches, founded in 1908 in response to "industrial problems" like child labor, unsafe workplaces, seven-day workweeks, and poverty wages. NCC's expanded social creed added civil rights violations, war, poverty, and other social concerns.

Protestant churches, especially the mainline denominations, were the largest source of NWRO funding, contributing 47 percent of their 1968 budget. Additional significant funding came from the Interreligious Foundation for Community Organization (IFCO), created in 1967 by several of the liberal Protestant churches of NCC. Under the direction of Rev. Lucius Walker, it was designed to be the first foundation directed and controlled by people of color, bridging mainline churches and community groups led by people of color. IFCO gave NWRO $500,000 over four years (1967–1971). After NWRO's founding director and primary fundraiser George Wiley left the organization in 1972, denominational funding dropped precipitously. It was completely gone by the end of 1973.[11] As

---

[9] Guida West interview of Beulah Sanders, July 9, 1983, New York City, Guida West Papers, Smith College Archives, box 11, folder 2, audio file and transcript.

[10] "About the National Council of the Churches of Christ in the USA," https://nationalcouncilofchurches.us/about-us/.

[11] West, *National Welfare Rights Movement*, 30–31. The drop in church funding was in part due to the departure of George Wiley, previous director of NWRO, who had brokered many of the fundraising relationships.

the newly elected chair of NWRO, Sanders urged the Protestant churches to help create "Friends of NWRO" chapters for non-recipients. Her hope was that this support at the grassroots level would aid in revitalizing the movement of poor women.[12]

Sanders was invited to speak to NCC at their general assembly in Houston in this moment of leadership transition and budget crisis. Yet she spent almost none of the speech talking about direct financial support. She had a more challenging demand. When she said that churches "didn't come through" for the poor in 1972, she was talking about the recent reelection of Richard Nixon on an anti-welfare, "law and order" platform. When she said NWRO was "expecting more from them" in the years ahead, NWRO's financial crisis was certainly on her mind, but her theory of the role of the Church in social change was not limited to financial support.

Sanders's Speech to the Churches

Sanders started by establishing her authority, making it clear that she spoke not just for herself and not just for welfare recipients, but for the poor. She stated that, as the leader of the "only nation-wide poor people's organization in this country, I represent all of those poor people who are on welfare and many who are not." From the start, Sanders made the point that the poor are not external to the Church. They are "people who believe in the Christian way of life ... whose nickels and dimes and quarters have built the Christian churches of America." The poor are not separate from the body of Christ or Christian living. They are not external objects of charity, service, or pity. And they are not unchristian. Sanders continued, "Because we believe in Christianity, we have continued to support the Christian churches. And I am saying to you here and now that we fully expect the Christian churches to support us."[13]

Before she got to what she meant by churches supporting the poor, Sanders showed NCC the process of her own thinking, where she came from, and how she got to her conclusions, particularly concerning who the poor are and why they are poor. She turned the assembly into a classroom to teach history, dispel myths about welfare, and interpret scripture,

---

[12] West, *National Welfare Rights Movement*, 186.

[13] Beulah Sanders, "Speech to NCC, Houston, December 1972," Guida West Papers, Smith College Archives, box 11, folder 1, transcript.

pointing out that these are all things with which church leaders should be familiar—"all of you have studied history"—and then called the Church to act in accordance with this understanding.

She took time with the NCC to observe US capitalism's manipulation of the poor along racial and ethnic lines, because she knew that, despite being fundamental to the lives of congregations and congregants, churches had not integrated it into their conception of poverty:

> This country was discovered and founded by poor people who had been rejected by the rulers of their countries for religious and financial reasons. Most of them came here from the jails of Europe. Many of them were indentured slaves. Not black men and women but white. They worked for years to earn their freedom. Later came the Indian slaves and the black slaves. Still later came the Chinese, Filipino, Japanese and Mexican immigrants by those seeking cheap labor. On the East Coast we imported the Irish, the Italians, the Germans, the Slavs, and Negroes from the South as cheap labor and strike breakers. We still import some of these in order to get cheap domestic or migrant labor.[14]

She argued that this history of migrations, unfree and semi-free labor relationships, and the development of the United States' particular forms of race and racism all shaped the US economy and facilitated capitalism's dependence on under-waged workers and poverty. She connected this immigration and racialization history to the necessity of poverty for capitalism:

> Our way of life has been built on making sure that we have a large number of poor people who are desperate enough to work for barely enough to keep body and soul alive, and another group behind them who have even less and must rely on the goodness and kindness of the affluent. Thus we continue to guarantee both poverty and cheap labor.[15]

---

[14] Sanders, "Speech to NCC, Houston, December 1972."

[15] Sanders, "Speech to NCC," 2. Sanders's assessment of the role of poverty in disciplining labor sounds like the work of Francis Fox Piven and Richard Cloward. The three of them collaborated around welfare rights organizing in New York. It

In Sanders's view, the "goodness and kindness of the affluent" played a particular role in the maintenance of this system, keeping a reserve of poor workers ready to serve the needs of low-wage employers. Churches had historically taken on this "goodness and kindness" role, helping sustain the system of exploitation.

Sanders argued that, instead of blaming the economic system, churches bought into ideas about the poor that blame the poor for their own poverty. Hard work, perseverance, faith, and a little charity are the answers. They promoted a kind of struggle theology—hard times are God's test of your faith. Tithe, pray, buckle down, save, and work. Churches positioned themselves as "the affluent," responsible only for "goodness and kindness." But Sanders said you cannot pull yourself up by your bootstraps if you do not control your economic conditions.

> All of our land belongs to somebody who demands a fortune for its use or purchase. Somebody else decides whether or not the factory will be opened or closed and whether or not you will be allowed to work there. The conditions of life have changed. The rules, the ethics, must also change.[16]

Romantic ideas about hard work and farming one's own land did not match the lived realities of 1972.

To the extent that churches are cultivators and disseminators of "rules and ethics," Sanders is calling them to make sure the "rules and ethics" they promote are a good fit for the actual conditions of life. Sanders is right that rules and ethics are tied to social, economic, and political conditions, but they tend to be tied to those conditions in the service of the owning classes. Just as the Church has tended to support capitalism's poverty wages by supplementing them with the "goodness and kindness of the affluent," the Church has contributed "rules and ethics" that justify the existence and persistence of poverty. If bootstrap morality and struggle theology don't help people figure out how to live in an economy where people have little

---

is striking that Cloward and Piven's writing about that organizing history almost entirely fails to mention Sanders by name or acknowledge her leadership. Frances Fox Piven and Richard A. Cloward, *Poor People's Movements: Why They Succeed, How They Fail* (New York: Vintage Books, 1977).

[16] Sanders, "Speech to NCC," 1.

control over the terms of employment, access to land, and cost of housing, then churches should stop promoting those theologies.

For Sanders, the reelection of Richard Nixon was a key piece of evidence that churches were moving toward ethics that blessed inequality and served the needs of the wealthiest. Just a month before the assembly, Nixon had won in 49 of 50 states on an anti-welfare, law-and-order platform. She charged, "Some of you turned your backs on the poor people of this country," when you voted for Nixon.[17] His official campaign slogan, "Now, More Than Ever" echoed his unofficial emphasis on "law and order." Sanders pointed to the ways he "publicly called welfare recipients lazy and unwilling to accept menial employment" and promised "more punitive welfare legislation."[18]

Nixon's "law and order" rhetoric was not new. It had been used by the opponents of civil rights activists in the 1940s and 1950s and in the presidential campaign of Barry Goldwater in 1964.[19] As in previous periods, it was not principally about crime and disorder but had always been code for a range of anxieties about ideas and people framed as un-American, unchristian, and immoral. Nixon's campaign focus was successful in tapping into the fears of white Southerners and many white working-class Northerners, casting the social movements and civil rights gains of the 1960s as threats to American values.[20] The legacy of Nixon's "law and order" campaign can be seen in the entrenchment of mass incarceration, erosion of welfare for poor families, and racialization of crime.

---

[17] Sanders, "Speech to NCC," 1.

[18] Sanders, "Speech to NCC," 1.

[19] Naomi Murakawa, "The Origins of the Carceral Crisis: Racial Order as 'Law and Order' in Postwar American Politics," in *Race and American Political Development*, ed. Joseph E. Lowndes, Julie Novkov, and Dorian Warren (New York: Routledge, 2008). The equation of segregation with law and order and of integration with disorder and chaos, even if not called "law and order," goes back to Reconstruction.

[20] "Nixon recognized this connection when he privately reviewed one of his campaign's hard-hitting television ads in 1972 about urban crime and remarked that "[this] hits it right on the nose. It's all about law and order and the damn Negro-Puerto Rican groups out there." Josh Zeitz, "How Trump Is Recycling Nixon's 'Law and Order' Playbook," *Politico Magazine*, July 18, 2016. https://www.politico.com/magazine/story/2016/07/donald-trump-law-and-order-richard-nixon-crime-race-214066.

Sanders flipped the rhetoric of "law and order": The poor, who are called criminal and lawless, are actually the ones maintaining law and order. "We believe in law and order," she said, giving the example: "When welfare officials and police officials threatened us with midnight raids on our homes to see if a man was there, we went to [the Supreme] Court to defend our right to privacy."[21] She framed NWRO as the upholder of both social order and American ideals, working to enforce the law in the streets, in welfare offices, in the courts, and in the legislature. "We have taken the welfare department and H.E.W. into the courts to force them to carry out the law."[22] NWRO's campaign tactics often took existing legislation and regulations and insisted that responsible agencies follow the law.

> When the legal process breaks down or moves too slowly to meet urgent human needs, we have taken to the streets. We have demonstrated to call both public and official attention to the violations of the law being carried on by public officials. In my opinion this is support for law and order. What we insist upon is that the laws of this land be carried out whether they affect the rich or the poor.[23]

This portrayal of NWRO's work pushed back on the use of "law and order" to criminalize welfare recipients and poor people. She framed the poor as guarantors of liberty, endowed with the rights of citizenship, and upholders of Christian values. "The laws of this land provide certain inalienable rights to all Americans. We are Americans. We insist that those rights belong to us."[24]

Sanders used the Cain and Abel story to describe a right relationship between the Church and the poor, using Cain's question to God, "Am I my brother's keeper?" (Genesis 4:9–12). Sanders answered Cain for those gathered at the general assembly: "You and I call ourselves Christians. We are our brothers' keepers whether we always like it or not." She offered a structural rather than an interpersonal interpretation of the text. The

---

[21] Sanders, "Speech to NCC," 4.
[22] Sanders, "Speech to NCC," x. HEW was the Department of Health, Education, and Welfare (1953–1979).
[23] Sanders, "Speech to NCC," 4.
[24] Sanders, "Speech to NCC," 5.

Church is Cain. The poor are Abel. That is not a charity relationship; it is a family relationship.

We need to be our brother's keeper in ways that go beyond charity. She took what Christians say they agree with—being their brother's keeper—and pushed them away from reading it as God encouraging them to practice the "goodness and kindness of the affluent." She took what they said they agreed with and challenged them to interpret it as structural care and the systemic meeting of needs. She was saying that here is what it actually looks like to be one's brothers' keepers: *Care for the poor isn't just interpersonal, but also how we organize our economy and society. It's who we vote for. We are our siblings' keepers, whether we want to be or not.* Christian support for Nixon in the election just a month earlier was evidence of a failure to be their siblings' keepers. They were not practicing what they were preaching.

Sanders asked churches to support the poor and welfare recipients in three ways. The first was material: "calling on all Christians to support their brothers and sisters who are in trouble whether that trouble be economic or physical or emotional." Second, she also asked that they "spread the truth about the welfare problems in this country," resisting the lies about poverty and welfare she had spent the first half of the speech unpacking and reframing. Churches are responsible for participating in pushing back against the criminalization of the poor. And third, their support should include legislative advocacy: "We expect the churches and their members to oppose local, state, and federal legislation that oppresses poor people, Black people, Chicano people, Indian people, Puerto Rican people, and all other people."[25]

She also made an appeal for churches to deepen their relationship with NWRO as an organization. After describing the three ways churches needed to support the poor, she pointed out that collaborating with the welfare rights movement would be a way of accomplishing all three. Importantly, churches would be collaborating with NWRO's leadership of poor Black women. The organization was a source for assessing legislative priorities (as one of the "most effective monitoring of social legislation of any group in the country"), for learning about the welfare system and the realities of poverty, and for resisting law and order theologies that cast the poor as unchristian, un-American, and immoral. And Sanders emphasized that a relationship with NWRO reminds churches that the poor are part of the

---

[25] Sanders, "Speech to NCC," 5.

body of the Church, supporting it through tithing and service, rather than being objects of charity beyond its walls: "We ask for your moral, personal, and financial support in this battle for bread, dignity and justice for all of our people. If we fail in our struggle, Christianity will have failed. For you are your brother's keepers."[26]

Sanders the Ethicist

Being poor helped Sanders have a better theoretical understanding of poverty and the system that upholds it. But it was not only her plight as a poor mom that made her leadership significant. In the dominant way of thinking about poor people, they are the source of poverty, not the solution to it. If poor Black women are the problem, then poor Black women are not the solution. Society does not allow them to be both.

Sanders's scholarship was not limited to knowing what it means to be poor or how to make a way out of no way. She had an analysis of the historical development of capitalism, how it creates poverty, and why it depends on the poor as a source of low-wage labor. Her analysis also included insights into what it looks like for there to be a right to welfare and to end poverty for poor families. Sanders rejected the idea that poor people are the source of poverty and put forward a restructured economy and society as the solution to poverty.

Sanders added theology to this political assessment of poverty's source. Scriptural injunctions to care for one another are in conflict with the ideological tradition that treats poverty as un-American, unchristian, immoral, and sometimes unlawful. Even where accommodations are made for the honorable poor of our national origin stories, to remain in poverty goes against America's perception of its own exceptionalism. Churches are susceptible to this line of thinking about poverty, and this is why Sanders spent time exposing the ways the economy depends on there being low-wage workers and a reserve of poor people. The poor are not apart from or outside the economy, society, or churches. Those who think of the poor as being apart from them are actually dependent on poverty and poor people. Preachers, social workers, employers, and so on—all depend on the poor. We are actually deeply interdependent. Social workers' livelihoods are tied to poverty. Church pews are full of poor people. She

---

[26] Sanders, "Speech to NCC," 5.

knows how much in tithing comes from the poor, often tithing problems away. Churches have been some of the most taxing: not just once a year but every Sunday, all 53 Sundays in 1972. Low-wage employers depend on poverty to discipline their workers. By not separating the poor from the whole—economically, socially, or theologically—Sanders pointed us away from charity and toward the right to fare well. There are resonances with Melissa Snarr's observation, "A theological vision of interdependence can open our eyes, not only to the lived reality that we all do and should receive numerous forms of welfare (provisions for well-being) that arise from our interdependent relationships, but also to the practices of solidarity that are necessary in light of this vision."[27]

Although Sanders spent her time in the speech positioning NWRO as the upholders of civil law and order, her social ethical arguments put the leadership of the welfare rights movement as the upholders of God's law and order, too. She called the Church to care for one another in structural, kinship ways. She rejected charity approaches to poverty that position the poor outside of the Church and outside of the economy. Her call to the churches to participate in the welfare rights movement was a call to join the struggle against poverty and not the struggle against those who are poor.

Sanders drew together history, biblical studies, and social sciences as all pointing to reasons not to vote for Nixon. What churches said they were about did not match what they did. Their ethics should point them in one direction, but that's not how they voted in 1972. Their vote was inconsistent with their proclaimed value of care for the poor. But their vote was consistent with the tendency for the Church to serve the interests of the existing social and economic order. This is why she started a speech about the role and responsibilities of the Church with a history of how the economy creates and depends on poverty, race, and a correlating set of morals and ethics.

Conclusion

Gary Dorrien observes that social ethics began with the "idea that Christianity has a social-ethical mission to transform the structures of society in the direction of social justice."[28] The work of social ethics crossed bound-

---

[27] C. Melissa Snarr, *All You That Labor: Religion and Ethics in the Living Wage Movement* (New York: New York University Press, 2011), 62.

[28] Gary Dorrien, *Social Ethics in the Making: Interpreting an American Tradition* (Malden, MA: Wiley-Blackwell, 2009), 1; 6.

aries of academy, church, and public. Although Sanders spent most of her time in the public sphere—demonstrations in the streets, in welfare offices, in the courts, and in the legislature—this speech is one of many examples of how her thinking extended into the sphere of theology, with big implications for how the Church is supposed to engage with the world.

In part, Sanders is missed as a religious leader because scholars confine religious leadership to those involved with churches or religious movements and confine welfare rights activism to secular political history. Civil rights movement scholarship has sometimes allowed its figures to occupy both spaces, particularly ordained men like King. Womanist scholars have expanded that body, with particular attention to Black women. Marcia Riggs's *Can I Get a Witness?* centered the religious character of the leadership of Black women's activism as both historically and theologically significant; these leaders include Septima Clark, Ella Jo Baker, and Fannie Lou Hamer. Riggs's work is both "reconstruction and retrieval" of significant but under-documented leadership. She pointed to how their activism included interpreting "the relevance of their spiritual experiences and belief systems for the Church, community, and society."[29] Similarly, Katie Cannon's scholarship expanded the canon of authoritative sources of Christian ethics by documenting the ways womanist scholars "in church, academy, and society" were "doing social analysis and proposing alternative vision for the future on the basis of their best creative impulses, their retrieval of Black women's history as sources, and their reinterpretation of methodologies and doctrines."[30] We see Sanders as a leader whose work needs retrieval and reconstruction, both for her historical significance and because her contributions continue to be relevant today. Sanders expands the canon of Black freedom struggles, Black-led class-based organizing, and religious leadership as movement leadership.

Like King, Sanders was a scholar of her own movement. She did theology from the midst of struggle. To the extent that she shows up in the histories of the welfare rights movement, her religious contributions are entirely excluded. We want to claim her for the tradition of Christian social ethics. In just one speech, she demonstrated her analysis of the social location of the poor and implications for the social obligations of

---

[29] Marcia Riggs, ed., *Can I Get a Witness? Prophetic Religious Voices of African American Women: An Anthology* (Maryknoll, NY: Orbis Books, 1997), xi.

[30] Katie G. Cannon, *Katie's Canon: Womanism and the Soul of the Black Community* (New York: Continuum, 1995), 76.

the Church. She understood the body of Christian churches as maintainers of the status quo and yet bound to scriptural obligations to participate in the transformation of society. She saw how Christians are vulnerable to the ideological worldview that made Nixon popular. She called churches closer to a social interpretation of the injunction to be our "brother's keeper," including through a closer relationship between the Church and social movements led by the poor, like welfare rights.

PART II

ГЛАВА II

5

Faith and Labor:

Organizing for the Kingdom of God on Earth

K. B. Brower

If you are reading this, you are probably just as worried as I am about the rise of Christian nationalism, its history, and the ongoing implications for working people, people of color, and femme, queer, trans, and nonbinary people. Perhaps you have also noticed that, lately, our organizing movements aren't exactly winning all the time, and that Christianity is being dangerously claimed and deployed by far-right nationalist forces in the United States and around the world today. In this chapter, I offer examples of people coming together to *win real change* for their communities and to consider how they can make possible forms of both social and personal transformation that challenge Christian nationalism. Past liberation struggles teach us that when worker organizations and religious institutions join together to build coalitions for justice, the effect of their coalition is forceful, deep, and creative. Recently, we have been a far cry from engaging widely in such partnerships, and the power of Christian nationalism along the US far right continues to grow. The struggle to resist these conditions requires us to work together across labor and religion, and for real enduring alignment.

But *how we work together,* our method and the strategies we use, matter. In this chapter, I show that part of the reason our movements are not winning is because many faith-based and social justice movements are "mobilizing" without organizing. I learned the difference between mobilizing and organizing during my fifteen years as a union organizer and through several life-changing campaigns alongside my organizing mentor Jane McAlevey. Mobilizing is when we spend our time gathering up the people who already agree with us to participate in protest and public actions. Mobilizing does not expand our base, and it does not attempt to change people's hearts and minds in any enduring way. Organizing is how we move people who don't agree with us already, and it is how we expand our base of support.

That Donald Trump won a second term in the Oval Office should make clear to us just how critical it is that we figure out how to change people's hearts and minds and how important a role workers' organizations and religious institutions will play in bringing about such changes. This chapter tells three stories to illustrate differences between mobilizing work and organizing work and what is at risk when faith and labor work in silos. We have the chance to challenge Christian nationalism with deep organizing and serious base-building, fostering instead coalitions of churches that stand with working people and the oppressed. Although I'm largely hoping to make a strategic intervention by telling these stories, I also hope to show how organizing and social movements make spiritual interventions in people's lives.

Under capitalism, people are made to be alienated, isolated, and disempowered. Capitalism commodifies everything, holding nothing as sacred, not even human dignity or the condition of the planetary climate. Under these conditions, working people often are either underemployed or working multiple jobs to make ends meet. Union organizing is a way of re-sanctifying the workplace, our communities, and the world. Organizing helps people understand, in an embodied way, that they are interconnected and interdependent.

Here's the beauty of organizing: You cannot win alone. If you go to your boss alone to demand respect or a raise to your salary, little to nothing changes about the conditions under which you work and live. However, if you and all your coworkers join together to approach your boss and demand change, the boss is forced to listen. Workers can win only when they learn to drop their prejudices against their coworkers and others, hear out one another's stories, and fight the boss together.

While writing this chapter, I have been in the throes of a campaign with a community college union, a campaign that beautifully illustrates the work of organizing as a transformative spiritual intervention. This union is a "wall to wall" organization, one that represents everyone from the highest paid tenured faculty member to the lowest paid facilities worker. As you can imagine, there are some big and often antagonistic dynamics at play between these groups of workers. The workers in these respective positions find themselves highly racialized and gendered, and the school administration has done its best to instill divisions between the workers based on race, ethnicity, and job title. If these workers do not figure out how to step beyond their biases and mistrust, none of them will win the improvements they're seeking. When workers decide to form a union, they decide that they are worth more than capitalism and whatever their boss says they are. They collectively agree to refuse the free market as the ultimate determinant of their value and worth. They make spoken and unspoken agreements that there is something beyond the so-called invisible hand of the market—and that they will have one another's backs in the fight to protect the dignity of their lives and labor. At its best, building a union re-sanctifies people's lives and helps them see themselves, one another, and their work as worthy and sacred. Through organizing, working people embody and enact real interdependency, together discovering possibilities for re-sanctifying their worlds.

When 5,000 Mercedes-Benz factory workers in Alabama were heading into their union election in the months before this writing, a longtime friend and comrade of mine who was working on the campaign forwarded screenshot messages of a local reverend urging the workers to vote *No* to forming a union. This was not the first time in my years as an organizer that I witnessed clergy stand on the side of the employer against the interests of working people—and I doubt it will be the last time. It is no mere coincidence that this pastor was taking a stand against the Mercedes workers in their union election, which was largely focused on winning living wages and an end to disrespect and discrimination. If you were the CEO of Mercedes in a state where 86 percent of adults identify as Christian,[1] and you saw workers across the South successfully joining unions and negotiating for higher pay and a voice on the job, wouldn't you enlist the clergy?

In this chapter, I share three campaign stories to illustrate what is at stake in establishing solidarity between working people and the church for the sake of union organizing. These stories offer textured accounts of what happens when we are unable to find ways of working together that are both strategically and spiritually transformative. However, the stories also reveal glimpses of what happens when we do.

A few years back, I was working on a campaign in DuBois, Pennsylvania, a very small rural town in Western PA, where a group of about 300

---

[1] Pew Research Center, "2023–24 US Religious Landscape Study Interactive Database," 2025.

nurses at a hospital were trying to form a union. These nurses had called the union office complaining about unsafe staffing levels that were putting their patients in danger. The nurses had begged management for more staff and better nurse-to-patient ratios for years without being listened to, and they were eager to do something to change their working conditions. Now, everyone knows that Pennsylvania is a battleground state and that these tiny towns, like DuBois, population of 8,000, play an outsized role in electoral politics and their news cycles. In fact, if, in 2016, just *one* of the right swing counties in Pennsylvania had swung away from Trump, he would not have won Pennsylvania and would not have become president. Christian nationalist forces fix their sights and formidable financial resources on dominating these little counties, where the vast majority of residents belong to some kind or denomination of Christian church.

The nurses had grown quite literally sick and tired of their hospital putting profit over their own well-being and the health and safety of their patients. They had learned the hard way that their bosses would listen to them only when forced to do so. In response, the nurses quickly began a process that is often quite grueling for workers in this country—the process of organizing a union. When any worker in any work site in the country decides to form a union, the first thing the employer does is hire a union-busting law firm to come in and coach management on how to effectively divide the workers and ensure they vote *No* to the forming of a union. Now, this small hospital hired nearly a dozen full-time union busters, spending millions of dollars to enable hospital management to undermine the workers' interests and sabotage their union organizing campaign. The hospital bosses did not hire just any union busters. They employed the infamous Peraino brothers, who were involved in organizing the deadly 2017 White supremacist "Unite the Right" rally in Charlottesville, Virginia. Much has been written about the Peraino brothers' links to right-wing extremism and Christian nationalist movements, and a quick internet search yields some frightening information about their political undertaking.[2] So why were these extremists brought on to bust the union campaign of a group of nurses organizing at a small hospital in a rural county of Pennsylvania?

---

[2] Ernest Owens, "Mazzoni Staff Forced Firing of Alt-Right-Supporting Anti-Union Consultants," *Philadelphia*, September 11, 2017, https://www.phillymag.com/news/2017/09/11/mazzoni-center-anti-union-consultants/.

Conservative and far-right groups understood that the political landscape of Pennsylvania would undergo tremendous shifts if workers like these were able to form unions and gain a voice in the decision-making of their employers. If the nurses won a union and started to achieve improvements and other demands at the hospital, these successes might inspire nurses at nearby hospitals and other workers in the region to organize, giving labor a foothold in this small town and in the politics of local communities. Sometimes, it seems as if the ultra-right actually recognizes the potential politicizing force of unions better than much of the social-justice left. That's why this Pennsylvania hospital spent a fortune to convince the Peraino brothers to take a break from plotting white supremacist rallies in order to dissuade this small group of nurses from joining together.

In rural Pennsylvania, immigrants and communities of color are often scapegoated for the hardship of white working-class people, and white workers internalize a lot of this propaganda as historical truth. People need to make sense of their suffering, and the far right provides them with a convenient answer in racist fear-mongering. However, through the process of organizing a union, workers can become clear on exactly who is to blame for their low wages and unsafe staffing conditions. They can see firsthand the lengths to which their employers will go in order to protect their financial bottom line and to refuse workers a voice. This is often the first promising step in a complex politicizing process that can dramatically shift the perspective and political commitments of the workers, through which workers start to realize that their immigrant neighbors or night-shift coworkers are not to blame for their suffering in the workplace and their wider world.

Now the nurses that I organized with were incredibly dedicated and hardworking workers who gave the best of themselves to their patients. They were largely evangelical Christians, and faith was at the core of their lives. When the union busters crafted a strategy for getting workers at the hospital to vote *No* in the union election, they exploited the workers' core beliefs and sought to exacerbate existing prejudices. They did not just stick with the usual union-busting lies about the hospital shutting down or the union stealing workers' money. Instead, they fabricated a story that the union funded abortions. The union busters put together an entire website to delegitimize the union organizers, calling us communists and highlighting our support for undocumented workers. They used Christian language about protecting what's sacred, encouraging workers to maintain the so-called innocence of their relationship with each other and their community, and preventing the union from getting in the way. The union busters' basic message was, "You don't want these outside commie, atheist, immigrant-loving, abortionists to come in and take what's sacred to you." The union busters bought burner phones and texted the nurses pretending to be organizers, sending messages to confuse and scare the nurses. A few of the nurse leaders said that they were followed home by the union busters after their shifts and felt scared for their lives. The union busters held regular captive audience meetings in the hospital and quickly drove a wedge between us and the nurses. When it came time for the nurses to vote on whether to form a union, two-thirds of the nurses voted *No*. When a majority of workers vote against organizing in a union election, that's the end of the road—no union, no voice, everything back to how it was. A few weeks later, a few of the key nurse leaders were fired.

This campaign made it clear how deeply the far right understands the potential power and politicizing force of organized workers. It also illustrates the strategic importance of engaging workers in conversations about their faith. How might our organizing efforts have unfolded differently if we had outsmarted the union busters and instead had begun our own campaign through a dialogue with workers centered in religion and their faith commitments?

Faithful and Effective Organizing

The next story comes from a campaign I worked on alongside my mentor, Jane McAlevey, who wrote about this story in her book *No Shortcuts: Organizing for Power in the New Gilded Age*.[3] Jane, a crew of organizers, and I were working with a group of about 1,000 nurses at a hospital in North Philadelphia. In many ways, the beginning of their story is similar to the preceding, granted the differences of organization size and political geography. The North Philadelphia nurses called up the union because of unsafe staffing levels in the hospital and stagnant wages. They had tried advocating for more staff and better nurse-to-patient ratios for years but had hit a wall. The hospital served thousands of North Philadelphia residents from low-

---

[3] Jane McAlevey, *No Shortcuts: Organizing for Power in the New Gilded Age* (New York: Oxford University Press, 2016).

income communities of color, and the group of nurses was racially and ethnically diverse. There were deep divisions among the nurses, divisions largely based on issues of race. A majority of the day-shift nurses were white, while the night-shift nurses were predominantly people of color. Women and people of color were often making less than their male and white counterparts, and staffing levels varied across the hospital based on who was favored by proximity to management.

As a veteran union organizer, Jane had already learned the lessons we learned in rural PA about the unique priority of addressing workers on matters of faith and engaging their faith leaders. Under Jane's leadership, we promptly started talking with the workers about their religious commitments, their faith communities, and the clergy who occupied positions of authority in their lives. In these conversations, we talked with the nurses about the importance of building relationships outside of the hospital, and how much more power they could build if they worked in partnership with clergy and lay members of their faith communities. Before we started asking the nurses to set up meetings with these faith leaders, we mapped out the largest and most powerful religious institutions and congregations across the city, prioritizing them in our outreach. The nurses then set up meetings with their own pastors, imams, and rabbis, and asked for their support in the campaign for fair wages, safe staffing practices, and livable working conditions.

Unsurprisingly, this hospital also hired a union-busting law firm, spending over a million dollars to arm management and undermine the organizing efforts. The union busters used many of the same tactics described in the first story, including captive audience meetings, baseless lies, and direct threats. They attempted to pit the workers against each other based on race. However, the union busters were ultimately unsuccessful. The workers built deep solidarity with each other through their organizing campaign, especially with their faith leaders and the wider community. Because of this solidarity-building, the union busters could not break through to divide workers. When things got scary or confusing, the workers felt moral clarity and had the support of their clergy to buoy them. When it came time for the union election, the nurses voted overwhelmingly to form their union.

After workers win their union election, they immediately start the process of negotiating their first union contract, where they can struggle for better wages and working conditions. How much they win in the negotiations process largely depends on the power and unity the workers have built by organizing. When the nurses started their first round of bargaining, they held these negotiations in one of the largest predominantly Black North Philadelphia churches, with the full support of the head pastor and the congregation. This really changed the dynamics of the negotiations process. When you have a pastor, or an imam, or a rabbi coming in and opening your meetings with prayer, the struggle for justice is situated within ancient and ongoing traditions of liberation. Imagine the employer being forced to enter a sanctuary of worship to refuse a group of nurses adequate money for patient care, just after these bosses have given themselves enormous bonuses.

Throughout the negotiations, the nurses collected dozens of letters of support from their faith leaders and delivered them to the CEO of the hospital. The nurses also developed a bargaining platform that included "common good" demands, which are demands that impact patients and the broader community. This approach is called "bargaining for the common good," and has been adopted by coalitions of unions, community groups, and faith groups across the country. Bargaining for things like safe staffing levels and language equity for patients creates a deeper investment for clergy and congregants who have been or might one day be patients of that hospital. After a difficult and long campaign, which included the nurses taking a vote to authorize a strike, the nurses were able to win significant wage increases, improved staffing, equity for women and people of color, and more.

This story offers at least two important lessons for labor organizers and religious leaders. First, it shows the power of thoughtfully addressing workers' religious traditions and strategically engaging their faith communities, including the deep bonds of solidarity that can be formed in that process. The second lesson is about how we apply the method of organizing within faith-based movements instead of merely mobilizing.

Many faith-based organizations and social movements are unfortunately preoccupied with the work of mobilizing clergy and communities that already agree with their principal causes. This means that the organizations and movements are most often not devoted to the work of expanding the base of support for their causes and initiatives. Philadelphia has a particularly strong interfaith coalition that does both mobilizing *and* organizing work but has still struggled to engage the largest and most powerful congregations in the city. When we performed our strategic analysis of the most powerful religious institutions and faith leaders in Philadelphia, we found that the vast majority of them were not involved in the preexisting coalition. This is not unique to Philadelphia. Often, some of the largest congregations in major cities do not self-identify as progressive and would be hesitant to join an interfaith group that they view as overtly political or left-leaning. In addition to these ideological differences, some clergy of color view such interfaith coalitions as being hegemonically constituted and directed by white congregations and communities. If the existing interfaith coalition had tried to engage these powerful clergy of color, they probably would not have gotten in the door. But union members—the nurses themselves—are members of these very congregations. A clergyperson is unlikely to ignore requests for a meeting from an active member of their congregation. Accordingly, our strategy in the campaign was to mobilize the already organized union members to approach their clergy in support of their collective bargaining power. During these meetings, union staff would accompany nurses to meet with their clergy, but the workers themselves would lead and shape the conversation with their religious leaders.

By organizing in this way, the union of North Philadelphia nurses made possible exactly what is feared by the likes of those right-wing extremist union busters in rural Pennsylvania. Through an organizing campaign that thoughtfully engaged the nurses around matters of religious commitment as well as the struggles in their workplace, these workers were able to step aside from prejudices and existing assumptions about each other, learn one another's stories, and build bonds of trust and solidarity that withstand propaganda and sabotage. I saw Republican-registered nurses go through political transformations, and I know at least a few who recently voted for Kamala Harris. Surprising wins and transformations are possible when labor and religion seek strategic partnership and spiritual alignment.

The Power of Faith and Labor Partnerships

Jane and I learned a lot from our campaign with nurses in North Philadelphia. In its wake, Jane wanted to see what might be possible if we scaled these methods from this specific campaign across the efforts of an entire union. In her last year of life, while she was in treatment for terminal cancer, Jane went back to the union that first trained her as an organizer. SEIU 1199 New England is a union in Connecticut that represents about 29,000 healthcare workers. It has a long history of militant organizing, striking, and fighting for racial and social justice. Martin Luther King Jr. called SEIU 1199 his favorite union because of its fighting legacy. With the support of the UC Berkeley Labor Center, Jane headed back to Connecticut to launch a campaign with SEIU 1199 that would experiment with the same methods across a union of 29,000 workers. When Jane asked me to come along for the campaign, it was an easy yes.

The president of the union, Rob Baril, is a visionary leader who tells the story of how, a few weeks into the pandemic, he got a call from a union member who told him, "Rob, I killed my mother." This nursing home worker had contracted the coronavirus at work and brought it home. In those first few months of the pandemic, nurses were being given trash bags as personal protective equipment (PPE), while the fourteen billionaires in Connecticut were making record profits.[4] Connecticut has one of the highest levels of income inequality and wealth gaps in the entire country. That disparity, and the grief of many union members like the one who reached out to Rob, is the backdrop for this campaign.

Rob knew that the workers would be capable of winning only so much if they fought alone. SEIU 1199 is a union that isn't afraid to stand up for a fight. The workers regularly participate in strikes, campaigns of civil disobedience, and other direct actions. Yet, even as one of the strongest unions in the country, SEIU 1199 members were watching their raises get eaten up by rent and cost of living increases during the pandemic. So, in 2024, SEIU 1199 brought hundreds of union members out on leave and trained them to have effective conversations with their coworkers about the importance of building relationships with their faith communities. Through member-to-member conversations, they tracked where hundreds of union members worshiped and who among them had connections with local clergy and other religious leaders.

Over the course of just a few months, union members worked with SEIU 1199 organizers Wen Zhuang and Isaiah Martinez to set up meetings with about forty-five clergy leaders in the Hartford and Waterbury areas. The union members shared their stories with the clergy, welcomed feedback about what clergy and their congregants understood to be necessary changes to the healthcare system, and then asked for the support of these

---

[4] Hedge Clippers, "Hedge Papers No. 43: Connecticut Billionaires and Their Lucrative Loophole," *Hedge Papers*, no.43, February 7, 2017, https://hedgeclippers.org/hedge-papers-no-43-connecticut-billionaires-and-their-lucrative-loophole/.

religious communities. All but one clergyperson agreed to participate in the campaign. Of those forty-five clergy, only a handful are part of the local interfaith organization, and they did not necessarily identify as progressive.

When we asked some of the clergy why they were not part of the interfaith alliance, they were candid about being wary of joining an organization that they perceived to be predominantly white in makeup and in vision. The local interfaith group does phenomenal work, but because of limited capacity and resources, it has often relied on recruiting clergy who already identify as progressive and self-select into the organization. If interfaith organizers had attempted to approach this group of clergy, they would have encountered resistance. However, when the clergy's own congregants came to them to share their stories of short staffing and low wages, the clergy were determined to join the fight. The union and the interfaith alliance are now working as partners in the fight for racial and economic justice and are able to bring together groups of clergy and workers who otherwise would continue to work in their silos.

The kickoff of the campaign was attended by thirty clergy, and every single clergy member signed the open letter to the governor of Connecticut, outlining the union's demands. I have never been in a more Spirit-filled space. The union members spoke powerfully about how God called them to organize for a world free from oppression and injustice. The clergy shared scripture and personal accounts of how the healthcare system affected their own family members and congregants. The kickoff left everyone in that room feeling fortified for the fight ahead.

Organizing as Embodied Interdependence

Organizing makes an important strategic intervention under capitalism, but I think we tend not to recognize and properly consider the role of organizing as a form of spiritual intervention. Under US capitalism, working-class people spend a majority of their waking lives at work—somewhere around *two-thirds* of their lives. And yet workers are still barely making ends meet.[5] Most working-class jobs are deeply alienating and

---

[5] Elise Gould and Josh Bivens, "There's No Debate: Measurable Income Inequity Has Skyrocketed in Recent Decades," Economic Policy Institute, January 18, 2024, https://www.epi.org/blog/theres-no-debate-measurable-income-inequality-has-skyrocketed-in-recent-decades/.

disembodied places. I have organized with Amazon workers who are told when they can and cannot use the bathroom. I have organized with nurses who don't take lunch breaks because they are afraid to leave their patients even more short-staffed. I have organized with janitors who sleep in the stadium they clean so they can work 80+ hours a week and send money home to their families. I have organized with women who are being regularly assaulted by their managers but cannot speak up out of fear of losing their jobs. Working people's bodies and movements are constantly monitored and policed.

Furthermore, when we consider the work we are doing or the goods we are producing, we are deeply alienated from the services and products we are providing. We are often forced to produce or sell goods we know are not healthy or good for the world. We watch with horror as our bosses value their own profit over the people we are serving, putting lives and health at risk daily. Unless we have strong unions (only 10 percent of workers are unionized), our bosses make all these decisions without even thinking to consider our input.[6] This leaves us feeling powerless, alienated, and expendable.

Capitalism makes everything a commodity: our time, our labor, our bodies, and the earth. It is a system that depends on the de-sanctification of our worlds. It is peculiar to hear so-called experts talk about our society as secular, especially when capitalism installs an entire cosmology through which we perceive and devalue ourselves, each other, and the purpose of life. Has capitalism not become our religion?

Religious institutions and unions are the two organizations that can help to re-sanctify the world and challenge capitalism. Workplaces and houses of worship are the only two places where masses of people from different social positions come together and encounter one another on a regular basis. These institutions importantly shape our politics and our worlds. At the intersection of these places, we can organize before and beyond our efforts to mobilize, working to change people's hearts and minds.

When I worship with my own community, I seek in prayer a place that counters the logic of capitalism and proclaims that I matter, that I am whole, and that my worth can be determined only by God. For a moment, I am suspended from the alienation and isolation of capitalism.

---

[6] Bureau of Labor Statistics, "Union Members—2024," January 28, 2025, https://www.bls.gov/news.release/pdf/union2.pdf.

I get a temporary taste of the Promised Land, of the world for which we are organizing. Unfortunately, this moment of suspension is only ever temporary under the conditions of capital, as most of us head back to work on Monday to feel commodified and deformed all over again.

When workers decide to organize a union, they're saying, "I'm worth more than what the boss has said that I am. My work has dignity. My life and the lives of my coworkers have dignity. We believe it can be different than this." One of the most beautiful parts of an organizing campaign is the real interdependence that gets embodied and practiced. Workers feel this in their bones. This interdependence comes with a realization that, if they want a higher wage, they cannot do it alone. When you start to feel powerful and connected in the place where you spend a majority of your life, it has resounding impacts on your life outside of work. Any union organizer can tell you stories of people being profoundly transformed in the process of organizing a union. In multiple union-organizing drives of which I have been a part, women have decided to leave their abusive husbands at the end of the campaign. Workers come out as queer during campaigns. Workers run for local elected office. Workers chant into megaphones, participate in civil disobedience, and, together, do things they never imagined possible on their own.

The left, in large part, seems to have lost sight of the importance of religion in organizing and liberation struggles. Others have written more eloquently than I am able about the misinterpretation of Marx's famous characterization of religion as "the opium of the people," and about the serious strategic mistake of ceding religion to the right. My organizer friends and I talk a lot about how the labor movement has become a place of hyper-secularism, disconnected from spirit and Earth. The entire social justice movement has been experiencing widespread burnout of organizers and incredibly high turnover. The labor movement tends to fail at providing people with a more encompassing and intimate cosmology and does not usually attempt to embrace people's religion and spirituality or to address deeper existential questions. This is not only a social problem; it is a serious strategic mistake.

There are examples that point the way forward, beautiful examples like The Landless Workers' Movement (MST) and other Latin American liberation struggles, particularly in Brazil, Mexico, and Nicaragua. Landback campaigns and Indigenous-led movements for climate justice and tribal sovereignty have woven together spirit, land, and justice for decades.

But the left in the United States has not picked up on these lessons widely enough yet. Meanwhile, the majority of people in this country are still religious, and even the starkest projections show that a majority of people in this country will in fifty years still identify religiously with Christianity or Islam.[7] With the spread of right-wing evangelicalism and the eclipse of some of the more progressive Christian denominations, I can't help wondering what form of Christianity will prevail in the coming century.

In our moment of accelerating climate catastrophe, of existential dread about the future of this planet, and of widening political divides, people are looking for answers to what's happening to them. Those nurses in rural Pennsylvania watched the mining and manufacturing industries in their communities collapse, and many lost their homes, their land, and so much of what they held sacred. They wanted someone to blame and some way to make sense of their suffering, and Trump and the Christian-right gave them those answers. People are going to continue to seek answers as climate collapse continues and inequality worsens. As a result, people will continue joining religious traditions and political sects that can provide ready-made answers for them. We on the left had better figure out how to counter such ideology with our own life-affirming and justice-seeking visions of religious identity.

Together, religious traditions and the labor movement could build enough power to transform the political landscape of this country, but we have a lot to learn from each other. The labor movement needs faith traditions to answer these bigger, existential questions, and to reach people's hearts and minds. In turn, faith traditions have a lot to learn from the labor movement about what it looks like to actually put theological conviction into concrete practice.

So, where do we go from here? I do not have the answers, but I have learned some lessons over the years about what it takes to build power and win concrete changes for working people. If you are a person of faith who is worried about the future of the planet and our society, about the rise of Christian nationalism and the abusive distribution of wealth, I would encourage you to get involved with base-building organizations that do serious *organizing* before and beyond any mobilizing, so that, together, we

---

[7] Pew Research Center, "The Future of World Religions: Population Growth Projections, 2010–2050," April 2, 2015, https://www.pewresearch.org/religion/2015/04/02/religious-projections-2010-2050/.

can really put our faith into action. If you are an organizer, I invite you to think about how your own faith or spirituality informs your work and how to build strategic long-term alliances between religious institutions and labor organizations. On days when it gets hard, we must lean on each other and root ourselves in the practices and traditions that ground and inspire us. For me, that means doing my best to follow prayerfully in the footsteps of a Palestinian Jew named Jesus, who not only believed that another world is possible but that, every moment that we stand together and see each other as holy, we create a little pocket of the Kingdom of God on Earth.

6

Teaching Community Organizing in Theological Education:

Pedagogical Conundrums and Delights

Cynthia Moe-Lobeda

The educator has the duty of not being neutral.
—Paulo Freire[1]

Ten years ago, I was invited by a network of faith-based community organizers working within the Evangelical Lutheran Church in America (ELCA) to accompany them as a theologian. They were developing ministries around the United States that were grounded in the arts of community organizing and were aligned with liberative movements in their communities. All had been trained by one of the major broad-based community organizing networks.[2] They were daring, courageous, and insightful, and they were committed to teamwork, an antiracism lens, accountability, and exploring the gospel as a foundation of liberation. Participating in their twice-yearly gatherings from Washington, DC, to Detroit to Seattle, engaging with them in theological reflection, and sharing respect, love, laughter, pain, and evaluation with them was a treasure trove of learning, growth, and joy for me.

---

[1] Myles Horton and Paulo Freire, *We Make the Road by Walking: Conversations on Education and Social Change* (Philadelphia: Temple University Press, 1990).

[2] Faith in Action (formerly Pacific Institute for Community Organization), the Gamaliel Foundation, the Industrial Areas Foundation, and DART Network (Direct Action Research and Training).

Another seminary professor, whom I had not previously known, the New Testament scholar Ray Pickett, who taught about Jesus as a community organizer, had also been invited to accompany this network. Two years into that sojourn, we both found ourselves on the faculty of Pacific Lutheran Theological Seminary (PLTS), a small progressive Lutheran seminary in Berkeley, California. Before long, the PLTS faculty had integrated a required course in faith-based community organizing into the ethics curriculum for MDiv and MA students. Ray and I knew that it should be designed and taught by community organizers. Thus was born the ever-evolving course, now in its seventh year and eighth iterations, explored in this essay.

For me, co-creating this course was a next step in a trajectory born in my high school years, when—although a straight-A student—I came to disdain traditional education (including the high school education I was experiencing) for inculcating conformity with the US imperialist political economy and the militarism that protected it. Later, while working and living in Central America, I was trained briefly in Freirean methods of liberative education and worked with campesinos enacting it. I have long held that education can be liberative or reinscribe systems of oppression and that traditional institutional education tends toward the latter. When I began my doctoral work at Union Theological Seminary, I had no intention of going into teaching. My purpose was to plumb the depths of Christian traditions for power to resist the foul matrix of exploitation that shapes our society. However, studying with James Cone, Delores Williams, Beverly Harrison, Larry Rasmussen, Vincent Wimbush, and others convinced me that I could do that resistance work through teaching, writing, and public speaking. As a result, I have found myself in traditional educational institutions, seeking to cultivate knowledge, skills, and moral-spiritual agency for resisting and dismantling systemic injustice and building more equitable, ecological, and radically democratic alternatives.

Daunting challenges accompany that aim. Note two: One is the vast degree to which white supremacy linked with wealth-based supremacy, both embedded in predatory capitalism, have infiltrated and undermined the profound gifts of the human intellect and education designed to develop it. A second is the lure of isolating intellectual work—including theory— from actual engagement in practices of social transformation and isolating spirituality from the same. Mountains of intellectual energy and creativity within the academy are wasted on theorizing that stays within intellectual candy stores.

So I am hungry to develop ways of cultivating the mind/heart/soul/spirit/body for ministry that (1) confronts and counters the forces of white supremacy and wealth-based supremacy, (2) empowers movement toward a post–predatory capitalist economy, and (3) puts the gifts of intellect and spiritual maturity in service of liberatory practice. The PLTS course in community organizing—I have come to realize—is an experiment in these aims.

This essay describes, assesses, and then builds on that experiment in teaching community organizing in a seminary context as a required course for all students in the MDiv and MA programs. The essay's first section identifies presuppositions undergirding the course and key questions flowing from them. The second section traces the development of the course through its iterations, focusing on evaluations by students and faculty and on the revisions catalyzed by those evaluations. The third section draws on three bodies of theory to augment, challenge, and expand the conclusions and revisions already enacted.

My purpose in this chapter is to harvest from this experience all that can be learned that would be useful to our team at PLTS and to others seeking to integrate community organizing into theological education in order to prepare leaders in the church for dismantling systemic injustice and building more life-giving alternatives.

Presuppositions and Ensuing Questions

Presupposition regarding Context

Many parts of the church—including seminaries—are replete with people who proclaim "social justice" as a core value.[3] We adopt powerful statements on social justice, sing that "even the stones will cry out for justice," and claim that seeking justice is a vocation of the baptized. We relish liberative readings of the Magnificat and God's drowning of the mighty and elevating the poor. We develop what we call "social justice ministries." This is all necessary; it is vital. The statements, hymnody, liberative text study, ministries of feeding and sheltering are crucial.

---

[3] This is true also of broader society. However, in this essay, the focus is the church.

However, they are accompanied by travesty. The travesty is that justice is "valued" and acclaimed but often not enacted, and justice is claimed without adequate sense of what injustice is and how it functions and stays intact. Moreover, many "social justice" ministries are, in fact, charitable services such as feeding and sheltering ministries without an enacted justice orientation. The travesty has varied facets:

- assuming that verbiage is adequate
- conflating justice with acts of service to marginalized people
- inadequate understanding of systemic injustices and their roots

This travesty is not unique to our society. Antonio Faundez in his *Learning to Question* (written with Paulo Freire) writes:

> One of the things we learned in Chile in our early reflection on everyday life was that abstract political, religious, or moral statements did not take concrete shape in acts by individuals. We were revolutionaries in the abstract, not in our daily lives. It seems to me essential that in our individual lives, we should day to day live out what we affirm.[4]

How can theological education in community organizing enable people to enact the justice that they profess?

Theological Presupposition regarding Purpose of Theological Education

From a perspective of Christian ethics, a central purpose of theological education is equipping people to perceive God's revelation so that we may love and heed God. We heed God by receiving and trusting God's justice-seeking, Earth-honoring love and then aligning life—both individual and societal—with the stream of God's creating, healing, liberating presence and activity on Earth. Theological education is meant to equip us to know, love, and heed the Holy One.

---

[4] Paulo Freire and Antonio Faundez, *Learning to Question: A Pedagogy of Liberation* (New York: Continuum, 1989), cited in bell hooks, *Teaching to Transgress* (New York: Routledge, 1994), 48.

Heeding God hinges on the understanding of what God is forming human beings and society into and what God is doing. I will go with the ancient claim, articulated by second-century theologian Irenaeus of Lyons, that God's purpose is to bring all of creation into communion, including communion with God. Irenaeus is not alone in this understanding. It has been articulated variously throughout time, including in recent decades. As stated by theologian Willie James Jennings, speaking of Jesus: "And now in him we see what God wants: communion." The "original trajectory of ... God" is "to gather together ... reforming us as those who ... gesture communion with our very existence.... This ... is God's dream."[5] Theological education, thus, ought to cultivate communion and equip people to go forth and cultivate communion. Communion indicates life that breeds inclusive belonging, justice, compassion, and ecological well-being.

However, communion is shredded by various forms of injustice that enable some to accumulate power or privilege at the expense—sometimes brutal expense—of others. The interlocking forces of white supremacy, wealth-based supremacy, and predatory capitalism (noted above as challenges to liberatory education) are mainstays of injustice in our time. Therefore, if it is to cultivate communion, theological education must counter these forms of injustice that shred communion.

How can theological education in community organizing cultivate the mind/heart/soul/spirit/body for ministry that confronts and counters the forces of white supremacy, wealth-based supremacy, and predatory capitalism so that people may realize the communion that God gives?

These two presuppositions have heightened my desire to incorporate community organizing into theological education. The questions flowing form these presuppositions inform this quest to learn from and strengthen our experiment in doing so.

Evolution of the Course

This course began as an experimental collaboration between Pacific Lutheran Theological Seminary (PLTS) and the Organizing for Mission Cohort (OFM) of the Evangelical Lutheran Church in America (ELCA) to

---

[5] Willie James Jennings, *After Whiteness: An Education in Belonging*, Theological Education between the Times (Grand Rapids: Eerdmans, 2020), 107.

provide a formal five-day training program as a requirement for all seminarians enrolled in degree programs and for clergy and lay leaders nationwide. A five-person planning/teaching team included the two seminary professors noted above and three highly experienced community organizers trained by one of the major networks. The course covered the basic tools of faith-based community organizing with additional sessions on biblical and theological perspective, all done with a racial equity lens. The aim was *preparing participants to lead ministries that work for justice and compassion using the disciplines of community organizing.* A secondary aim was for certain practices at the heart of community organizing—in particular one-to-ones, listening campaigns, and relationality—to influence the seminary culture. The course was held in January of the seminarians' first year. The pedagogical approach was that of a traditional five-day training program and included engaging in a community "action" in the Bay Area with a local Gamaliel affiliate. The initial iteration included fifty participants composed of PLTS students, one ELCA bishop, synodical staff, and other clergy and lay leaders from around the country.[6] The course was fully in-person except for the one year it was online due to COVID restrictions.

Evaluation took four forms: two formal evaluation sessions each day by the planning/teaching team, a post-training written evaluation by participants, a post-training listening session with participants who were seminary students, and a final formal evaluation by the planner/teachers.

Evaluations by participants ranged from highly appreciative ("the course was life-transforming") to highly critical, with criticism coming disproportionately from the seminary students for whom the course was required. Primary concerns included: (1) agitation: while a few students experienced powerful shifts, a larger number experienced it as damaging or unjust;[7] (2) students were confused by uncertainty about the purpose of the training as it seemed to be preparing them to be full-time organizers, which was not their intention; (3) power dynamics in the room whereby seminarians felt unsafe to be fully vulnerable because the room included people who could wield power over them in their movement toward ordination (e.g., bishops, synodical bishops and staff, senior clergy).

---

[6] "Synod" refers to a geographic region of the ELCA.

[7] "Agitation" is used in community organizing to signify a method of intentionally asking probing questions that challenge the agitatee to live more fully into their actual values, and to recognize where she/he/they are not doing so.

Instructors' evaluations called for: (1) better integration of theological and biblical reflection into the other aspects of the training; (2) more attention to the role of liturgy and other aspects of worship life in the practice of organizing; and (3) less didactive pedagogy.

In response to these evaluations, substantive revisions were made with each iteration of the course. As a result, the most recent iteration (January 2024) was the most successful in terms of students experiencing powerful transformative learning as manifest in their: (1) using course learning in subsequent semesters in coursework and contextual learning; (2) bringing course learnings into play in the life of the seminary; (3) their evaluative and informal comments about the course and about their intentions to make use of it in ministry.

What has shifted to render this kind of success? Six primary reorientations now shape the approach and content of the course.

- It has been reconceived not as a five-day training but as a five-day course that includes training modules. This allows for a far less didactive and more liberative pedagogy, and frees the course from some of the constraints imposed by the five-day training model.[8]
- It is grounded intentionally and strategically in relationality, and more specifically in building a trustworthy community of learners that chooses honestly to share vulnerabilities and "what gets in the way of ..." in ministry that is aimed at social justice.
- It is designed explicitly to prepare seminarians to use the learning in justice-oriented congregational ministry, rather than using a design for training community organizers.
- It is planned and led by a seminary professor, with key sessions led by practicing pastors who are trained in community organizing and who lead justice-oriented ministries and by professional community organizers working in congregational contexts. The professor's primary foci are creating an ethos of relationality and trustworthy daring community, grounding all aspects of the course theologically, and integrating the sessions taught by others.
- It is reorganized around three major components: the "why" of engaging in ministry that seeks transformation toward more

---

[8] For example, the course gives up some skill-building sessions (called "trainings" in traditional community organizing) to allow more time for biblical reflection, theological reflection, grounding, prayer, etc.

compassionate, equitable, ecologically sane communities and world; the "why" of using the arts /tools of community organizing; the "what" and "how," which is learning particular tools of community organizing (one-to-ones, power analysis, listening campaigns, etc.).
- While the course is open to practicing ordained and lay leaders who are not enrolled in the seminary's degree programs, it is not open to bishops or bishops with responsibility for approving candidates for ordination.

These reorientations have meant a number of shifts in who leads sessions and what they share with students, session content, key concepts, and the role of agitation.

We now bring in practicing pastors with on-the-ground experience leading faith-based efforts to dismantle systemic injustice to lead sessions on arenas in which they are highly gifted and experienced. Most of them are also trained in faith-based community organizing. We ask them to begin with stories of how they came to rely on and relish the arts of community organizing in ministry, and stories of how they have enacted in ministry the particular topic of their session. These topics include:

- Trainings in basic skills of community organizing including one-to-ones, listening campaigns, building a team, propositions;[9]
- Linking social justice work with pastoral care;
- Biblical reflection focused especially on Jesus as a community organizer;
- Integrating liturgy, preaching, biblical and theological reflection with other aspects of worship and congregational life, and deeply with the arts of community organizing practiced with liberative aims.

We now have sessions dedicated to dynamics that commonly "get in the way" of active engagement in social transformative public engagement for leaders in Christian communities. Those dynamics include the

---

[9] "Proposition" in community organizing discourse refers to the practice of inviting another person to engage in a particular endeavor (e.g., to join a campaign for changing a law, join a leadership team, support an organization, or to assume some other responsibility) that will enable them to put into practice something that they value or work in community with others to achieve something that they value.

false narrative that power is bad, the false narrative that "self-interest" is selfishness and is contrary to neighbor-love, the tendency to claim values such as justice but not embody them in public life, and the need to be liked. Sessions centered in biblical reflection and sessions of theological reflection are related explicitly to the sessions on skill building.

The reorientations have meant conceiving key concepts in a new way. We refer to one-to-ones as "sacred encounters" and treat them as such. Propositions are now "sacred invitations." Organizing is considered "sacramental organizing," and accountability triads are "sacred circles." Tools of community organizing are seen also as tools for following Jesus and for building others' capacities for following Jesus.

Finally, the reorientations have led to a change in the role of agitation. Agitation has tremendous value and can be life-shaping in a positive and empowering way. When well done and landing well, it exposes the (often unconsciously held) lies or myths that we tell ourselves about ourselves, our roles, our power, or our worthiness. These lies may: (1) strangle one's power; (2) get in the way of following Jesus; (3) lure one away from one's purpose; (4) impede one's capacity to be part of the body of God's justice-seeking love on Earth; (5) obscure self-interest and prevent one from honoring it. Agitation not only exposes such lies, but also propels people to recognize and embody truths that counter the lies.[10] In this sense, agitation may be an invaluable tool for helping another person become the person whom God is creating them to be. It is a way in which the Spirit works through one person to form another, a means of spiritual formation.

However, agitation also can be wounding or alienating when: (1) the agitatee is in a vulnerable or traumatized state due to factors outside of the course/training;[11] (2) the agitator's judgment is off and the agitatee then feels publicly and falsely accused by a powerful person in front of people whose respect the agitatee values;[12] (3) the agitatee is in the room with people who have power over their future; (4) the agitator has not yet

---

[10] Agitation may be perceived theologically in various ways, but discussing them is beyond the limits of this essay.

[11] Exhaustion; struggling to afford rent, food, tuition; suffering from frequent micro-aggressions, lack of health care, and the dangers of living as a Black, Brown, Indigenous, queer, or differently-abled person are examples.

[12] "Off-judgments" are more likely to be made by inexperienced trainers, trainers too motivated by "getting in an agitation," or trainers who do not know the group well.

established relationship with the agitatee; (5) the agitatee is in the course not by choice, but because it is required; (6) the stage has not been set regarding the reasons for and fruits of agitation. Therefore, we are developing ways to expose disempowering "lies" and motivate living according to truths that counter them without using traditional techniques of agitation. This is a challenging pedagogical conundrum.

Learning from Theory

For the sake of future efforts to integrate community organizing into theological education, what more can be learned from this seven-year experiment if we hold it in the light of insights from the following theoretical fields?

- Feminist and antiracist internal critiques of classical broad-based community organizing;
- critical pedagogy theory, especially as developed by womanist, feminist, eco-womanist, and eco-feminist scholar-activists;
- decolonial theory as seen in selected works of Linda Tuhiwai Smith.

We bear in mind, in particular, the questions posed: How can community organizing in theological education: (1) enable people to enact the justice that they profess and (2) cultivate the mind/heart/soul/spirit/body for ministry that counters the forces of white supremacy, wealth-based supremacy, and predatory capitalism so that people may live into God's purposes of communion?

The guideposts suggested below are but a tiny taste of contributions these fields could make to the teaching of community organizing in theological education. This account is an illustrative glimpse and does not claim to be comprehensive.

Feminist and Antiracist Internal Critiques of
Classical Broad-Based Community Organizing

Community organizing has shifted in the last four decades. This has happened as a result of leadership arising from communities of color and women who prioritize an antiracist or feminist lens. Additionally, their internal critique of the methods, assumptions, principles, priorities, and power arrangements characteristic of organizing from its inception through the late 1980s has helped bring this shift in organizing.

Antiracist critique has focused on the dominance of leadership by white organizers, their reticence to centralize racism and other issues facing communities of color, and the dissonance between the strategies and leadership cultures typical of community organizing, on the one hand, and the strategies and leadership cultures of many communities of color, on the other. Feminist critiques, as summarized by Rinku Sen, had "four targets: community organizing overemphasizes intervention in the public sphere, does not allow organizers to balance work and family, focuses on narrow self-interest as the primary motivator, and relies on conflict and militaristic tactics."[13]

Partly as a result of these critiques, formal community organizing is evolving. Networks have formed that are led by women, people of color, and queer people.[14] The major traditional networks and many of their affiliates have more BIPOC and women in leadership roles and are addressing racism.[15] Some organizing communities are incorporating self-compassion, self-respect, and work/life balance into the culture of organizing.

These critiques and developments suggest guidelines for the teaching of community organizing in theological education.

- Course planning and teaching should be led or co-led by people of color and women.
- An antiracist focus and a feminist lens should be central in the course.
- The course should explicitly foster a sense of community that attends to the emotional, spiritual, and material well-being of participants, including cultivating capacity to know and meet one's needs.

Critical/liberative Pedagogy Theory

The movement of critical pedagogy "emerged from a long historical legacy of radical social thought and progressive educational movements, which aspired to link practices of schooling to democratic principles of society and

---

[13] Rinku Sen, *Stir It Up* (San Francisco: Jossey-Bass, 2003), liv.

[14] A first was the Center for Third World Organizing in Oakland.

[15] See, for example, the Gamaliel affiliates Genesis and Poder en Accion, and the Midwest Academy.

transformative social action in the interest of oppressed communities."[16] It involves diverse movements, perspectives, and schools of thought.[17] In very general terms, they share the aim of enabling students to become "empowered subjects, achiev[ing] a deepening awareness of the social realities that shape their lives and discover their own capacities to recreate them."[18] They share, too, the intent of equipping people to "challeng[e] asymmetrical relations of power and transform the fundamental sociopolitical and economic structures that reproduce inequities."[19]

Community organizing education within theological education, as we are designing it, shares these two aims. Critical pedagogy theory yields two valuable guideposts for meeting them:

- Integrate more theory than is typical of much training in community organizing, including the version of it developed at PLTS, and link theory inseparably with action.
- Bring to the fore forms of knowing other than cognitive reason—personal narrative, the body as epistemological subject, and earth as teacher.

Community organizing tends to emphasize practice over theory, and many activists caution about the danger of theory unlinked to practice. Moreover, seminary students often push for more practice and less theory in theological education. Critical pedagogy, too, recognizes the danger of theory divorced from liberative action. However, as influenced by Paulo Freire, one of its seminal thinkers, critical pedagogy also insists on the necessity of theory. bell hooks says it well: "We must continually claim theory as a necessary practice within a holistic framework of liberatory activities."[20] While acknowledging that "elite academics" may threaten

---

[16] Marta Baltodano, Antonia Dardar, and Rodolfo Torres, "Critical Pedagogy: An Introduction," in *Critical Pedagogy Reader*, 3rd ed., ed. Marta Baltodano, Antonia Dardar, and Rodolfo Torres (New York: Routledge, 2017), 2. The essay (1–23) provides an excellent succinct account of the historical legacy of critical (liberative) pedagogy.

[17] Notable has been the role of the Highlander Folk School and its founder Myles Horton.

[18] Baltodano, Dardar, and Torres, "Critical Pedagogy," 14.

[19] Baltodano, Dardar, and Torres, "Critical Pedagogy," 13.

[20] hooks, *Teaching to Transgress*, 69.

liberative struggles by constructing theory "in ways that make it a critical terrain which only the chosen few can enter," she insists that the "anti-intellectualism [that] declares all theory as worthless" also sabotages liberative struggle.

Theory typically presupposes cognitive reason as the mode of knowing. Yet feminist, womanist, eco-feminist, and eco-womanist theorists of critical pedagogy problematize the epistemological privileging of cognitive reasoning. They insist on epistemologies that centralize other forms of knowing, including personal narrative, the body as epistemological subject, and Earth as teacher.

Decolonial Theory through Work of Linda Tuhiwai Smith

Dangers accompany the use of decoloniality discourse by a white settler-colonial person, especially without also advocating for land rematriation/repatriation.[21] Yet, I—a person of white settler-colonial heritage—do use this body of theory and language for two reasons. One is the need for a decolonial lens in efforts to dismantle ongoing colonialism. Second, people who have "benefited" materially from centuries of colonialism also have been colonized materially and spiritually by its chains, demands, mind-

---

[21] The term "decolonial" is used in varied ways, at times juxtaposed with anti-colonial or postcolonial. Some theorists assert that "decolonial" should be used only with reference to efforts to repatriate land stolen in the colonial enterprise: "Decolonization brings about the repatriation of Indigenous land and life; it is not a metaphor for other things we want to do to improve our societies and schools. The easy adoption of decolonizing discourse by educational advocacy and scholarship, evidenced by the increasing number of calls to 'decolonize our schools,' or use 'decolonizing methods,' or 'decolonize student thinking', turns decolonization into a metaphor." See Eve Tuck and K. Wayne Yang, "Decolonization Is Not a Metaphor," *Decolonization: Indigeneity, Education, and Society* 1, no. 1 (September 8, 2012), 1. I respect this position. Yet I also see that some Indigenous scholars and scholars from other colonized communities use "decolonize" much more broadly to apply, for example, to the "unlearning of settler colonial mentality." See Lily Mendoza, "Transdiasporic Indigeneity and Decolonizing Faith," in *Decolonizing Ecotheology: Indigenous and Subaltern Challenges*, ed. S. Lily Mendoza and George Zachariah (Eugene, OR: Pickwick, 2022), 155–78. I recognize also the tremendous insight and agency offered by applying "decolonize" beyond explicit land rematriation/repatriation, especially to epistemologies and their material implications.

sets, and bodily formative influence. The poet and seminal decolonial and anti-colonial thinker, Aimé Césaire, described the "mutually dehumanizing consequences of colonization" on the colonizer as well as the colonized.[22] The decolonial theorist Linda Tuhiwai Smith also acknowledges that, in "colonialism ... it is not just the Indigenous populations who had to be subjugated. Europeans also needed to be kept under control, in service to the greater imperial enterprise."[23]

From Smith, we may learn four aspects of decolonizing minds and action, and thus also decolonizing theological education. All four bear insight for designing community organizing in theological education.

First Aspect: One aspect of decolonization implied by Smith is gaining a "more critical understanding of [colonialism's] underlying assumptions, motivations, and values."[24] I refer to these assumptions as myths. They include:

1. the assumed superiority of people identified as white;
2. the assumed superiority of people with economic wealth relative to people without it;
3. the inevitability of economies that prioritize wealth concentration through maximization of profit, consumption, and growth over human and ecological well-being and equity;
4. the separateness of the human mammal from the rest of creation, with the former having singular claim to subjectivity and moral standing, and the latter assumed to exist for the sake of the former;
5. the assumed epistemological superiority of cognitive reason over other forms of knowing.

These are unacknowledged building blocks of the intellectual paradigms and epistemologies—including within theological education—spread by colonialism.[25] Horrors upon horrors have issued from these myths and

---

[22] Keith Walker, "Transformational and Enduring Vision of Aimé Césaire," *PMLA* 125, no. 3 (May 2010): 756–63.

[23] Linda Tuhiwai Smith, *Decolonizing Methodologies: Research and Indigenous Peoples: Research and Indigenous People*, 3rd ed. (London: Zed Books, 2021), 26.

[24] Smith, *Decolonizing Methodologies*, 22.

[25] These five assumptions are integral to the colonial enterprise beginning in the fifteenth century. They are among its central ideological pillars. They are key instruments of the hegemonic power of white supremacy, wealth superiority, and racialized capitalism to shape life today.

related ideological coding that structure society in the Western world. These myths are powerful foundations of injustice and obstacles to communion. Their impact is not only on how we think, but also on who we unconsciously experience ourselves to be; our sense of reality, values, and who or what is worthy; and our enactment of these.

Even where they have countered these myths explicitly, theologies and theological education have been informed by them and may implicitly have reinforced them. This presents an astounding and challenging conundrum: These myths, while implicitly foundational to North Atlantic Christian theology and how it is taught (theological education), thwart the very purpose of theological education, the cultivation of community along the lines of God's justice-seeking Earth-honoring love. Moreover, these myths have forged the deadly trajectory on which humanity races—a trajectory toward unimaginable climate catastrophe that destroys communion and is imbued with racism and economic violence.

The challenge to community organizing courses in theological education is daunting. *If theological education is to help people know and be in communion with a God who hungers for communion in the Earth community, then the theological education must eschew and undo myths that obstruct or damage communion.* How can community organizing in theological curricula help to dismantle these myths and their material manifestations? How ought we conduct community organizing courses in theological education in ways that will counter the epistemologies and worldview that inhere in the DNA of theological reflection as shaped by these abiding myths?[26] This is a matter of life and death because our knowing of the very force that could heal and liberate us (God) is profoundly truncated by assumptions that undergird theology and life lived under the influence of white supremacy, wealth supremacy, profit-maximizing late capitalism, and human exceptionalism.

Second Aspect: A second aspect of decolonizing minds and actions implied by Smith is understanding how these myths infiltrate people's heads and hearts.[27] From there, we may understand more fully by what processes they have entered into theological education. According to Smith,

---

[26] Cynthia Moe-Lobeda, "Faith and #BlackLivesMatter: Future Directions and Current Directives for White Folk," *Currents in Theology and Mission* 49, no. 1 (January 2022).

[27] Smith, *Decolonizing Methodologies*, 25–26.

one means by which they get into our minds is the dominance of Western knowledge. "Knowledge and the power to define what counts as real knowledge lie at the epistemic core of colonialism."[28] Jamaican anti-colonial writer Sylvia Wynter agrees: "Empire's most powerful apparatus is the education system."[29]

Where do these myths hide (reside unrecognized) in theological education and, in hiding, shape us unconsciously (get into our heads)? Do they hide in what are assumed to be valid sources for doing theology (e.g., the "Wesleyan Quadrilateral")? Do they hide in the predominant whiteness of theological faculties, authors footnoted in theological writing, and invitees to contribute to edited volumes? Do they hide in the epistemological assumptions guiding assignments, grading, and accreditation? Do they hide in the financial models, investments, and pay scales of educational institutions?

Third Aspect: A third aspect of decolonizing is recognizing the impact of the colonizing myths. What behaviors, attitudes, and beliefs do they invite? How do they shape lives, societies, and, in the case of this essay, theological education and the practice of faith? For example, how has white supremacy informed and deformed ecclesial structures? How has it informed and truncated our capacity to know (be in relationship with) God and cultivate communion? In *After Whiteness*, Willie James Jennings argues that theological education has been profoundly "distorted" by being "born in white hegemony," which mitigates against "communion."[30]

Fourth Aspect: These three aspects of decolonizing—recognizing the myths, how they infiltrate minds and lives, and their impacts—are essential. Yet getting out from under the power of these myths also requires action that contradicts (defies, resists) them. That action is the fourth aspect of decolonizing. Types of action range broadly, from land repatriation/

---

[28] Smith, *Decolonizing Methodologies*, xii.

[29] Sylvia Wynter, "Unsettling the Coloniality of Being/Power/Truth/Freedom: Towards the Human, After Man, Its Overrepresentation—An Argument," *CR: The New Centennial Review* 3, no. 3 (2003): 259. See also Max Liboiron, *Pollution Is Colonialism* (Durham, NC: Duke University Press, 2021), 54. Speaking of dominant (Western) science, he writes: "A single knowledge becomes the touchstone for all other knowledge systems, which either can dismiss and erase other forms of knowledge or can place those knowledges in the waiting room of modernity as late, quaint, cute, curious, undeveloped, and consumable for settler desires."

[30] Jennings, *After Whiteness*, 5, 6, 10.

rematriation to new forms of education, to shifts in research methods, to public policy advocacy, to many other actions at levels of individual behaviors, social structures, and consciousness.

This brief foray into decolonial theory provides a guidepost for the teaching of community organizing in theological education. It is this:

- Community organizing in theological education will be designed to expose these five myths; help students recognize how they lodge themselves in our minds and actions and how they shape consciousness, behaviors, and systems; and equip students to practice defying these myths.

The guideposts suggested by this inquiry into three bodies of theory confirm the reorientations that we made in response to course evaluations. And they push for further revisions and developments in the course. By what pedagogical moves will we: (1) integrate theory regarding social change more fully into the course in ways that empower effective action; (2) strengthen the antiracist and feminist lenses; and (3) build student capacity to recognize the presence, functioning, and impact of white supremacy, wealth supremacy, predatory capitalism, and human exceptionalism in ways that foster moral-spiritual power for countering these forces?

In Sum

I have viewed the evolution and evaluation of an experiment in teaching community organizing as a required course in seminary education, noting presuppositions, questions, and some personal history motivating the experiment. Drawing on three bodies of theory, I have suggested guidelines for further efforts to incorporate community organizing into theological education for the purpose of preparing leaders in the church to resist and dismantle systemic injustice, build more equitable and life-giving alternatives, and lead others in this work as an integral dimension of faith. This venture into intersections of community organizing, theological education, and those three bodies of theory is but a glimpse of all that could be learned by exploring those intersections more fully.

I close with a response from my gut when I ask myself: "What has been key to this course becoming as meaningful and effective as it appears to have been in its most recent iteration? What must we be sure to retain as we go forward?" My sense is that all six "reorientations" noted above and the shifts that flowed from them have worked synergistically. All are vitally important. At the heart of them is students interacting honestly with each other and with the pastoral practitioners whom we brought in to lead sessions and who deeply value using community organizing in their ministries related to social justice. Central to these practitioners' impact is our request that they open with a personal story of why community organizing is vital in their ministry and how they came into that practice, and our request that they share very honestly about the fruits of this work and the challenges they have faced.

7

Is, Ought, and How:

Intertwining Social Ethics and Social Movement Theory for Social Change

C. Melissa Snarr

Community organizing networks regularly train their adherents to analyze the "is" of their communities (what challenges, embedded resources, and power dynamics are present?) and place these descriptions in conversation with the "ought" (what should our community be like, which values should be primary, and who should hold what kind of power?).[1] In the process, professional organizers craft immersive workshops for burgeoning community leaders that incorporate significant skill building in "how" communities move from the "is" to the "ought." How do people identify common issues, build collective will, grow leaders, leverage power, and sustain social change? Fortunately, theological education is finding a renewed place for these kinds of workshops and community-organizing partnerships as academic institutions seek to be more pragmatic, practical, and effective in their professional formation. As discussed by others in this volume, these collaborations represent one vital vector in the formation process of professional and grassroots Christian social ethicists.

---

[1] Institution-based community organizing (IBCO) networks with roots in Saul Alinsky–style organizing, such as the Industrial Areas Foundation, Gamaliel, and Faith In Action, regularly host extended training workshops for leaders (often 5–10 days). This type of training looks different from other organizing traditions. Still, intentional work on strategy, tactics, and collective formation is a regular part of most national community organizing networks related to abolition, immigration, reproductive rights, queer inclusion, and so on.

Within this chapter, however, I argue for revitalizing another collaborative vector within the academy to aid Christian social ethicists and their students in understanding "how" to bridge the gap between the "is" and "ought" in our beautiful and suffering world. Over the past several decades, I have taught at the intersection of religion, politics, and social movements in a university divinity school while engaging transdisciplinary conversation partners through my research on social ethics and social change. Out of this experience, I contend that those of us working at the intersection of Christian social ethics and organizing/social movements would be well served by engaging in the vibrant field of social movement theory, primarily based in sociology.[2]

As I elaborate below, increasing conversation among social movement theorists, Christian ethicists, and movement leaders can sharpen our analyses around the why and how of conscientization, collective political identity, issue framing, and much more. Certainly, Christian social ethicists also offer insights to social movement theorists, for example, nuancing their analysis of religious resources and discussing the development of moral reasoning. But in this essay, I focus on encouraging Christian social ethicists and their students to amplify another avenue for understanding how to weave together questions of "what the world is" and "what it should be" with "how we change it."

Historical Origins

The academic field of Christian social ethics emerged through collaborations among Christian professors, ministers, and Progressive Era activists in the late 1880s. Turn-of-the-century progressive religious academics, pastors, and advocates interpreted their religious commitments as demanding theological and social analysis and action to address the "social problems" of the day.[3] Moreover, many progressive religious leaders argued that, to understand and counter poverty, illiteracy, disease, racism, sexism, war, and so on, they needed to embrace emerging academic disciplines like sociology, political economy, and political science to examine the dynamics

---

[2] Social movement theorists (sometimes also called collective behavior theorists) are also located in political science or other transdisciplinary academic programs.

[3] Gary Dorrien, *The Spirit of American Liberal Theology: A History* (Louisville, KY: Westminster John Knox Press, 2023), 25.

of social sin and understand how to change social structures. For example, challenged by the brutal poverty in Hell's Kitchen, New York, Walter Rauschenbusch, one of the popularized figures of the (white) social gospel movement, undertook a dramatic reworking of his theology and theory of social change in part by engaging political economists like Richard Ely and studying the municipal socialism movement in Birmingham, England.[4] Early Black social gospellers and abolitionists, such as Reverdy Ransom, Richard R. Wright, Jr. and more, were greatly indebted to the groundbreaking work of the sociologist W. E. B. Du Bois, with his redefinition of racial consciousness and leadership in the early civil rights and pan-African movements.[5] Social ethics and sociology intertwined in their early development and drew together analysis of social issues, ethical claims (often theological), and social change strategies.

As Gary Dorrien has thoroughly documented, "No field operated with a concept of social structure until the social sciences were invented in the 1880s. The social gospel founded the field of social ethics and arose together with sociology, the social sciences, socialism, trade unionism, corporate capitalism, and the first protest organizations devoted to racial justice."[6] Establishing Christian social ethics within academic institutions, Francis Greenwood Peabody (Harvard), William Jewett Tucker (Andover), and Graham Taylor (Chicago Theological) designed new courses and founded departments that embraced an inductive methodology focused on social movements' efforts to address social issues. They joined forces with political economists such as Ely and Richard Sanborn, who argued that "to learn patiently from what *is*—and to promote diligently what *should* be—this is the double duty of all the social sciences."[7] Peabody, Tucker, Taylor, and others expanded the scope of this duty to (a) understand the nature of the social structural challenges before them, (b) learn from the ethical analysis/

---

[4] Paul T. Phillips, *A Kingdom on Earth: Anglo-American Social Christianity, 1880–1940* (University Park: Penn State University Press, 1996), 199. Paul Minus, *Walter Rauschenbusch: American Reformer*, first ed. (New York: Macmillan, 1988), 73.

[5] Gary Dorrien, *The New Abolition: W. E. B. Du Bois and the Black Social Gospel* (New Haven, CT: Yale University Press, 2015), 158ff.

[6] Dorrien, *The Spirit of American Liberal Theology*, 131. He crucially notes that Black social gospel academics did not pursue theology at the time but instead built on the legacy of W. E. B. Du Bois and trained in sociology.

[7] Gary Dorrien, *Social Ethics in the Making: Interpreting an American Tradition* (Malden, MA: Wiley-Blackwell, 2009), 18.

practices of movements, and (c) mobilize Christians and their churches for social change.[8] To serve this educational and missional end, "Social Ethics" and "Christian Sociology" departments emerged in universities and seminaries in the early twentieth century as scholars and religious leaders sought to understand and intervene in the social questions of the day.

Divergences and New Collaborations

This historical taproot of Christian social ethics entailed collaborating with and studying social movements in a decidedly transdisciplinary manner. Yet institutional shifts and the secularization of the social sciences over the last century have led to a radical decline in the collaboration of Christian social ethicists and social scientists, particularly within sociology departments.[9] Broader dynamics related to the role of ethical imperatives in sociology, scientific positivism, and secularization theories portended the move of Christian social ethics out of colleges of arts and sciences to university divinity schools and independent seminaries. Overall, religion also became viewed as less relevant to studying "modern" societies in universities. As sociologist José Casanova summarizes, the dominant European assumptions in sociology fed a secularization theory that took "a plausible historical narrative of particular European socio-historical developments [and] transformed them into a universal teleological grand narrative.... Alas! This teleological projection of increasing secularization and religious decline has not been confirmed by general historical developments around the globe in the last fifty years."[10]

Sociologist Christian Smith underscores how this embrace of secularization theory impoverished social movement theorists' capacity to see and analyze the role of religion in progressive social change.[11] In his groundbreaking essay, "Correcting a Curious Neglect, or Bringing Religion Back

---

[8] Dorrien, *Social Ethics in the* Making, 18.

[9] Dorrien points to the demise of Peabody's social ethics department at Harvard as one specific example that, even with its particularities, embodies these larger shifts (Dorrien, *Social Ethics in the Making*, 33).

[10] José Casanova, *Global Religious and Secular Dynamics: The Modern System of Classification*, Brill Research Perspectives (Leiden: Brill, 2019), 3.

[11] Christian Smith, "Correcting a Curious Neglect, or Bringing Religion Back In," in *Disruptive Religion: The Force of Faith in Social-Movement Activism* (New York: Routledge, 1996), 1–13.

In," Smith identifies the influence of structural-functionalism (in the 1940s–70s that viewed religion as a "source for consensus, integration, and equilibrium") and rational actor theory (among early US social movement theorists with embedded views of religion as irrational and emotional), alongside secularization theory, as marginalizing the analysis of "disruptive religion."[12] Finally, and especially important to our conversation, Smith sees the "fragmented nature of contemporary academic inquiry" as a primary culprit that distanced scholars in the sociology of religion from those in social movement theory. For example, until the mid-1990s, three separate organizations with their own journals focused on the sociological analysis of religion; thus, "any interesting social movement studies produced over the years by students of religion had minimal chance of influencing social movement scholars. Potential intellectual 'cross-pollenization' was structurally impeded."[13]

As scholars have challenged the dominant assumptions of these formative theories, new space has opened up among sociologists of religion and some social movement scholars to study the role of religion in organizing social change. Smith, Aldon Morris, Belinda Robnett, and James Aho broke new ground in the cross-pollination within sociology, soon followed by influential theorists such as Sharon Nepstad, Richard Wood, Mark Warren, Pierrette Hondagneu-Sotelo, and Tina Fetner and a more recent generation of scholars such as Grace Yukich, Ziad Munson, Ruth Braunstein, Rhys Williams, and Jonathan Coley.[14] Yet there remains a significant chasm

---

[12] Smith, "Correcting a Curious Neglect," 2–3.

[13] Smith, "Correcting a Curious Neglect," 3.

[14] Aldon D. Morris, *The Origins of the Civil Rights Movement* (New York: Free Press, 1984); Christian Smith, *The Emergence of Liberation Theology: Radical Religion and Social Movement Theory* (Chicago: University of Chicago Press, 1991); Belinda Robnett, *How Long? How Long? African American Women in the Struggle for Civil Rights* (New York: Oxford University Press, 1997); James A. Aho, *The Politics of Righteousness: Idaho Christian Patriotism* (Seattle: University of Washington Press, 1990); Mark R. Warren, *Dry Bones Rattling: Community Building to Revitalize American Democracy*, Princeton Studies in American Politics (Princeton, NJ: Princeton University Press, 2001); Richard L. Wood, *Faith in Action: Religion, Race, and Democratic Organizing in America* (Chicago: University of Chicago Press, 2002); Sharon Erickson Nepstad, *Convictions of the Soul: Religion, Culture, and Agency in the Central American Solidarity Movement* (New York: Oxford University Press, 2004); Tina Fetner, *How the Religious Right Shaped Lesbian and Gay Activism* (Minneapolis:

between those who study the role of religion in community organizing/ social movements sociologically and Christian ethics more generally. Structurally, university divinity schools and independent seminaries that still house Christian social ethicists are largely divorced from the sociological study of religion. Unlike the social science of psychology, which continues to be embraced by theological education through pastoral care/theology areas, rare is the contemporary seminary or university divinity school that hires a sociologist or someone with cognate training in sociology. This siloing and erasure make it even less likely that social ethicists and social movement scholars will collaborate across the disciplinary divide.[15]

I consider this to be a great loss. Those of us who work at the intersection of social ethics and organizing/social movements could greatly benefit from engaging with the vibrant field of social movement theory. We are already seeing a revitalization of Christian ethicists who are studying community organizing and social movements as part of their normative methodologies (e.g., Traci West, Rebecca Todd Peters, Keri Day, Vincent Lloyd, Luke Bretherton, Yvonne Zimmerman, Kyle Lambelet, Kristin Heyer, Nikkia Robert, and colleagues in this volume).[16] Expanding our transdisciplinary

---

University of Minnesota Press, 2008); Pierrette Hondagneu-Sotelo, *God's Heart Has No Borders: How Religious Activists Are Working for Immigrant Rights* (Berkeley: University of California Press, 2008); Ziad W. Munson, *The Making of Pro-Life Activists: How Social Movement Mobilization Works* (Chicago: University of Chicago Press, 2010); Grace Yukich, *One Family under God: Immigration Politics and Progressive Religion in America* (New York: Oxford University Press, 2013); Ruth Braunstein, *Prophets and Patriots: Faith in Democracy across the Political Divide* (Oakland: University of California Press, 2017); Ruth Braunstein, Todd Nicholas Fuist, and Rhys H. Williams, *Religion and Progressive Activism: New Stories about Faith and Politics* (New York: NYU Press, 2017); Jonathan S. Coley, *Gay on God's Campus: Mobilizing for LGBT Equality at Christian Colleges and Universities* (Chapel Hill: University of North Carolina Press, 2018).

[15] This is particularly true at independent seminaries. Yet in the last two decades, university divinity schools have greatly limited or eliminated their full-time sociologists, with the number of psychologically trained faculty far outnumbering them.

[16] Traci C. West, *Disruptive Christian Ethics: When Racism and Women's Lives Matter* (Louisville, KY: Westminster John Knox Press, 2006); Kristin E. Heyer, *Kinship across Borders: A Christian Ethic of Immigration* (Washington, DC: Georgetown University Press, 2012); Yvonne C. Zimmerman, *Other Dreams of Freedom: Religion, Sex, and Human Trafficking* (New York: Oxford University Press, 2013); Luke Bretherton, *Resurrecting Democracy* (Cambridge: Cambridge University Press,

conversation partners could enable Christian social ethicists to sharpen and enhance conversations around vital *how* questions: How do movements emerge? How are we moved and sustained to act? How should we talk about social issues? How should we choose tactics? How does activism form us? With attendant concepts like resource mobilization, conscientization, bridge leaders, collective political identity, framing, and so on, social movement theory offers interpretive schema and grounded data that can help social ethicists analyze the moral work of movements.

How ... Do Movements Emerge?

Social movement theory (SMT), in part, developed as a focus within sociology to make sense of when, why, and how mass movements for social change emerge. "Classic" SMT wrestled with the rise of fascism in Europe and leaned heavily (drawing on Durkheim and others) on psychosocial explanations of people's alienation from social structures, which produced anomie that persons irrationally worked out through eruptions of protest and discontent.[17] In other words, this tradition argued that folks are alienated or anxious due to system strain and reach a boiling point. They act not so much for political goals, per se, but to manage the psychological tensions of a stressful situation. Although this perspective was discredited in the 1960s and 1970s, we can hear popular versions of this assumption in discussions of "irrational" Trump voters and insurrectionists. But classical SMT—and contemporary punditry—failed to account for at least two things: (a) the material and leadership resources required for movement emergence, and (b) that disruptive politics is a regular, rational part of political life rather than irrational and primarily aberrant.[18]

2015); Keri Day, *Religious Resistance to Neoliberalism: Womanist and Black Feminist Perspectives* (New York: Palgrave Macmillan, 2016); Rebecca Todd Peters, *Trust Women: A Progressive Christian Argument for Reproductive Justice* (Boston: Beacon Press, 2018); Joshua Dubler and Vincent Lloyd, *Break Every Yoke: Religion, Justice, and the Abolition of Prisons* (New York: Oxford University Press, 2019); Kyle B. T. Lambelet, *¡Presente!: Nonviolent Politics and the Resurrection of the Dead* (Washington, DC: Georgetown University Press, 2020); Nikia Robert, "Not Meant to Survive: Black Mothers Leading beyond the Criminal Line," in *Walking through the Valley*, ed. Emilie Townes et al. (Louisville, KY: Westminster John Knox Press, 2022), 107–22.

[17] Nepstad, *Convictions of the Soul*, 8.

[18] David A. Snow, *A Primer on Social Movements*, Contemporary Societies (New York: W. W. Norton, 2010).

"Resource mobilization" and "political process" theory emerged as a counter to this earlier perspective through particular attention to the Black Civil Rights Movement in the United States. Theorists in this tradition point out that grievances are everywhere and are often relatively steady (e.g., oppression of Blacks in the US). What varies is the amount of social and material resources available to an aggrieved group to help them launch an organized demand for change. This tradition emphasizes a rational actor model of political participation where the intentional, systematic cultivation and consolidation of money, organizations, and leadership enable the birth of movements. Rather than focusing primarily on the individual psychological attributes of adherents, these models emphasize the structural necessities of resources and political openings. The groundbreaking work of Aldon Morris pointed to the importance of the burgeoning Black middle class, key organizations, and localized leaders (with a particular emphasis on the relative autonomy of the Black church and its clergy).[19] Morris was an early ripple in a wave of work that emphasized the strategic rationality of the Black Civil Rights Movement (and others) and widened the conversation on how vital strategic alliances (with labor unions, etc.), infrastructure (alternate educational systems, etc.), and political opportunities (wars, policy shifts, etc.) were for countering dominant systems.[20] In this view, people, by and large, do not spontaneously and irrationally move toward concerted, sustained collective action. To act in the face of risk, they observe and assess the world around them, deciding whether their grievance is essential enough and whether their efforts will likely succeed.

Transdisciplinary conversations with these theoretical resources can amplify Christian social ethicists' emphasis on the crucial social structures necessary for alternate moral formations and power-building. These resources also help us greatly complexify questions like, "Why do people vote against their own interests?" and reengage the seemingly irrational behavior of our populist adversaries by inviting us to look at their long institutional and resource history (e.g., Christian capitalist nationalism as a highly networked and resourced counter to the New Deal).[21] More progressive institution-based community organizing networks, like the

---

[19] Morris, *The Origins of the Civil Rights Movement*.

[20] Doug McAdam, *Political Process and the Development of Black Insurgency, 1930–1970* (Chicago: University of Chicago Press, 1999).

[21] Darren Dochuk, *From Bible Belt to Sunbelt: Plain-Folk Religion, Grassroots Politics, and the Rise of Evangelical Conservatism* (New York: W. W. Norton, 2012).

Industrial Areas Foundation, have long emphasized the importance of "organized money and organized people" and local organizations relatively autonomous from the state or corporate sectors. Conversations with social movement theorists can expand this inquiry to help us focus on the larger institutional landscapes and accompanying spadework required to build resilient networks of resistance and liberation.

If resource mobilization theory invited scholars to study how movements have a material history, the "cultural turn" in 1990s social movement theory focused on the collective meaning work of movements. Scholars in this tradition emphasize that (a) values, motivations, and emotions are just as vital in the emergence of movements, and (b) they are often formed through movements rather than preexisting. Beliefs are not constant, simply waiting until material resources roll them up into movement emergence. Instead, movement leaders with cultural authority and insight help potential adherents make sense of the world through resonant metaphors, symbols, stories, emotions, experiences, art, music, and other creative cultural productions.[22] Sharon Nepstad notes that "like artists, protesters act as creative symbol makers, interpretive communicators, and emotional managers. They draw from tools, artifacts, and patterns of their existing cultural traditions to invoke indignation and compassion, recruit others, and to inspire resistance."[23] Cultural theorists do not set aside structural dimensions but rather turn attention to the cultural knowledge within structures and the agential work of leaders to navigate and transform them.

Social ethicists can benefit from even more conversation partners on how movements influence moral rationalities, legitimate alternative worldviews, and form the will toward social-political risk. For example, Ruth Braunstein's *Prophets and Patriots*, a comparative ethnography of Tea Party and Institutional Based Community Organizing (IBCO) organizations in the early 2010s, challenges many assumptions of conservative activists as religiously monolithic and avoidant of critical inquiry.[24] Through her analysis, Braunstein invites readers to wrestle with how moral worldviews are formed through organizational socialization processes, helping us better understand how we live such divided political lives. While SMT does not provide a handbook on launching a successful

---

[22] Nepstad, *Convictions of the Soul*, 9.
[23] Nepstad, *Convictions of the Soul*, 18.
[24] Braunstein, *Prophets and Patriots*.

movement, the field provides a vibrant complement to Christian social ethicists' social structural concerns and analysis by inviting us to engage and analyze data from actual movements, with their challenges, complexities, and creativity.

How ... Are People Moved to Act?

"Wait, they didn't have pro-life beliefs before they joined the Pro-Life Movement? And they still hold inconsistent views on abortion while they are in the movement?!" So started a robust classroom discussion on Ziad Munson's ethnographic and survey data on pro-life activists.[25] Munson's social scientific research showed that relational networks, personal invitations, familial crisis junctures, and cultural identity markers were more influential for becoming active in the pro-life movement than preexisting beliefs about abortion. He analyzes the "process of conviction," or conscientization, through mobilization rather than through prior beliefs predicting participation.[26]

"Micro-mobilization," in SMT, focuses on how people are drawn into movement activism. Largely discrediting isolated self-interest as the primary driver of participation, scholars have argued vigorously about the role of "biographical availability," "ideological compatibility," and "social networks" in the initial engagement with activism.[27] Smith's and Nepstad's studies of the Central American Peace Movement emphasize the profound influence of early family formation, cross-cultural experiences, and immersion in networks of alternative meaning-making for the "subjective engageability" of high-risk activists.[28] Grace Yukich's analysis of the New Sanctuary Movement discusses the importance of being invited into longer-term transformative relationships ("story-sharing") to re-form identities toward sustained collective action and risk.[29] Belinda Robnett is pointed in her counter of the patriarchally biased analysis of the Black

---

[25] Munson, *The Making of Pro-Life Activists*.

[26] Munson builds out a concept introduced in Carol J. C. Maxwell, *Pro-Life Activists in America: Meaning, Motivation, and Direct Action* (Cambridge: Cambridge University Press, 2002).

[27] James M. Jasper and Jeff Goodwin, eds., *The Social Movements Reader: Cases and Concepts* (Malden, MA: Wiley-Blackwell, 2015), 54.

[28] Nepstad, *Convictions of the Soul*.

[29] Yukich, *One Family under God*.

Civil Rights Movement when she argues that women who were "bridge leaders" did the cultural work of moving everyday folks from a personal racial identity to a political identity.[30] These bridge leaders were not the formal, charismatic leaders identified by popular analysis and previous theorists. Still, they were the ones who convinced people to take the risk to join the movement. Collective political identity had to be formed through one-on-one grassroots organizing that entailed great emotional work, often outside formal organizational structures.

As a Christian social ethicist, I find these discussions vital because they can shift limited conversations about whether ignorance, abstract selfishness, or individualized weakness of will keeps people from acting for social change. In reality, the number of people who join community organizing networks or social movements is relatively small; most people don't intentionally engage in active political change. Studying those undertaking this intentional action provides rich data on the complexity of moral and political formations that can challenge us to move beyond the short-term banking model within ethics education that assumes teaching right facts, theology, or even reasoning will lead to right action. Engaging with social movement theorists encourages social ethicists to continue thinking about formation for social change relationally, affectively, and institutionally so as to contextualize committed action, formation of the will, and the role of belief. Transdisciplinary conversation invites us to be explicit about what paideia for long-term structural change looks like.

How ... Should We Talk about Social Issues and Change?

Social movements are not about individual perceptions but rather the outcome of negotiated shared meaning. Thus, one of the primary tasks of social movement leaders is to "frame" or develop "action-oriented sets of beliefs and meanings that inspire and legitimate the activities and campaigns" of an organization.[31] These beliefs and meanings move beyond everyday interpretive processes to a collective action framing that seeks to "mobilize or activate movement adherents so that they move, meta-

---

[30] Robnett, *How Long?*

[31] Robert D. Benford and David A. Snow, "Framing Processes and Social Movements: An Overview and Assessment," *Annual Review of Sociology* 26, no. 1 (2000): 611–39, https://doi.org/10.1146/annurev.soc.26.1.611.

phorically, from the balcony to the barricades (action mobilization); to convert bystanders into adherents, thus broadening the movement's base (consensus mobilization); and to neutralize or demobilize adversaries (countermobilization)."[32] We can hear elements of these frames in the chants of "Black Lives Matter" or "Protect Kids Not Guns," or even "Make America Great Again." But ultimately, theorists in this tradition argue "frames" are not just slogans but are particular forms of persuasion that have three primary tasks: diagnostic (what's wrong and who's to blame), prognostic (what to do), and motivational (why now).[33]

Cultural creativity and nimbleness are essential as one navigates metabolizing grief into political grievance. Movement leaders must draw on the cultural and interpretive resources most relevant to a particular political landscape while shifting dominant perceptions and motivating action. As my ethnographic work on religious activists in the Living Wage Movement showed, leaders did this effectively not only by developing the phrase "a job should keep you out of poverty, not in it" but by emphasizing moral frameworks rather than getting caught up in debating numbers (exact living wage calculations, probable costs, etc.).[34] Through their framing, movement leaders challenged dominant assumptions about the amorality of the market by drawing on religious and "American" values that resonated across multiple constituencies. In reclaiming the term "living" wage, they drew on religious traditions that argued that flourishing, not just survival, should accompany working full-time and demonstrated that even those who "played by the rules" in the United States could not move beyond basic subsistence. The American Dream did not exist for the mythic two parents (working full-time on the minimum wage) with two kids; there would be no white picket fence for these working poor families. This diagnostic was intertwined with careful analysis of how politicians' choices not to raise the federal minimum wage beginning in the 1970s created the problem. This diagnosis led to the prognostic action for municipal living wage ordinances

---

[32] Rebecca Kolins Givan, Kenneth M. Roberts, and Sarah A. Soule, *The Diffusion of Social Movements: Actors, Mechanisms, and Political Effects* (Cambridge: Cambridge University Press, 2010), 36.

[33] Benford and Snow, "Framing Processes and Social Movements."

[34] C. Melissa Snarr, *All You That Labor: Religion and Ethics in the Living Wage Movement*, Religion and Social Transformation (New York: New York University Press, 2011), 37.

to counter national neglect. Although this framing certainly was not perfect (e.g., arguing for independence from the government that could undermine long-term social supports), the agential meaning-making from movement leaders shifted debates about municipal budgets and expanded a base to engage the labor market ethically.

The negotiation and development of frames constitute primary and often contested tasks of social movement leaders. These negotiations can foster collective identity or manifest splinters in power. In analyzing internal contestation over frames, social ethicists study conflicting values at stake, the art of moral negotiation, and perhaps identify a collaborative role in on-the-ground social change. In the New Sanctuary Movement, Yukich tracks the critical and challenging navigations of shifting the movement's framing from "welcoming the stranger" to emphasizing the unity of the "family of God" with an extension to not splitting up "mixed citizenship status" families.[35] Leaders sought to become more theologically inclusive by undoing the "othering" of undocumented immigrants as "strangers" while frame bridging to the culturally prolific emphasis on "family values." More recently, the work of Black female-identified movement leaders, particularly from Sister Song, shifted considerable public activism and debate from frames of "reproductive choice" or "reproductive health" to "reproductive justice."[36] Their impressive reframing extended from existing movement frames while moving away from primary emphases on lack of legal protections or lack of education/services to a more extensive structural analysis of what is required for marginalized women and their communities to exercise self-determination. Social movement theorists such as Meghan Daniel trace Reproductive Justice Movement leaders' innovation in ways that invite social ethicists to engage the extensive literature on the strategy work of the movement, which can be read alongside crucial primary documents and ethical analysis such as Loretta Ross's "Reproductive Justice and Intersectional Feminist Activism" and Rebecca Todd Peter's explicitly Christian *Trust Women*.[37]

---

[35] Yukich, *One Family under God*, 96ff.

[36] Meghan Daniel, "The Social Movement for Reproductive Justice: Emergence, Intersectional Strategies, and Theory Building," *Sociology Compass* 15, no. 8 (2021): 1–13.

[37] Loretta J. Ross, "Reproductive Justice as Intersectional Feminist Activism," *Souls: A Critical Journal of Black Politics, Culture, and Society* 19, no. 3 (2017): 286–314; Peters, *Trust Women*.

Social ethicists can build on our strengths in understanding and assessing moral argumentation by engaging social movement theorists' theoretical analyses and data on framing. The careful attention to the agential work of movement entrepreneurs can also help social ethicists keep the *social* primary in our work by foregrounding the navigations, negotiations, and tensions in how communities talk about moral goods. For example, while presenting an academic paper on the Living Wage Movement at the Society of Christian Ethics, I was asked whether movement leaders utilized the "parable of the laborers in the vineyard" (Matthew 20:1-26; where the laborers hired near the end of the day were paid the same as those hired earlier).[38] In returning to my sources, I realized that none of the key participants had ever drawn on that parable because, as one said, "you could also read the parable as breaking a union." It was not the job of the movement leaders to fight a biblical interpretation battle, instead they sorted through more resonant religious resources for their framing. In this way, social movement theory centers the agency and on-the-ground navigations of movement framers that can help social ethicists attend to the "how" with greater depth, empathy, and collaboration with organizers.

How ... Do We Enact the Fullness of Christian Social Ethics?

By encouraging academic conversation with the discipline of social movement theory, I do not wish to overshadow essential direct learning with the grassroots experience and wisdom of community organizers and movement leaders. Rather than use a zero-sum approach, I want to add another rich vein of analytical material and vital discussions that I hope Christian social ethicists will engage as they link the "is" and "ought" to the "how" in their work. In this limited space, I have offered just a few windows into the "how" questions of the field. Many more opportunities exist in social movement theory discussions of tactical innovation, sustaining engagement, developing leaders, navigating repression, and understanding movement cycles and decline.

As I close, I want to return us to academic ancestors who paid careful attention to movement leaders and everyday moral agency for social change. Katie Cannon, building on Beverly Harrison's "dance of redemption," chal-

---

[38] Snarr, *All You That Labor*, 47.

lenged our field to engage pedagogically in the tasks of "strategic options" and "re-reflection & strategic action" as part of the wise circular practices of Christian social ethics.[39] Cannon's chapter on teaching womanist ethics included a sample course assignment, "Model for Action," which even included budgetary and evaluation components. There are undoubtedly many ways to approach the tasks of Christian social ethics. Still, our forebears at the birth of our field and many of our brightest ancestors invite us to consider, methodologically, how we connect the is, ought, and how of ethical action and articulate our learning relationship with social movements. Social movement theory, with its focus on the agential, strategic, cultural (and often moral) work of movement leaders and organizations, offers a fertile conversation partner in a time where we need more wisdom and insight in the seemingly constant uphill journey toward justice, healing, and community flourishing. With social movement theory as a cognate disciplinary partner, I contend that Christian social ethics more systematically keeps the "how" foregrounded in our disciplinary tasks and helps hold us accountable to the complex and life-giving grounded work of social change.

---

[39] Katie Geneva Cannon, "Metalogues and Dialogues: Teaching the Womanist Idea," in *Katie's Canon: Womanism and the Soul of the Black Community*, rev. and exp. 25th anniv. ed. (Minneapolis: Fortress Press, 2021), 194.

8

In Search of Our Common Treasure:

A Womanist Approach to Antiracism Work

Malinda Elizabeth Berry

This essay assumes the origin story of social ethics that Gary Dorrien tells in *Social Ethics in the Making:* It is an academic field of study founded in the 1880s as part of the Social Gospel movement by scholars committed to "the distinctly modern idea that Christianity has a social-ethical mission to transform the structures of society in the direction of social justice."[1] In seeking to make a home for Christian ethics as an "ethically grounded social science" in liberal arts and seminary curricula, the early inventors of social ethics were keen to avoid the pitfalls of secularized sociology, with the hope of relating to society as something with a soul and orienting that soul toward the Reign of God in the modern world. Another essential feature of social ethics is the epistemological insistence that salvation has two inseparable dimensions to it: personal and social. In his historical account of social ethics' origins, Dorrien explains how three successive movements have championed social ethics' vision of social transformation: the Social Gospel, Christian realism, and liberation theology.[2] The unitive binary of salvation's personal and social character also relates to how learning works in social ethics classrooms.

As he reflected on the significance of pedagogy for social ethics in remarks made during a panel at the 2023 meeting of the Society of Christian Ethics, Dorrien boldly stated, "I believe that social ethics should mediate how social ethicists conduct advocacy, and I doubt very much that

---

[1] Gary Dorrien, *Social Ethics in the Making: Interpreting an American Tradition* (Malden, MA: Wiley-Blackwell, 2009), 1.

[2] Dorrien, *Social Ethics in the Making*, 674.

any of us are conducting too much advocacy."[3] His rationale is steeped, of course, in the historical and visionary roots of social Christianity. But his rationale is also based on the aspirations of critical pedagogy (Paulo Freire) and engaged pedagogy (bell hooks). Thus, there is a natural overlap and synergy between critically engaged pedagogies and the sites of church-academy partnerships that fuel social justice praxis.

Dorrien's panel presentation also described how important pedagogical commitments are to the work we do as ethicists. I share his analysis that, whether the students in question are preschoolers or postdocs, traditional approaches to education integrate learners into what Walter Wink calls the Domination System.[4] But, when social change and social justice ground the educational approach we take, then we—both teachers and students—become co-learners, explorers searching for transformation and freedom. I consider myself fortunate that my doctoral program required that I take a pedagogy class before being unleashed on students in my tutorial sections. This class introduced me to hooks's work on educational themes and gave me the courage and conviction to weave my beliefs about pedagogy into my theo-ethical method so that *what* I teach shapes *how* I speak, write, and profess. This is how I affirm hooks's sense that the work of teaching and classrooms themselves are at their best when we create spaces of "fierce engagement and intense learning."[5]

Formation and Frustration

I come to the subject of this volume as an "organizee" more than as an "organizer." That is to say, I have been part of grassroots organizing activities as a community member rather than as a movement or campaign leader. The movements I have participated in range in focus from peace and disarmament to teaching yoga in schools, from joining a national political campaign to participating in training courses (antiracism, circle

---

[3] Gary Dorrien, remarks made during a panel, "Organizing Visions: The Past, Present, and Future of Christian Social Ethics and Organizing Movements," presented at the Society of Christian Ethics Annual Meeting, Chicago, January 5, 2023.

[4] Wink writes, "I use the expression 'the Domination System' to indicate what happens when an entire network of Powers becomes integrated around idolatrous values." Walter Wink, *Engaging the Powers: Discernment and Resistance in a World of Domination,* Powers Trilogy, vol. 3 (Minneapolis: Fortress Press, 1992), 9.

[5] bell hooks, *Teaching Critical Thinking: Practical Wisdom,* Teaching Trilogy, vol. 3 (New York: Routledge, 2010), 5.

process, safe zone, nonviolent communication, etc.). Within these movements, my level of participation has varied, giving me a range of vantage points from which to observe that advocacy manifests in many different ways. As my own activism has ebbed and flowed over time, the paradigms of social change I am most drawn to are those that include three things: a clear metaphysical orientation, good pedagogy, and priorities that share easy alignment with biblically animated social Christianity.[6]

Participation in movements for social justice has significant formative power in people's lives, but it can be very easy to let that formation go unnoticed without deliberate and ongoing moral and critical reflection. This essay is about my search for a way to approach antiracism organizing that is metaphysically cogent, pedagogically winsome, and morally inspiring. I want to see antiracism efforts build on shame research and wrestle with internal critiques so that, in settings where people identify as biblically sophisticated Jesus-Followers, being antiracist is not simply a question of having the correct politics or intellectual analysis of race and power but having a story to tell about how participating in this movement is teaching them valuable lessons about wholeness.[7]

My interest in a better approach to antiracism education and movement building is predictably personal and political. I teach in a predominantly white institution that is a small, binational denominational seminary committed to Christian globalism. Our ethos is one where we think of ourselves as a learning community. It is both my alma mater and the primary theological school of my denominational tradition, Mennonite Church USA. In fact, my formal introduction to the faith-based wing of the antiracism movement occurred while I was a student, when I joined the seminary's antiracism team. This seminary is a place I know well, and I have observed and participated in its struggle to name, unmask, and engage its own racism.

About a year after the Black Lives Matter uprising of 2020, I found

---

[6] "Biblically animated" indicates my alignment with Wink's conviction: "It is my conviction that any attempt to face the problem of evil in society from a New Testament perspective must be bound up with an understanding of what the Bible calls the 'Principalities and Powers.' I am also convinced that no social ethic can be constructed on New Testament grounds with recognition of the role of these Powers in sustaining and subverting human life." Wink, *Engaging the Powers*, 3.

[7] For more background on the insights of shame research, see Bréne Brown, *The Gifts of Imperfection*, 10th anniv. ed. (Center City, MN: Hazelden, 2022). A recent, vocal internal critic of antiracism is John McWhorter, author of *Woke Racism: How a New Religion Has Betrayed Black America* (New York: Portfolio, 2021).

myself in an existential conflict with some of my white colleagues that was, of course, intersectional in nature. Along with race and gender, the interplay of ethnicity and denominational identity was shaping the conflict dynamic.[8] While I could make intellectual sense of what was going on—I teach a course called "Church and Race" in which we read Willie Jennings's *After Whiteness: An Education in Belonging* (Eerdmans, 2020)—that did not help me untangle the politics or relationships preventing open conversation about what was unfolding. Furthermore, my seminary, like many earnest organizations oriented toward social justice as a matter of Christian ethics, is committed to undoing racism and building intercultural competence.[9] Even so, our aspirations have not prepared us to (a) understand that the terrain of white fragility is part of the conflictual situations and (b) navigate this fraught territory with more courage than fear.[10]

---

[8] My institution is predominantly white and maintains strong ties to its affiliated denominations, Mennonite Church Canada and Mennonite Church USA. Our denominations are also predominantly white, and this whiteness includes strong subcultures with deep ethnocentric histories and patterns, including resistance to assimilation. Because my white mother comes from that lineage and my parents' professional lives were intertwined with denominational institutions, I have "power" as an insider relative to those who are white but do not share my ethnic connections. Sometimes white people around me "forget" that I am Black because I am so "Mennonite" (read: white?), raising a provocative and, I think, unresolvable question from an antiracist standpoint: as a Black woman who is a denominational insider, how much power do I have compared to white colleagues who may or may not be denominational insiders? My reality is that both my white mother and my Black father come from minority/minoritized communities that have seen themselves as irrelevant and inconvenient to the larger "American project," leading to a sense that survival in a world that would rather you did not exist depends on finding and staying connected to kin (whether chosen or biological) and keeping a low profile. In this way, being Black and being Mennonite (ethnically and ecclesially) are inseparable in my psyche and identity; they are two sides of the same coin.

[9] All employees participate in a multi-day antiracism training and complete an intercultural development assessment tool as part of their orientation. Teaching faculty and students also set annual intercultural development goals based on the profile generated by the assessment and informed by the institution's antiracism vision.

[10] White fragility refers to the emotional response some white people have when feedback about attitudes and behaviors related to racial bias challenge their identity such that they "perceive any attempt to connect [them] to the system of racism as an unsettling and unfair moral offense." Robin DiAngelo, *White Fragility: Why It's So Hard for White People to Talk about Racism* (Boston: Beacon Press, 2018), 2.

Reflecting on my faculty's gross lack of skill, I began to wonder: What kind of antiracism training, education, and discourse could help us—a group of *deeply* social-justice-minded Christian academics—figure out how to turn toward each other and work together to address the way race and perceptions of both interpersonal and systemic racism were showing up in our midst? My research into the roots and branches of the antiracism movement has failed to provide me with insights beyond "the work is messy." Even so, I believe we can rework our defensive postures and fashion tools to prune our antiracism efforts with the hopes of doing more effective, fruit-bearing work.

I believe profoundly that antiracism is important work for Christians to participate in because racism is a manifestation of the Domination System, a system that has held sway over human societies for millennia. When it comes to racism's place in that system, Wink cites slave rebellions and the abolition and civil rights movements as glimpses we have caught of God's domination-free order. Wink says, "Throughout the Era of Domination, egalitarian resurgences have appeared. . . . But none of them has been able to overturn belief in the fundamental right of some to dominate others."[11] In Wink's framework, the importance of Jesus is that his message reverberates in a "very specific context, even if it has been essentially the same context for five thousand years: the Domination System." He continues,

> *The gospel is a context-specific remedy for the evils of the Domination System.* This means that the overthrow of any particular manifestation of oppression can never satisfy the demands of the gospel if what replaces one form of domination is simply another. The gospel is thus permanently critical of every political program, reform, and revolution.

Even so, Wink hastens to add, we are able to make gains in helping God establish a domination-free order; we simply need to remember that this work takes time, and the groundswell is growing.[12] Wink's perspective gives renewed meaning to Jesus's followers as "The Way"; Christians are called to help keep the world on the widening path toward wholeness.

What follows is a brief description of two things that I wish had supported the pieces of training in which I participated, offered as analogies under the guiding image of a treasure hunt. Inspired by Layli

---

[11] Wink, *Engaging the Powers*, 46–49.
[12] Wink, *Engaging the Powers*, 48.

Phillips Maparyan's work in womanist thought, my ideas are Luxocratic. This aspect of womanism speaks to the primary concerns I have about metaphysics, pedagogy, and social Christianity. To be "ruled by Light" is to be guided by thoroughly egalitarian, benevolent, and nonviolent forms of spirituality and social organization that help us claim our luminousness. Maparyan explains that education and health, in their fullest meaning, are two things that facilitate Luxocracy, aiding us in discovering the treasure trove of possibilities that can be found within each person and together with others.[13] Maparyan's use of treasure conjures womanist books such as Alice Walker's *In Search of Our Mothers' Gardens,* Stacey Floyd-Thomas's *Mining the Motherlode,* and even Delores Williams's *Sisters in the Wilderness.* These works speak of womanism's cosmological values and concerns, which I discuss below, but they also exemplify womanism's literary and poetic methods that come naturally to those of us who favor speaking through image, metaphor, and analogy.

My imagination has settled on the search for treasure fed by Walker's essay "Looking for Zora," Toni Morrison's novel *Paradise,* and three parables from Matthew 13:44–46, 52, in which Jesus compares God's Reign to a secret stash of riches found in a field, a pearl of great price, and a housekeeper who can find anything you need from the depths of a capacious pantry. What exactly is this treasure? All good treasure hunts include elements of mystery; we will not know until we find it. I can say it has something to do with the "Why?" and "What?" and "How?" of antiracism organizing work. I turn now to offer you ideas and resources to help us in our search: a compass to answer why, a map to answer what, and good company to answer how.

A Compass: Spiritual Activism and Luxocracy

The compass I have in mind is the instrument that helps us know what direction we are going. When used with a paper map, a compass helps us correlate what is on a map with our actual surroundings. In our day and age, we rely on global positioning systems to help us with navigation, but

---

[13] As part of the Baháʼí Faith, Layli Phillips Maparyan draws on imagery from this passage from the Tablets of Baháʼuʼlláh, Lawh-i-Maqsúd 11: "Regard man as a mine rich in gems of inestimable value. Education can, alone, cause it to reveal its treasures and enable mankind to benefit therefrom."

it is often the case that antiracism work takes us into wild places that GPS cannot navigate accurately. Being able to use a magnetic compass, adjusted for declination, with a paper map is an important skill that takes practice to develop comfort and proficiency.

As far back as the 1840s, English speakers have spoken of using a "moral compass" as a parallel to the physical compass.[14] Basic dictionary definitions of the phrase describe a moral compass as the ability to distinguish right from wrong or as a set of values and beliefs that guide our behavior and inform ethical decision-making. With the fading of moral philosophy in higher education, social ethics sought to step into the gap and provide students with a means to calibrate their respective moral compasses, particularly by shining the light of compassion on the social evils hidden in plain sight.[15] This is why I believe that, when people of faith work for social change, it is critical that we orient ourselves toward our goals (i.e., treasure) with a metaphysical vision or framework. Such a vision and framework helps us find north and track which values help us navigate rough places.

As a doctoral student at Union Theological Seminary in the early 2000s, I was honored to be a student of the preeminent womanist theologian Delores Williams. One of the most important things I learned from her seminars, written feedback, and personal conversations underscored a truth we already know but often fail to manifest: A true wellspring of *deep* spirituality is necessary as we work for social change, whether we are in the streets of society, the halls of the academy, or the sanctuaries of the church. In academic terms, I could categorize this lesson as womanism siding with idealism against materialism, but that framing is too small. It is more appropriate to describe this lesson as one in womanist theopoetics and cosmology with a radical incarnationalist vision. As I have lived into what this means, I have found the language of "spiritual activism" to be an apt description of what Professor Williams meant when she added "demonarchy" to my theological vocabulary.[16]

---

[14] *Oxford English Dictionary*, s.v. "moral compass (n.)," December 2024, https://doi.org/10.1093/OED/4889340389.

[15] Dorrien, *Social Ethics in the Making*, 15.

[16] I am borrowing this phrase from Alastair McIntosh and Matt Carmichael's book *Spiritual Activism: Leadership as Service* (Cambridge: Green Books, 2016). On his webpage dedicated to the book, McIntosh explains, "Spiritual Activism [means]

Demonarchy is Williams's word for "the demonic governance of Black women's lives by systems ruled by white men *and* women using mechanisms of social control like racism, violence, violation, and death. Rooted in the history of slavery, demonarchy creates a matrix of oppression so that Black women are not simply trying to get out from under the thumbs of patriarchs but also out from under white supremacy and its minions of greed and violence. But the word also signals a cosmological understanding. As Williams explains demonarchy, she includes the "business of casting out the demonic—the socially, politically, economically, and spiritually demonic rule" that threatens the well-being of Black lives and the human spirit—this defines the liberating work of the church.[17] Williams is not alone in her view of womanism and spiritual activism.

In one of the most insightful and comprehensive introductions to womanist thought available, Maparyan, editor of *The Womanist Reader*, describes womanism not simply as evaluating reality through Black women's experience but as

> a social change perspective rooted in Black women's and other women of color's everyday experiences and everyday methods of problem solving in everyday spaces, extended to the problem of ending all forms of oppression for all people, restoring the balance between people and the environment/nature, and reconciling human life with the spiritual dimension.[18]

---

the spiritual underpinning of *action* for social and ecological justice. It is an *underpinning* because it is not sufficient to think of spirituality—that which gives life—as an optional 'dimension' or 'element.' If activism is not grounded in spirituality, it cannot be sustained in the long run: we either burn out or sell out as the oil of life runs low. We need replenishment from the wellheads of life itself. No matter what religious tradition we may or may not be coming from, this re-sourcing is a question of depth psychology and, we argue, ultimately one of spirituality" (emphasis his). See https://www.alastairmcintosh.com/spiritualactivism/.

[17] Delores S. Williams, "The Color of Feminism: Or Speaking the Black Woman's Tongue," in *Feminist Theological Ethics: A Reader*, ed. Lois K. Daly, Library of Theological Ethics (Louisville, KY: Westminster John Knox Press, 1994), 50–51, 55.

[18] Layli Phillips [Maparyan], "Introduction: Womanism—On Its Own," in *The Womanist Reader*, ed. Layli Phillips [Maparyan] (New York: Taylor and Francis, 2006), xx.

In practical terms, this work involves tasks and activities aimed at harmonizing and coordinating, balancing, and healing. In the opening chapter of her subsequent book, *The Womanist Idea*, Maparyan broadens this discussion by sharing her vision of and for Luxocracy. Her bold and exciting offering is not just a theory or philosophy of social change but a metaphysics that offers womanism to the world as an example of integrated politics and spirituality.

Maparyan expands the source material of womanism to place Walker's definition of "womanist"—from *In Search of Our Mothers' Gardens*—into a larger conversation that crosses the Atlantic Ocean and disciplinary lines leading to five interdependent characteristics of womanist thought. First, womanism is *anti-oppressionist* as it focuses our attention on transcending domination and oppression. Second, it is *vernacular*: "The soul of womanism is grassroots, identified with the masses of humanity" and is expressed in many ways, including trusting everyday people to both imagine and work toward social justice. Third, womanism is *nonideological* in the way it opts for decentralization and inclusion over rigid partisan lines: "Womanism is not a rule-based system, and it does not need to resolve internal disagreement to function effectively." Fourth, womanism is *communitarian*, following the principle of "commonweal," which is Maparyan's word for collective well-being. Black women's experience is the origin of a commitment to all livingkind with the purpose of realizing commonweal by reconciling humans across our divisions, humans and the natural world, and humans and the spiritual world. Fifth, womanism is *spiritualized*, which means that social and political activism includes an unequivocal belief in the spiritual realm of reality, a metaphysical realm that participates in our work for social justice. These characteristics also combine to set the terms of womanism's method for social change through nonviolent and assertive postures taken toward everyday activities that grow out of people's actual lives.[19] I offer them as the compass's magnet.

A Map: Engaged Pedagogy and Capacious Antiracism

Anyone searching for treasure needs a map. In my experience of antiracism training in four different settings over twenty-five years, there has always been a plethora of definitions and a dearth of maps (metaphorical or other-

---

[19] Phillips [Maparyan], "Introduction," xxiv–xxx.

wise). Maps help us identify our location in relation to our destination. Maps also help us visualize the fact that, because we all begin the search from different points of origin, our respective paths to the destination are going to be different as we navigate varying routes, terrain, and landmarks. Resourced by engaged pedagogy, the antiracism movement, especially in higher education, is a healthier and stronger movement when it has the ideological flexibility to guide people to a common destination without requiring everyone to travel to the same starting point and follow the same path.[20]

If we accept womanism's worldview, then it easily follows that racism is a Fallen Power in the grip of evil. "Evil is a contagion," Wink writes, adding, "No one grapples with it without contamination."[21] For this reason, the antiracism movement is at its best when it is awake to its own imitative resistance, the point when the movement takes on the characteristics of what it is trying to change. I am not calling for perfectionism but wholeheartedness, especially in the face of negative feedback from internal critics and fierce backlash from culture warriors. As tempting as it might be to interpret such responses as textbook examples of predictable pushback from the forces of whiteness, if we acknowledge that, like any reform movement, antiracism can become ideologically driven, then engaged pedagogy reminds us that curiosity is an indispensable teaching assistant and vulnerability a wise mentor. hooks distinguishes engaged pedagogy from conventional critical and feminist pedagogies in the way it regards teachers as healers and focuses on well-being. She writes, "Teachers must be actively committed to a process of self-actualization that promotes their own well-being if they are to teach in a manner that empowers students."[22]

---

[20] See Jack Niemonen, "Antiracist Education in Theory and Practice: A Critical Assessment," *American Sociologist* 38, no. 2 (June 2007): 159–77, https://www.jstor.org/stable/27700497. Niemonen writes, "Antiracist education appropriated the postmodern premise that Western epistemology is a form of hegemony that does not deserve its privileged status. Embodied in social scientific practices, Western epistemology imposes restrictions a priori on what constitutes knowledge, is fraught with problems of subjectivity and preferentiality, and should not be privileged as objective, factual, or universal. In extreme interpretations, Western epistemology represents little more than domination by Eurocentric white men. Here antiracist educators claim that whiteness determine what counts as knowledge and that ignoring alternative epistemologies is racism at work" (161).

[21] Wink, *Engaging the Powers*, 205.

[22] bell hooks, *Teaching to Transgress: Education as the Practice of Freedom*, Teaching Trilogy, vol. 1 (New York: Routledge, 1994), 5.

In antiracism training and education, there are many ways to offer people maps. One option is to practice transparency by sharing information about the ideological commitments of a training curriculum. Another option is to use training events as opportunities to teach people about the global nature of the antiracism movement.[23] In my own teaching, research, and campus-based antiracism organizing, I have found Alastair Bonnett's work to be invaluable in this mapmaking process. What my students and I find compelling about his work is the simple fact that Bonnett, a social geographer from the United Kingdom, situates antiracism as a global movement with both a past and an evolving present. He also describes how the movement's politics move in different directions leading us to a view of antiracism as necessarily capacious.[24]

Bonnett begins by defining antiracism as "those forms of thought and/or practice that seek to confront, eradicate, and/or ameliorate racism," which implies an ability to (a) identify the phenomenon of racism and

---

[23] On this point, I often reflect on a critical incident from my first experience in a Christian, faith-based antiracism training in the early 2000s. When I was growing up, my family, jointly headed by my Black father and white mother, described itself as "interracial" and my siblings and me as "biracial." An unspoken but implied value my family has held is that interracial families are a sign of God's reign because we embody a commitment to overcoming racism in its most intimate forms. This theo-ethical interpretation of my own existence meant I was primed to be "on side" in the work of resisting racism and "offside" in endorsing the simplified neo-Marxist and critical theorist racial analysis foundational for the training curriculum. In the first of three weekends of antiracism training, there was an exercise where I needed to identify as either one race or the other, which I refused to do. I also suspected that, if and when I was out of alignment with the contours of the training materials, then the implication was that I might be too cozy with whiteness. With census data reporting that the number of "mixed-race" people like me is on the rise in the United States, how can the story that white people are racist oppressors and people of color are victims of racism account for people falling in love and forming intimate bonds that produce children and successful long-term relationships across racial lines?

[24] Alastair Bonnett, *Anti-Racism*, Key Ideas (London: Routledge, 2000), 118. He writes, "Antiracist work is often propelled by a sense of urgency, a 'just do it' imperative that privileges action as the soul of 'the movement.' However ... the variety of pathways in antiracism means that it can be 'done' in a variety of, not always complementary, ways. Perhaps the most fundamental distinction that exists within this work is a political one: while some want to find solutions within the socio-economic status quo, and believe that modern societies can be reformed to create racial equality, others see antiracism as a revolutionary activity" (118).

(b) respond to it constructively.²⁵ He proceeds to outline seven different views of racism that help readers see just how infrequently we ask ourselves the moral question, "What do I believe is wrong about racism?" Bonnett pointedly notices, "Despite the fact that racism appears so unpopular a cause, evidence for its existence remains abundant. In this context, the question of how and why people *claim* to be against racism becomes important."²⁶ Thus, with Bonnett's prompting, we can have a deeper conversation about our hopes and dreams of a world without racism. When we take the time to "[explore] the genesis and forms of anti-racist activism and consciousness" that animate the movement, we feel less alone and more connected to our own motivations.²⁷ Bonnett does not view his list as exhaustive and notes that the views below often exist in concert with each other, which has been borne out in my years of using his text in my teaching. With this list as a basic map, groups can add their own reasons for why they claim racism is a Fallen Power that must be resisted. These additions serve as "topographical data" for the map.

Here is a summary of Bonnett's seven reasons often cited as evidence of racism's problematic nature that have led to various forms of antiracism awareness and activism.

1. *Racism is socially disruptive.* This view regards racism as a destabilizing influence on norms and values like healthy community relations, social cohesion, and national unity. When held by state agencies, this view is especially opposed to racism's power to cause conflict that wastes human potential and resources. Thus, racism is found to be antithetical to an integrated, peaceful, and tolerant society.
2. *Racism is foreign.* Here, racism is considered malignant and alien in its origins. This line of thinking can be found around the world. Some nations regard equality, tolerance, and pluralism as the benevolent ideas out of which their countries are born. Other nations, subjected to colonization or heavy Western influences, may view racism as symptomatic of their indigenous traditions being infected by foreign contaminants.

---

[25] Bonnett, *Anti-Racism*, 3.
[26] Bonnett, *Anti-Racism*, 4 (emphasis his).
[27] Bonnett, *Anti-Racism*, 4.

3. *Racism sustains the ruling class.* In this case, racism is seen as an ideology or social practice that is an important part of what keeps "the System" functioning, giving those with the most power in a given society the means of influence to stay in power. Thus, racism keeps the working class divided and fed on narratives steeped in conservative ideologies.
4. *Racism hinders the progress of "our community."* When a group oppressed by racism rises to resist it, that group often pairs its social analysis with an emphasis on self-interest. Understanding that "community" may or may not be a racial category, racism is at odds with "our community" because racism has the power to prevent "us" from realizing "our" potential economically, socially, and politically. If racism is dismantled, then "our community" will enjoy full participation in society, particularly in elite economic and occupational roles the community has been historically barred from.
5. *Racism is an intellectual error.* This view is linked to the discussions among academics and intellectuals who began labeling racism as "bad science" in the mid- to late-twentieth century. Antiracism advocates view themselves as cosmopolitan compared to racists who are unaware of other ways of being human.
6. *Racism distorts and erases people's identities.* Making a psychological turn, the concern with racism, inclusive of the harm of racism on its individual victims, expands to focus on what harm can happen to society if racially defined groups do not know "their own" history because their experience is marginalized (victim) or distorted (oppressor).
7. *Racism is anti-egalitarian.* While all streams of antiracism share this basic view, those that emphasize it draw on political and/or religious views that our inalienable human rights include the right to be free from being a victim of racism.

In addition to inviting antiracism advocates to consider what motivates their work, this list helps us begin to see tensions and even paradoxes that arise within this work.[28] The goal of such reflection is not to push toward ideological unity; rather, the goal is an awareness that antiracism is

---

[28] Bonnett, *Anti-Racism*, 4–7.

a wide-ranging space with many geographical features. As we explore it, we learn about ourselves, each other, racism, and what it means for us to search for treasure together.

Good Company: Antiracism Practice

The third resource in my analogy, good company, is both literal and figurative: We cannot do this work alone. The corporate and communal nature of antiracism work in a womanist way is not about the strength of numbers; it goes back to the compass and the metaphysics of it all. The treasure we are searching for teaches, heals, transforms, and frees us and our world. Searching for this treasure together is exercising our agency to be the change we want to see in the world, as the saying goes.

Another useful aspect of Bonnett's work is his thematic clustering of antiracism practices found around the world. This is not an exhaustive list of the "right" or "best" ways to be antiracist but examples of routes that everyday people in ordinary communities take each day. Giving people language and options to think through what is important to them honors their agency and avoids the ideological and dogmatic caricature of antiracism cited by a range of critics, including those who are sympathetic to antiracism's aims but frustrated by the ways some expressions of antiracism education follow patterns that eerily resemble evangelical Protestantism, becoming highly moralistic and insistent that there are right ways and wrong ways to be antiracist.[29]

- *Everyday antiracism* comprises the nonpartisan actions ordinary people take to oppose racial inequalities and discrimination found in everyday life and popular culture.
- *Multicultural antiracism* describes activities that range from focusing on creating social bonds that favor a combination of racial and ethnic diversity to examining how social power changes when culture and race overlap. All these activities affirm building multicultural communities, organizations, and coalitions as a way of challenging racism (understood as cultural exclusion) through positive cultural inclusion that builds friendship across racial and ethnic divisions.

---

[29] Niemonen, "Antiracist Education in Theory and Practice," 165ff.

- *Psychological antiracism* deepens the movement's general interest in attitudes and behaviors by confronting racism's impact on individual and collective consciousness. Racism is an evil disease that takes control of our minds and souls. If racism cannot be exorcised or cured, then shoring up personal identity against racist attacks becomes another line of defense.
- *Radical antiracism* has a wide range of expressions, but they are united by a common interest in using revolution to confront patterns of socioeconomic power and privilege that create and perpetuate racism.
- *Anti-Nazi and anti-fascist antiracism* are two forms of antiracism that have developed in Europe to specifically confront the ongoing political and cultural expressions of these movements. In the United States, this would be *anti-white supremacy antiracism* aimed at the formal (organized) and informal (personal prejudice) manifestations of white supremacy.
- *Representative organization antiracism* may combine the strategies above but is its own form of antiracism because it reflects a commitment to making social change by overhauling organizations and institutions to include and welcome the participation of those from racial groups previously excluded by policy and/or practice.[30]

Where the list of seven perspectives on the nature of racism helps us respond to the question, "What makes racism a problem?" this additional list serves to answer such questions as "If I oppose racism because it is socially disruptive, how do I act on that belief?" and "Why does my antiracism practice look so different from yours?" These questions make it possible for us to find our place in this movement for social justice without undermining our self-confidence.

Without meaningful ways to comprehend and distinguish differences within the antiracism movement, conflict quickly becomes personal and destructive, when someone says, for example, "I would rather be on my own than work with 'them.' " When we cannot agree on which way to turn because we are using different maps, then we have the means to disagree constructively and even bless each other if we decide to go in different directions. Traveling in good company affords us the possibility of staying

---

[30] Bonnett, *Anti-Racism*, 85–115.

connected even though we have each been shaped by intersecting social forces in our own particular and peculiar way because we believe, as a matter of conviction, that we each have something meaningful to contribute to a shared understanding of how God is using all of us to bring health and insight into a hurting world.

Conclusion

I harbor no illusions that this essay will lead to a sea change in how we educate, train, and form people to be advocates for antiracism. I do hope, though, that my presentation of antiracism from a womanist worldview invites us all to ongoing reflection on the meaning we find and the vision we hold up for social justice as people of faith.

9

We Want to Be Loving:

The Ethics of Reciprocity in Chicago's Response to Venezuelan Asylum Seekers

Christophe D. Ringer

From August 2022 to December 2024, nearly 47,000 migrants and asylum seekers, mostly Venezuelan, arrived in Chicago.[1] Migrants and asylum seekers arrived on buses and private charter flights sponsored by Texas Governor Greg Abbott. Images of men, women, young persons, and children sleeping in police stations throughout the city created a dramatic image of a social crisis. This humanitarian crisis occasioned me to rethink key aspects of how I teach Christian Social Ethics at Chicago Theological Seminary. This essay attempts to consider how political and geographic influences affect the relationship between classroom and community. This chapter begins with a descriptive account of the social crisis that motivates my reflections on pedagogy and concepts of justice. The second part moves to consider the concept of reciprocity as articulated by Tommie Shelby and bell hooks. Finally, I augment these accounts with Edward Soja's theory of spatial justice to develop an eschatological approach to Christian Social Ethics that is pedagogically responsive to the local context in which I teach.

---

[1] Nell Zalzman, "Two Years after Migrants Began To Arrive, Many Have Settled in Chicago Even as Some Continue to Struggle," *Chicago Tribune*, September 13, 2024, https://www.chicagotribune.com/2024/09/02/two-years-after-migrants-began-to-arrive-many-have-settled-in-chicago-even-as-some-continue-to-struggle/.

Chicago Theological Seminary: History and Pedagogy

It is important to note that CTS has significant history with social ethics. In 1892, Graham Taylor accepted a call from CTS to serve as professor of a new experimental field called Christian Sociology. Taylor was convinced of the value of sociology for the advancement of theological education and for the capacity of churches to build up the Kingdom of God.[2] For Taylor, the experiences of the social world are the primary texts in which to teach from the "ground up and not from the clouds down."[3] One of the many lasting legacies of Taylor was the establishment of the Chicago Commons, a settlement house designed to offer services and build relationships of solidarity with immigrant and working-class residents. Taylor's presence instantiated an ethos regarding social ethics at CTS that continues to be informed by local community issues. This ethos is also evident as CTS became deeply involved in the racial politics in the surrounding community.

In the wake of the civil rights movement and the emerging Black Power movement, CTS became more involved with urban issues. The students, faculty, administration, and board of directors began to engage issues related to economic opportunity, housing, and education with the Black community. Rev. Archie Hargraves, director of the Center for Black Religious Studies, describes this as the "blackening" of CTS.[4] The engagement with the Black community on Chicago's South Side was expressed through Operation Breadbasket, The Woodlawn Organization, and the Kenwood-Oakland Project, which included work with a youth organization, the Blackstone Rangers.[5] This involvement represented another significant engagement for CTS in its surroundings. I recount this brief history to note that engaging the crisis of Venezuelan migrants and asylum seekers is part of the institutional legacy and ethos of CTS.

Geographically, CTS is located on Chicago's South Side. The seminary is largely associated with a group of seminaries located in Hyde Park, and it has a significant relationship with the University of Chicago. However,

---

[2] Gary Dorrien, *Social Ethics in the Making: Interpreting an American Tradition* (Hoboken, NJ: Wiley-Blackwell, 2010), 42.

[3] Dorrien, *Social Ethics in the Making*, 43.

[4] Perry D. LeFevre, *Challenge and Response: The Chicago Theological Seminary Story, 1960–1980* (Chicago: Exploration Press, 1999), 130.

[5] LeFevre, *Challenge and Response*, 141.

our actual address places us in the Woodlawn community and bordering South Shore. The South Shore community was an early site of significant resistance to the presence of asylum seekers, who, at the time, were largely referred to as migrants in the local media.

The current methodology I use to teach "Introduction to Christian Social Ethics" draws from several methodological influences. The first is an emphasis on assisting students in understanding the complex relationships between moral context, moral norms, and interpretations of moral fulfillment. The second draws from a tradition of moral inquiry that uses empirical tools to ask "What is going on?" and then subsequently "What shall we do?" from a theological perspective. The third influence is critical theory and pedagogy that is concerned with mutual transformation of knowledge and the social world. And this assumes that persons are shaped and shape the social worlds we inhabit. The latter point is important as critical pedagogy also includes a self-awareness of the ways in which education oriented toward social justice can also serve as a site that reproduces dominant class interests.[6] The course is organized thematically. I take up various social justice issues while illustrating various methods in the field. Thus Laura Stivers's *Disrupting Homelessness* and Miguel De La Torres's *The US Immigration Crisis: Toward an Ethics of Place* were taught on separate weeks as two distinct social justice questions. However, the crisis of Venezuelan asylum seekers presented new pedagogical challenges as different geographic and cultural histories of injustice were clashing in real time.

Anatomy of a Social Crisis

A key aspect of my pedagogy in teaching Christian social ethics is gaining a historical understanding of contemporary social issues. Thus, when engaging questions of the "border crisis," it is important to understand the history of US policies that contribute to the destabilizing of economies that contribute to pushing populations away from their home countries.[7]

---

[6] See Peter McLaren, "Critical Pedagogy: A Look at the Major Concepts," in *The Critical Pedagogy Reader*, ed. Antonia Darder, Rodolfo D. Torres, and Marta P. Baltodanao (New York: Routledge, 2017).

[7] See the report Juan Gonzalez, "The Current Migrant Crisis: How US Policy toward Latin America Has Fueled Historic Numbers of Asylum Seekers," Great

Scholars such as De La Torre are helpful in challenging the norm of hospitality that many liberal Christians have been shaped and formed to invoke in response to undocumented immigrants.[8] The norm of hospitality tends to mask awareness of and complicity in the various US economic and military policies that contribute to the perennial so-called border crises. In this instance, this means attending to the sanctions the United States placed on Venezuela in 2006 due to human rights violations and lack of cooperation with US counterterrorism efforts.[9] These sanctions barred the Venezuelan government from accessing US financial systems and froze bank accounts as well as blocked oil imports. The sanctions were kept in place under the Obama administration and aggressively tightened by Donald Trump, resulting in an increase in disease, mortality rates, and widespread hunger that have accelerated migration.[10]

On May 4, 2023, hundreds of community residents attended a meeting at South Shore International College Preparatory School to hear the city's plans to house asylum seekers at a former South Shore High School.[11] I was present at the meeting. There was sharp resistance to city officials both for leaving residents out of the planning process as well for the historical disinvestment of the South Side.[12] There were certainly xenophobic

---

Cities Institute, October 2023. Also for broader background on US relations with the Northern Triangle, see Cristina Eguizábal, Matthew C. Ingram, Karise M. Curtis, Aaron Korthuis, Eric L. Olson and Nicholas Phillips, "Crime and Violence in Central America's Northern Triangle: How US Policy Responses are Helping, Hurting, and Can Be Improved," no. 34, Woodrow Wilson Center Reports on the Americas, December 18, 2014, https://www.wilsoncenter.org/publication/crime-and-violence-central-americas-northern-triangle-how-us-policy-responses-are.

[8] See Miguel A. De La Torre, "Conclusion: Against Hospitality," in Miguel A. De La Torre's *The US Immigration Crisis: Toward an Ethics of Place* (Eugene, OR: Cascade Books, 2016).

[9] See Diana Roy, "Do US Sanctions on Venezuela Work?" Council on Foreign Relations online, November 4, 2022, https://www.cfr.org/in-brief/do-us-sanctions-venezuela-work.

[10] Roy, "Do US Sanctions on Venezuela Work?"

[11] Zoe Pharo, "South Shore Residents Blast City's Plan to House Migrants at Repurposed School," *Hyde Park Herald*, May 5, 2023, https://www.hpherald.com/evening_digest/south-shore-residents-blast-city-s-plan-to-house-migrants-at-repurposed-school/article_c88111c0-eb95-11ed-9d16-47da2eaed89f.html.

[12] Pharo, "South Shore Residents Blast City's Plan to House Migrants at Repurposed School."

sentiments expressed such as signs reading "build the wall 2024" and calls to "close the border." However, I argue that this vocal community's response is not reducible to a xenophobic or predictable nativist response. Specifically at issue was the city's plan to use a former school at 7627 S. Constance as a respite center for migrants to live while awaiting more permanent shelter. This building is a representation of the wave of former Mayor Rahm Emanuel's closure of forty-nine public schools in 2013.[13] The city made promises to many Chicago communities that the buildings would be repurposed as community centers. A decade later, many of the buildings remain shuttered. The building was subsequently designated for additional police training in 2020 without community input.[14] The level of community resentment over the broken promises is such that a lawsuit was filed to prevent the city from using the location to house asylum seekers.[15] The building effectively became a symbol of disinvestment and disregard. A key statement made from a community resident in the May 4th meeting occasioned a conceptual shift in my thinking.

The contentious town hall meeting was an opportunity for residents to redefine the meaning of humanitarian crisis and name the problem of political reciprocity. Residents made it clear that the community is already enduring persistent high rates of violence, homelessness, poverty, and over-policing. A Black woman crystallized the sentiments in the room when she walked up to the microphone and with profound conviction and clarity stated, "We want to be loving. But part of love is reciprocity. And so, when you pick up one of them and feed them and house them, pick up one of ours and feed them and clothe them."[16] The people in the gym exploded

---

[13] For comprehensive local reporting on the legacy of these closings see WBEZ and Chicago Sun-Times, "Chicago's 50 Closed Schools," https://www.wbez.org/chicagos-50-closed-schools; and Eve L. Ewing, *Ghosts in the Schoolyard: Racism and School Closings on Chicago's South Side* (Chicago: University of Chicago Press, 2018).

[14] Maxwell Evans, "Closed South Shore School Will Become Police Training Center as City Council Approves Controversial Plan," Block Club Chicago, April 24, 2020, https://blockclubchicago.org/2020/04/24/closed-south-shore-school-will-become-police-training-center-as-city-council-approves-controversial-plan/.

[15] Emmanuel Camarillo, "Lawsuit Seeks to Stop Former South Shore High School from Being Turned into Shelter for Migrants: 'We were forced to do this,'" *Chicago Sun-Times*, May 11, 2023.

[16] Camarillo, "Lawsuit Seeks to Stop Former South Shore High School from Being Turned into Shelter for Migrants." Unfortunately I was not able to get her name.

with applause. Her words captured the deep anger directed at city officials for using underinvested communities as the first recourse to address an emerging crisis while demonstrating a lack of reciprocity for existing ones. Her words occasioned my engagement with the concept of reciprocity in the work of Tommie Shelby and bell hooks.

Visions of Reciprocity

Tommie Shelby's account of reciprocity is situated in a broader project that reframes the enduring social ills associated with America's "ghettos." Instead of the familiar debates between "behavioralists" and "structuralists," Shelby asks what justice personally and collectively requires of us.[17] In particular, Shelby critiques what he terms the medical model, which engages targeted interventions to reduce material disadvantages while leaving the basic structure of society unchanged. Moreover, such a model marginalizes the political agency of the persons it is designed to assist.[18] Instead, Shelby employs a social-injustice model that assumes citizens and government have a duty to ensure a just society. Here, Shelby adopts the familiar Rawlsian definition of society as a "fair system of social cooperation over time" that can be used to evaluate institutional arrangements.[19] As such, reciprocity is a matter of justice between persons who regard one another as equals. For Shelby, this is an intervention that can determine if the urban poor are doing their fair share (thus countering stereotypes of laziness) and receiving their fair share as equal participants in this system of social cooperation.[20] Shelby acknowledges three visions of reciprocity as it relates to the government.

Shelby's most thorough account of reciprocity is embedded in a broader account of the relationship of work and welfare benefits. It includes a review of three versions of reciprocity. The first account of reciprocity envisions a

---

[17] Cornel West interpreted the structuralist and behavioralist arguments as an ideological divide between liberals who emphasize full employment, health, education, childcare programs and affirmative action practices and the conservatives who champion the Protestant ethic rooted in self-help programs, Black business expansion, and non-preferential job practices. See Cornel West, *Race Matters* (New York: Vintage Books, 1995), 18.

[18] Tommie Shelby, *Dark Ghettos: Injustice, Dissent, and Reform* (Cambridge, MA: Harvard University Press, 2016), 2.

[19] Shelby, *Dark Ghettos*, 20.

[20] Shelby, *Dark Ghettos*.

benefactor and a debtor, a scene in which society provides a benefit, and each member of society returns the debt by working.[21] The second is imaged as a market of mutual advantage, in which government provides benefits to citizens in exchange for social meaningful work. And the third vision of reciprocity is predicated on fairness; in this version citizens contribute labor to the public good, assuming the benefits of social cooperation. I find this option compelling, since Shelby claims that government also has an obligation to provide work for those willing and able to work. Shelby's account of reciprocity addresses the relationship of work to welfare benefits, and I find it helpful as I think through the social tension between current residents and recent residents on Chicago's South Side.

The critique leveled by residents is that the city has produced an unjust distribution of benefits, resources, and opportunities along the lines of race and geography. This occasions both political and moral problems. The first is that the city continues to reproduce an unjust relationship between residents and the city by attempting to use under-resourced communities to house and serve new populations. More specifically, such actions position communities to both receive fewer resources and shoulder more burdens than more affluent communities. This is a double failure of reciprocity. At this point, it is important to connect the question of reciprocity to the work of bell hooks.

I interpret the work of bell hooks as being part of a tradition of contemporary agapism in which love is central to justice.[22] hooks makes two primary claims about the virtue of love. The first is drawn from the work of M. Scott Peck (with influences from Eric Fromm), who defines love as "the will to extend oneself for the purpose of nurturing one's own or another's spiritual growth" that is marked by both intention and action.[23] In particular, love includes a mix of ingredients such as "care, affection, recognition, respect, commitment, trust as well as open and honest communication."[24] Her account is an important critique of the confusions

---

[21] Tommie Shelby, "Justice, Work, and the Ghetto Poor," *Law and Ethics of Human Rights* 6, no. 1 (2012): 201.

[22] I use the phrase "contemporary agapism" in contrast to Nicholas Wolterstorff's "modern-day agapism," which describes modern accounts of love that are unable to satisfactorily integrate the demands of justice into love. See Nicholas Wolterstorff, *Justice in Love* (Grand Rapids: Eerdmans, 2015), 1–62.

[23] bell hooks, *All About Love: New Visions* (New York: Harper Collins, 2001), ix.

[24] hooks, *All About Love*, 5.

that often attend our use of the term love, especially when it only indicates a feeling or an emotional investment without any other qualities. As it relates to the migrant crisis, I found the interpretation of hooks's work by Michael J. Monahan compelling.

Michael Monahan argues that a key quality of hooks's account of love across her corpus is that of reciprocity. Specifically, loving other persons requires the acknowledgment and respect of their personhood, and in return one's own personhood is clarified in the process of being loved. Here, Monahan is worth quoting at length. He states:

> Genuine service not only demands that I acknowledge and respect your subject-hood in serving you, but that my own subject-hood is made even more clear to me in the way that you, in loving me back, honor and serve me. We each come to give our subject-hood to the other reciprocally, and so have our own subjecthood given back to us in a more fully-realized way. All of this furthers our education for critical consciousness, as well, for in serving each other, we come to learn more not only about the other, but also about ourselves.[25]

The process of gaining clarity about one's own subjectivity in the case of Venezuelan migrants and asylum seekers is important.[26] Journalist Natalie Moore contributes to this critical consciousness by recalling the history of Blacks migrants from the South facing stiff resistance when they arrived in Chicago.[27] The interactions between current residents and new arrivals are often mediated by distorting representations.

A good example of distorting perceptions is evidenced on a radio talk show, the David Seaton Show, on the Chicago-based station WVON. WVON is a significant station because it represents a genuine Black public sphere that addresses issues pertinent to Black Chicagoans primarily

---

[25] Michael J. Monahan, "Emancipatory Affect: bell hooks on Love and Liberation," *CLR James Journal* 17, no. 1 (Fall 2011): 108.

[26] I use the term "subjectivity" to describe the complex ways in which our internal lives are shaped by the structures of our social world and as an equivalent to Monahan's "subjecthood."

[27] See Natalie Y. Moore, "Black Chicago, Let's Check Our Attitudes on Migrants," *Chicago Sun-Times*, October 19, 2023.

on the South and West sides.²⁸ As such, the call-in format provides a window into perspectives that residents hold on migrants. During one broadcast in March 2024, Seaton poses the question "What should we do with migrants?"²⁹ He suggested several options: (1) deport them; (2) give them work authorizations; or (3) care for them in shelters. One caller by the name of Angel says, "Trump says he's going to deport these illegal immigrants," and asks, "Do we not send Venezuela billions of dollars every year?" Seaton acknowledges that Trump's sanctions contributed to crashing the Venezuelan economy and was the catalyst for this migration. The caller, Angel, immediately says, "No, Biden invited them in!" Another caller Deborah argues that migrants should be helped in their own states, sent to Republican states to work in agriculture, or "let Trump come in and do what he has to do."³⁰ Both callers represent a refusal to acknowledge the role of the United States in creating the conditions for the surge in migrants from Venezuela.

Eschatology, Spatial Justice, and the Common Good

At this point, I want to develop an account of the common good rooted in spatial justice that engages eschatology as a form of practical reason.³¹ In *Seeking Spatial Justice*, Edward Soja develops an account of spatial justice rooted in the claims that we are spatial beings as well as social beings. As such, we are embedded in geographies from birth. This addresses the conceptual oversight in accounts of social existence that only feature societal and historical forces. Soja's account is particularly relevant to the migrant crisis, as racialized political economies shape geographical landscapes and the built environment. These processes occasion uneven development,

---

²⁸ Edmund Ramsay, "WVON Radio and the Black Public Sphere" (DePaul University). https://communication.depaul.edu/academics/digital-communication-and-media-arts/student-resources/complete-your-degree/Documents/Project%20Examples/EdRamsay_WVON%20Radio%20and%20the%20Black%20Public%20Sphere.pdf.

²⁹ The David Seaton Show, WVON, March 15, 2024, at 45:00, https://www.facebook.com/share/v/1AqyXnscMp/.

³⁰ The David Seaton Show, WVON, March 15, 2024, at 33:50.

³¹ This account builds on my initial engagement *with this theme in Necropolitics: The Religious Critique of Mass Incarceration in America* (Lanham, MD: Lexington Books, 2021).

which produces consequential inequalities that "have deeply oppressive and exploitative effects, especially when maintained over long time periods and rooted in persistent divisions in society such as those based on race, class, and gender."[32] The migrant crisis represents the simultaneity of uneven development in Chicago and unjust relationships with Latin America. This still requires a bridge to the idea of the common good.

I find David Hollenbach's *The Common Good and Christian Ethics* to be a persuasive account of the common good. He is attentive to the ways that sustained disinvestment perpetuates poverty and the short-lived responses to the social unrest disinvestment produces are not "commensurate with their seriousness."[33] This adequately captures the sense of frustration for residents in the South Shore community meeting. I highlight key points in his account of the common good. First, the common good is one that members both create and benefit from together. Specifically, the common good consists of adequate housing, accessible jobs, quality education, childcare, and healthcare that citizens require to live in dignity. Second, society is related through forms of mutual interdependence. Hollenbach rightly argues that urban and suburban communities are not independent variables but are in a relationship marked by unequal interdependence based in nonreciprocity and inequality that affects both geographic regions. This holds especially true for the relationships between the North, South, and West sides of Chicago. Hollenbach is careful to note that such relationships are mediated through political, economic, and cultural institutions that affect issues such as "land use, zoning, housing and the funding of education opportunities."[34]

This account is rooted in two related aspects of justice: contributive and distributive. Contributive justice calls on all citizens to build up these aspects of social life appropriate to their capacity while distributive justice concerns the allocations of goods for the well-being of its members.[35] When citizens fail in their contribution, it is a failure of solidarity, and

---

[32] Edward W. Soja, *Seeking Spatial Justice* (Minneapolis: University of Minnesota Press, 2010), 73. Also see Edward W. Soja, *Postmodern Geographies: The Reassertion of Space in Critical Social Theory* (New York: Verso Books, 1989), 76–93.

[33] David Hollenbach, *The Common Good and Christian Ethics* (Cambridge: Cambridge University Press, 2002), 34.

[34] Hollenbach, *The Common Good and Christian Ethics*, 174–75.

[35] Hollenbach, *The Common Good and Christian Ethics*, 196.

institutional arrangements that deprive persons from sharing in social goods is a failure of distributive justice.

Eschatology, as I am using I it here, then, integrates space, time, and judgment in the task of practical reason.[36] From this perspective, to discern "what is going on?" one must simultaneously attend to spatial and temporal injustices within the city of Chicago as well as between the United States and Venezuela. Within Chicago, there is a historical failure of reciprocity along the lines of distributive justice through disinvestment and a contemporary failure of contributive justice in the reluctance to initially require more affluent communities to care for migrants and asylum seekers. The failure to recognize the role of US policies in producing this profound surge in new arrivals opens the door for misunderstandings and inadequate moral judgments from long-term residents. Moreover, it impedes the ability to love one's neighbor justly, for the necessary critical consciousness that bell hooks articulates is compromised. In attending to the historical, the spatial, and the demand of realizing the common good, there is the potential to provide a Christian social witness as it relates to new arrivals from Venezuela.

---

[36] For my initial engagement with this claim see "Tangle of Perils: The Eschatological Dilemma of Black Families in America," *Concilium: International Journal of Theology* 2 (2016); and "The Eschatological Production of Mass Incarceration," in *Necropolitics: The Religious Crisis of Mass Incarceration in America* (Lanham, MD: Lexington Books, 2021).

10

To Be Foils, Not Fooled:

The Insistent Practice and Insurgent Pedagogy of Christian Social Liberation Ethics for Colleagues, Church, and Community

Stacey Floyd-Thomas

When I think about the work of my friend and fellow Christian social ethicist Gary Dorrien, I can easily say that I have always been encouraged by and even enamored of the ways he has upheld the clarion call of justice in his formulation of ethics. Although we could not be more dissimilar in our phenotypical backgrounds and social realities, what has helped us bridge that great divide has been a shared sense that, for Christian social ethics to be relevant, it has to be rooted in Scripture and must eventually be realized in society. Even as I am inspired by the prolific and profound work of Dorrien as a colleague, I have set out on my own journey guided by womanist ways of thought, being, and action in an American society and culture deeply saturated with misogynoir and have felt myself increasingly drawn to advance a concept of "just ethics" as a reframing of our shared field of study and disciplinary concern.

Simply put, just ethics as I see it is not just sociopolitical, it's also scriptural. This assertion forms the bedrock of a rich and robust understanding of justice, one that recognizes the inherent interconnectedness of faith and action, of divine mandate and social transformation. To separate the ethical pursuit of justice from its scriptural moorings is to sever it from its deepest source of inspiration and prophetic power. Just ethics, therefore, must be understood as both deeply rooted in sacred texts and actively engaged in the messy realities of the sociopolitical world, especially at the time of writing this in the ongoing age of Trumpism.

Too often, discussions of ethics are confined to knee-jerk questions of right and wrong within the largely secular context of the public sphere, as if deeper, more meaningful considerations of freedom, human flourishing, fairness, and equity among a host of other concerns somehow could be divorced from the spiritual and theological traditions that have shaped our moral imaginations for centuries, if not millennia. As I recently have written in my own work, *When the Good Life Goes Bad: The US and Our Seven Deadly Sins*, the simultaneous secularization and devaluation of ethics not only impoverishes our understanding of justice but also weakens our capacity to pursue it with the kind of unwavering commitment it demands.[1] The scriptures of various faith traditions, particularly within the Abrahamic lineage, are replete with calls for justice, not as abstract ideals but as concrete demands woven into the very fabric of religious life. From the Hebrew prophets' fiery pronouncements against oppression to Jesus's radical teachings on love and compassion, Scripture provides a consistent and compelling mandate for ethical action in the world.

However, to claim that just ethics is scriptural is not to suggest an overly simplistic application of ancient texts to contemporary problems. To say that just ethics is scriptural is in no way to try to recast and replicate for the Religious Left the "bibliolatry" that defined the Christian fundamentalists' evangelical project of the past century of hiding a brutally conservative political agenda in priestly robes. To the contrary, scriptural interpretation centered in and seeking justice is a complex and nuanced process, requiring careful attention to historical context, sociopolitical structures, literary genre, human difference, power dynamics, and the ongoing dialogue between tradition and experience. Moreover, the Scriptures themselves often present diverse, sometimes conflicting, perspectives on justice, reflecting the inherent complexities of ethical decision-making as a perennial and difficult reality. What returning to Scripture as a seedbed for contemporary Christian social ethics *does* offer, however, is a framework for ethical reflection, a set of guiding principles that can inform our engagement with the social and political issues of our time. These principles—such as the inherent dignity of all human beings, God's preferential option for the poor and marginalized, and the call to challenge unjust systems—provide a moral compass for navigating the incessantly confusing complexities of modern social life.

---

[1] Stacey M. Floyd-Thomas, *When the Good Life Goes Bad: The US and Our Seven Deadly Sins* (forthcoming 2026).

Just ethics, or perhaps we should say *JUSTethics*, therefore, is not simply about adhering to a set of restrictive rules or dogmatic doctrines. It is about cultivating a way of seeing the world, a perspective that recognizes the inherent worth and interconnectedness of all creation. It is about developing a "preferential option for the poor," as liberation theologians have articulated, so that our actions are always oriented toward the needs of the most vulnerable. It is about recognizing that injustice is not merely a matter of individual failings but is often embedded in social structures and institutions. *JUSTethics*, then, demands that we not only act justly in our personal lives but also work to transform the systems that perpetuate inequality and oppression.

This is where the "sociopolitical" and the "social gospel" dimensions of enlightenment and empowerment, faith and formation, meaning and method spring forth a *JUSTethics* as both crucial and urgent. Scriptural principles must be translated into concrete action in the world. This requires engaging with the political process, advocating for just laws and policies, and challenging those in power who abuse their authority. It also requires building coalitions with others who share a commitment to justice, regardless of their religious or political affiliations. *JUSTethics* is not a solitary pursuit. It is a collective project, demanding collaboration and solidarity across lines of difference.

This chapter takes up the crux of Gary Dorrien's scholarly telos as a project not simply for the failed project of the Enlightenment but also for the ethical undermining of Christian socialism.

Toward this end, there is a need for a metaethical framework for answering theo-ethical questions with logic and epistemological insight with regard to what is *fitting* or *good* for society as well as what is *freedom* or *responsibility* for moral leadership within the collegium, church, and society. As exemplified in Antonio Gramsci's explanation of traditional intellectuals—those who are the deputies not of democracy, as they may portend, but are managers and enforcers of the ruling class elite and the governmental power structure such that intellectual and moral leadership is only bestowed upon those who pay allegiance and patronage to social influence and political administration—traditional intellectuals, made up of philosophers and clergy, are a remnant of a noblesse oblige.[2] Capital is king and God is government.

---

[2] Antonio Gramsci et al., *Selections from the Prison Notebooks of Antonio Gramsci*, 1st ed. (New York: International, 1971).

Dorrien extends the critical pedagogy of bell hooks and Paulo Freire: "Education is never a neutral process. Education either integrates students into the dominant system, facilitating conformity to it, or is a practice of freedom that seeks to transform the system."³ This is evident within the mandate of the Social Gospel, as the democratic principle of paideia is implied in Micah 6:8 / Luke 4:18–19. By privileging the biblical critique of oppression, forgoing the serenity of the status quo, and linking divine justice to social justice, I will outline an insurgent pedagogy as that which forms moral theologians to interrogate the intersections of race, gender, class, embodiment, and ecology, as informed by Dorrien's work and call to disavow ties to the "lost causes" of the empire, and take up instead the struggle for success of both the social gospel and the very soul of democracy and ourselves.

Dorrien's Definition of Christian Social Ethics

As articulated in *Social Ethics in the Making: Interpreting an American Tradition*, Gary Dorrien's approach to social ethics offers a significant contribution to the field of moral inquiry.⁴ He moves beyond traditional ethical frameworks that focus primarily on individual behavior, expanding the scope of ethical analysis to encompass the complex interplay between individuals, institutions, and social structures. Dorrien's vision of social ethics is not simply about personal morality. It is about understanding and transforming the very fabric of society.

A key element of Dorrien's approach is his emphasis on the evaluation of social practices, institutions, and policies through a moral lens. He argues that ethical reflection must extend beyond individual actions to include a critical examination of the systems that shape our lives. This involves analyzing the ethical implications of social structures, such as political systems, economic models, and legal frameworks. Dorrien recognizes that these structures are not neutral; they embody particular values and often perpetuate existing power dynamics. Therefore, social ethics, in Dorrien's view, must be concerned with how these structures affect the pursuit of justice and the common good.

---

³ Gary Dorrien, *A Darkly Radiant Vision: The Black Social Gospel in the Shadow of MLK* (New Haven, CT: Yale University Press, 2023), 359.

⁴ Gary Dorrien, *Social Ethics in the Making: Interpreting an American Tradition* (Malden, MA: Wiley-Blackwell, 2009).

Dorrien's understanding of the common good goes beyond a simple aggregation of individual interests. He is concerned with the "good in common," a concept that emphasizes the interconnectedness of individuals and the importance of creating a society where all can flourish above and beyond the more typical formulation of the "common good." This requires a commitment to addressing systemic inequalities and working toward a more just distribution of resources and opportunities. To this point, Dorrien's social ethics is inherently concerned with issues of power and justice insofar as it seeks to uncover the ways in which power operates within social structures and to challenge those structures that perpetuate injustice.

Crucially, Dorrien highlights the relational dimension of social ethics. He recognizes that ethical reflection cannot be divorced from its historical, theological, and philosophical context. Toward this end, he emphasizes the interconnectedness of these disciplines with material conditions and sociopolitical landscapes. Social ethics, for Dorrien, is not an abstract theoretical exercise but a deeply grounded engagement with the realities of human existence. It requires understanding how historical forces, theological traditions, and philosophical ideas have shaped our understanding of morality and justice. Furthermore, it requires recognizing how these ideas are embedded in and influenced by the material conditions of life.

For Dorrien, social ethics is not simply a descriptive endeavor. It is also a prescriptive one. It is concerned not only with understanding how society works but also with how it ought to work. He envisions social ethics as a vital tool for individuals to understand and engage their society, empowering them to contribute to the creation of a world that embodies their highest ideals and virtues. In this sense, social ethics becomes a practice of critical reflection and transformative action. It is a way of working toward a more just and compassionate world, a world that reflects the values of human dignity and social solidarity. Dorrien's work provides a valuable framework for navigating the complex ethical challenges of our time, reminding us that the pursuit of justice and the common good requires not only individual moral reflection but also a sustained engagement with the social structures that shape our lives.

Enlightenment, Education, and Ethics

Throughout modern history, the role of education was enlightenment. The great books and philosophies of Descartes, Locke, Kant, Goethe, Voltaire, Rousseau, Montaigne, and Adam Smith, among others, provided the blueprint to not merely make enlightened thinking a process but a project, the very persona or institution that was synonymous with education. However, the Enlightenment Project, despite its lofty aspirations of advancing society through education, seems to have eluded its proponents, as the movement's overemphasis on rationality, neglect of emotional and cultural dimensions, and unbridled optimism inadvertently contributed to societal challenges and imbalances. This has led many postmodern critics, such as Jacques Derrida, Michel Foucault, Jean-François Lyotard, Jean Baudrillard, and Richard Rorty, to argue that the Enlightenment ultimately failed in fulfilling its educational promise.

In fact, if we may have learned anything in the classical history of the "Academy" of ancient Athens—ironically known as Plato's Academy—we have learned that it served as a crucial nexus in the interconnected evolution of philosophy, religion, and mathematics. Within this intellectual hub, these fields were intricately interwoven and explored in conjunction with one another, reflecting Plato's profound belief in the mathematical essence of existence. He utilized geometry as a central instrument for philosophical investigation, ultimately viewing mathematics as a means to comprehend the divine structure of the cosmos. Despite its significant ideological contributions to modern society—such as the promotion of individual liberty, rational thought, scientific progress, a focus on human rights, and the foundation for modern democracy—its limitations can be characterized as what were once considered its virtues:

1. *Excessive emphasis on reason*: The Enlightenment's focus on rationality sometimes led to a disregard for emotion, intuition, and other nonrational aspects of human experience, which are essential for a holistic understanding of the world.
2. *Eurocentrism*: The movement was primarily a European phenomenon, and its universalist claims often overlooked the diverse perspectives and experiences of the two-thirds world, the global south, and all non-white and non-Western cultures.
3. *Egotistic optimism*: The Enlightenment's belief in progress and the perfectibility of human nature has been criticized as overly optimistic, as it failed to anticipate the negative consequences of industrialization, colonialism, and other societal changes that followed.

The slippery slope of siloed scholarship and the solipsism of white normative ideologies both failed to produce anything other than the status quo of illusory white patriarchal supremacy and flatlined the long moral arc of the universe that was to lead toward a more just union rather than "a more perfect" one, as Martin Luther King Jr. once imagined. This disjuncture and disconnect from the Kantian notion that what enlightens us educates us and raises us up and out of the banality of immaturity, the discombobulation of chaos, and the clarity of civitas in fact becomes disorienting and beyond the pale. Its pedagogical dimension that was to be instructive for progress and intrinsic for putting knowledge to work for the good of the society in reality faltered grossly in providing Diderot's Plan of a University or of a Public Education as a "strategy with which to secure and consolidate the path of reason, and to protect it against dogmas and prejudices against it."[5] However, the free access to reason and rationality that was to wrest us out of Plato's cave of illusion and misperception and make mere mortals paragons of virtue and pillars of society has, in fact, shown us that, despite the proclamations of these self-appointed philosopher-kings, we have not only failed to escape the stronghold of institutionalized ignorance and self-delusion; we have become villainous in claiming our vainglory.

Calling Out the Failure of the Enlightenment and Miseducation of Ethics

The Cartesian logic known as the "cogito"—"I think, therefore I am"—has held the intellect and the intervention of education captive in a self-imposed cave shaped by Calvinist orthodoxy and the Protestant work ethic. In this country, Calvinist orthodoxy of the privileged class of Christian cultism has claimed a predestined righteousness, while the Protestant work ethic has pathologically posited that there is a greater propensity for diligent work and success through faithful participation in the civil religion of our land. This religious disposition affords democracy and rights to life, liberty, and the pursuit of justice to only the few forefathers who wanted to protect their

---

[5] Carlota Boto, "The Age of Enlightenment and Education," *Oxford Research Encyclopedia of Education*, February 23, 2021; Accessed January 28, 2025, https://oxfordre.com/education/view/10.1093/acrefore/9780190264093.001.0001/acrefore-9780190264093-e-1469.

property and progeny through an unjust privilege that has been packaged as the arduous labor and self-control that is fundamentally socially acceptable and divinely ordained. Nevertheless, these white lies linked and locked against those who are Black, Brown, young and old, female and nonbinary people, who are proof positive that the third world, that is, the minoritized perspective that claims universal enlightenment and entitlements, is actually not only a minority opinion but a miseducated reality in need of scrutiny and rebuttal from various perspectives, including ethical analysis, theological critique, sociopolitical and economic research that refutes its validity by bearing historical evidence that undermines its foundations and promotes greater enlightenment and rights to those in need of protection. As theologian Joerg Rieger confesses:

> For a long time, theology seemed most at home in the proverbial ivory towers of the academy, where its influence once used to be considerable. Whenever theology ventured outside of the academy, it often linked up with another set of ivory towers, symbolized by church steeples. There, too, it used to have some influence. As both the academy and the church made efforts to escape from their respective ivory towers—often by making common cause with business ventures, corporations, and politics—theology has tried to join, lagging behind in many cases. But rebellion against ivory towers is not revolution, even if it is directed against traditional Eurocentric (or Americentric) ideals. Nor does this kind of rebellion necessarily lead to transformation.... Contrary to common belief, none of these ivory towers ever existed in isolation in the first place.... For organic theologians, the question of context, therefore, is not about "lifting up" specific minority contexts (for instance, with the intent of including them into the dominant system), nor is it about volunteering their time for any enterprise (even the most bizarre) which is vaguely subversive. Rather, the question of context is about locating hegemony and power differentials with an eye toward liberation.... Nothing less is [our] task.[6]

---

[6] Joerg Rieger, *Theology in the Capitalocene: Ecology, Identity, Class, and Solidarity* (Minneapolis: Fortress Press, 2022), 7–10.

Herein, as ethicists taking up where even a liberation theology leaves us, we first must free ourselves from the Cartesian captivity, or cogito impetus, and render it obsolete and subject to an Ubuntu perspective of "I am because we are" or a Buberian religion of right relationship on how we relate to one to another, consciously and unconsciously. This rebirth of critical analysis as it reconciles itself to cultural awareness is the critical agency and attention to the fact that what makes us human and ordained as good is not an us-versus-them but an I-Thou (as opposed to I-It). Moral leadership, then, can then only be deemed as divinely legitimate when it pursues liberation, no matter the profession, for such liberation is cultivated by co-creation and the work of human flourishing as a philosophical or theological good.

From positions of prominence, power, and privilege—be they the assumed objectivity of academia, the moral authority of religious institutions, or the inherent advantages of a dominant social class—we are compelled to confront the ethical foundations of our lives. This necessitates a profound self-examination, echoing the urgent questions posed by Howard Thurman, mystic, theologian, and influential figure in the Civil Rights Movement:

> With full intensity we seek, ere the quiet passes, a fresh sense of order in our living. A direction, a strong sure purpose that will structure our confusion and bring meaning in our chaos. We look at ourselves in this waiting moment—the kinds of people we are. The questions persist: what are we doing with our lives?—what are the motives that order our days? What is the end of our doings? Where are we trying to go? Where do we put the emphasis and where are our values focused? For what end do we make sacrifices? Where is my treasure and what do I love most in life? What do I hate most in life and to what am I true? Over and over the questions beat in upon the waiting moment.[7]

When thinking about the pedagogical impact of Dorrien's approach to ethics, Thurman's words, like the historical materialism of womanist ethics, are concerned with the material realities of the world and how our faith commitments and intellectual ability compels us to be historically relevant

---

[7] Howard Thurman, *Meditations of the Heart* (Boston: Beacon Press, 2023), 12.

rather than conducive to the comfortable assumptions of our privileged positions and grapple with the fundamental questions of purpose, values, and commitment. Dorrien, as an allied academic with the capital of demographics, academy, and clerical status, lives in the way of Glenn Stassen's *Thicker Jesus* and David Gushee's *Defending Democracy from Its Christian Enemies* and is in the thick of "deep solidarity," of which Joerg Rieger speaks, by compelling us to examine not just what we do, but why we do it, and to consider the ultimate impact of our actions on the world around us when speaking from the center on behalf of the margins.[8]

As if taking cues from the failure of the Enlightenment, peril of the privileged, and the confession of a corrupted Christianity that begs Thurman's most searing question as to "what is the word of Jesus Christ to those whose backs are against the wall," Gary Dorrien also posits,

> "I am myself" lacks the emotive force of the cross, but it strikes me first while walking home from a talent show rehearsal at Forest School Number Two. I turn this sentence over and over in my mind, saying it aloud, punching the first word, then the second, then the third, then the second half of "myself," then two-word combinations of the phrase, trying to catch hold of the "I" of self-consciousness. It puzzles me that I cannot do it. How can my self—this immediate "I" who spends so much time alone with his thoughts and baseballs—be so elusive? I feel the slippery problem of identity, but have no language for it and do not try to discuss it with anyone. These experiences are glimmers of the unlikely Christian Left intellectual that I became.[9]

Whether discussing the great books or philosophies of the great thinkers that constitute the Enlightenment canon or the problem of personal piety or privilege that claims heavenly virtue where they may not

---

[8] See the representative texts: Glen H. Stassen, *A Thicker Jesus: Incarnational Discipleship in a Secular Age* (Louisville, KY: Westminster John Knox Press, 2012); David P. Gushee, *Defending Democracy from Its Christian Enemies* (Grand Rapids: Eerdmans, 2023); and Joerg Rieger and Rosemarie Henkel-Rieger, "Deep Solidarity: Broadening the Basis of Transformation," *HTS Teologiese Studies / Theological Studies* [online], 73, no. 3 (November 24, 2017).

[9] Gary Dorrien, *Over from Union Road: My Christian-Left-Intellectual Life* (Waco, TX: Baylor University Press, 2024), 2.

be of any earthly good, Dorrien's stance, like that of all ethicists who avow linking intellectual enlightenment to socio-spiritual empowerment, does not intend to diminish the supposed aims of collegiate enlightenment or Christian evangelism of its most meaningful aspirations but rather to assess its impact. Ethicists, particularly those who believe in our civilization's endurance, emphasize the need to overcome our inclination to revere esteemed intellectuals without question and recognize that bad faith has been a necessary component in fostering the pursuit of knowledge (enlightenment as education) or understanding (theology). Even the most brilliant minds or pietistic souls are capable of significant errors, and, as history demonstrates, some of the era's most influential thinkers and theologians inadvertently undermined the very values of freedom, faith, reason, and redemption they sought to uphold. Failing to challenge their ideas-turned-ideology has perpetuated divisions among those tasked with defending civilization and Christianity. To avoid the potentially catastrophic consequences of this division, we must be willing to critically examine our intellectual heritage, acknowledging its limitations and learning from its mistakes.

A thoroughgoing citizen of faith and reason assumes an aim not merely to introduce and theorize issues of justice and salvation but to offer solutions and encourage a more discerning approach to the ideas that shape our world in a social divinity and a salvific democracy. This is what I call the *JUST*ethics that will afford what Bev Harrison, Dorrien's institutional predecessor on Union's legendary faculty, once deemed as undoing the injustice that history has done. This is the "fierce urgency of now" of which Martin Luther King Jr. spoke.[10] This is "US" in terms of what Maya Angelou prophetically and poetically proclaims to be "these yet to be united states."[11] In turn, this necessitates the *JUST*ethics of an insurgent pedagogy informed by the metaethics of a Christian socialism infused by moral leadership (Micah 6:8), the social gospel that orients us (Luke 4:18), the social activism that organizes us (Micah 6:8), and the Christian socialism that optimizes our faith, fortitude, and ethics (Habakkuk 2:1-4).

---

[10] Martin Luther King Jr., "I Have a Dream." March on Washington for Jobs and Freedom, August 28, 1963, Lincoln Memorial, Washington, DC.

[11] Maya Angelou, "These Yet to Be United States," in *Complete Collected Poems of Maya Angelou* (Norwalk, CT: Easton Press, 2005).

Insurgent Pedagogy

As an instructive and urgent approach to liberationist education, I envision insurgent pedagogy as a teaching-learning dynamic that equips those engaged within it with the tools to critique and disrupt oppressive systems while emphasizing the immediacy of addressing social inequalities. By empowering learners to challenge the status quo and take action for change, insurgent pedagogy cultivates a sense of urgency in the pursuit of a more just and equitable society.

As exemplified by Gary Dorrien, insurgent pedagogy seeks to disrupt traditional power dynamics within contemporary educational spaces. For instance, while they stem from different disciplines and social locations, the work of Black feminist theorist bell hooks and the work of Gary Dorrien as a white cis-gender male Christian social ethicist converge to offer a powerful and liberating approach to pedagogy. Whereas hooks's emphasis on "education as the practice of freedom" resonates with Dorrien's focus on social justice as an integral component of Christian faith, both advocate for a pedagogy that transcends mere information transmission. Instead, their work fosters critical consciousness that empowers individuals to challenge oppressive structures. Dorrien's call for a relational social ethics that acknowledges the interconnectedness of individuals and social systems aligns with hooks's concept of "engaged pedagogy," which prioritizes dialogue, vulnerability, and the recognition of diverse experiences. By integrating hooks's emphasis on personal transformation with Dorrien's focus on social change, liberationist educators can create learning environments that not only empower students intellectually but also inspire them to become agents of social justice, working toward a more equitable and compassionate world. It is the practice that resonates with hooks's call in *Teaching to Transgress* for "education as the practice of freedom," a space where students and teachers "transgress" the established boundaries of conventional learning.[12] This transgression, hooks argues, is essential for creating a "democratic classroom" where "everyone's voice matters." Furthermore, as bell hooks asserts:

---

[12] bell hooks, *Teaching to Transgress: Education as the Practice of Freedom* (New York: Routledge, 1994).

The academy is not paradise. But learning is a place where paradise can be created. The classroom, with all its limitations, remains a location of possibility. In that field of possibility we have the opportunity to labor for freedom, to demand of ourselves and our comrades, an openness of mind and heart that allows us to face reality even as we collectively imagine ways to move beyond boundaries, to transgress. This is education as the practice of freedom.[13]

In *Pedagogy of the Oppressed*, Paulo Freire emphasizes the "banking model" of education and advocates for a "problem-posing" approach in which the oppressed become active participants in their own liberation.[14] Like Freire's, Dorrien's work also recognizes the importance of empowering individuals but extends this focus beyond the traditionally marginalized. Dorrien suggests the necessity to focus on those who shape the thinking of others. He engages not only with those directly experiencing marginalization but also with those within institutions like the academy and the church who, even if privileged, can become agents of change. This aligns with Freire's concept of *conscientização*, or critical consciousness, which is not limited to any one group. Dorrien's approach, therefore, might be seen as an attempt to cultivate this critical consciousness even within spaces of privilege, recognizing that dismantling oppressive systems requires a multipronged approach that includes influencing those who hold positions of power. It's not simply about what Freire did for the marginalized, but also about what is necessary to transform the systems that perpetuate marginalization, a task that requires engaging with the privileged as well.

Insurgent pedagogy further extends and expands the strategies and philosophies of resistance inherent in the tradition of "fugitive pedagogy." In *Fugitive Pedagogy: Carter G. Woodson and the Art of Black Teaching*, Jarvis Givens contends that Black education always already was a subversive enterprise since its inception in this nation. African Americans pursued education through clandestine means, often in defiance of law and custom of Jim and Jane Crow segregation, even under threat of racist terrorism and violence. They developed what Jarvis Givens defines as "fugitive

---

[13] hooks, *Teaching to Transgress*, 207.
[14] See Paulo Freire, "The 'Banking Concept' of Education," in *The Pedagogy of the Oppressed* (New York: Herder and Herder, 1970), 58.

pedagogy"—a theory and practice of Black education epitomized by Carter G. Woodson, the groundbreaking historian, legendary educator, and founder of Black History Month.[15] Givens shows that Woodson and his contemporaries succeeded because of the ontological worldview of Black teachers to which he belonged. As a precursor to insurgent pedagogy, Givens chronicles how the ambitious efforts of Woodson combated what he famously called the "mis-education of the Negro" by helping teachers and students see themselves and their mission as set apart from the depravity, division, and destructiveness of an anti-Black world. Without question, insurgent pedagogy firmly builds on this foundation.

In light of these works that now make up history, we might ask, *Why write another vision when the visionary died? Why stand from the safe place of the rampart when the world is on fire?* The faithfulness of the desperate father in Mark 9 and the determined Canaanite woman, castigated as having the status of a dog, in Matthew 15, gave them the divine power to bend the moral arc of the universe toward justice. Like these clouds of biblical antiquity and civil rights, scribes like Dorrien know full well that, while the visionary dies, we are the ones they saw. We are the inheritors of their dream. As King's rampart was a mountaintop experience, he saw a better world, in fact a world house, a beloved community with all of us in it. Whether in jail cells, at kitchen tables, behind pulpits, in prayer closets, on the streets, or in the Oval Office of the White House, King wrote the vision into books, sermons, policies, and laws, and we are those words made flesh. Though we are not Kings, we can be inspired and instructed in the insurgent pedagogy of the likes of our co-sojourner Gary Dorrien and take up our post, pen, podium, and pulpit to use our agency as the kin-dom of God. We are the very substance of divine faith, the evidence of what many before us hoped for the future.

It is time for us to take good care in our calls, confessions, and lovecraft. Let us not be fools held captive in our towers. Let us foil the evil of our day by doing justice, loving mercy, and walking humbly with the God, whose spirit gives us perspective and power to make our lifetime the appointed time to not merely save souls but to free minds and lives in the process.

---

[15] See Jarvis Givens, *Fugitive Pedagogy: Carter G. Woodson and the Art of Black Teaching* (Cambridge, MA: Harvard University Press, 2021).

The Social Gospel as Orienting Insurgent Pedagogy

The Spirit of the Lord is upon me,
because he has anointed me
to bring good news to the poor.
He has sent me to proclaim release to the captives
and recovery of sight to the blind,
to set free those who are oppressed,
to proclaim the year of the Lord's favor.

—Luke 4:18–19

Dorrien looms large as a prominent interpreter of the Social Gospel movement, not merely as a fossilized historical artifact but as a living theological tradition with enduring relevance. His work offers a nuanced understanding of the movement, moving beyond simplistic characterizations and highlighting its complexities, internal tensions, and persistent contributions to American religious and social thought. Dorrien's interpretation emphasizes the Social Gospel's prophetic critique of social injustice, its commitment to implementing God's will on Earth as it is in Heaven, and its enduring legacy for contemporary struggles for social transformation.

Dorrien argues against the common misconception of the Social Gospel as a naïve and ultimately failed attempt to Christianize society. He acknowledges the movement's idealistic fervor and its occasional oversimplification of complex social problems. However, he also stresses the profound theological and ethical insights that emerged from the Social Gospel's storied engagement with the ravages of industrial capitalism, poverty, and social inequality during the late nineteenth and early twentieth centuries. Dorrien emphasizes that the Social Gospel was not simply a sociological application of Christian principles, but a deeply theological project rooted in a profound understanding of the nature of God and humanity.

Central to Dorrien's interpretation is the Social Gospel's emphasis on the immanence of God's Kingdom (or as I would contend in a womanist mode, Kin-dom). This concept, often misunderstood as a utopian vision of a perfect society on earth, is better understood as a call to action in the present. The Social Gospel theologians believed that God's reign was not solely a future reality but was already breaking into the world through acts of justice and compassion. This immanent eschatology fueled their commitment to social reform, as they sought to create social structures that reflected the values of the Kingdom: justice, peace, and love. Dorrien highlights how this emphasis on immanence distinguished the Social Gospel from more traditional forms of Christian social ethics, which often focused on individual piety and deferred social transformation to a future, otherworldly realm.

Dorrien also underscores the Social Gospel's prophetic critique of social injustice. The movement's theologians, deeply influenced by the Hebrew prophets, saw themselves as voices crying out against the systemic injustices of their time. They challenged the prevailing social order, which they saw as deeply flawed and incompatible with the teachings of Jesus. They condemned the exploitation of workers, the vast disparities of wealth, and the rampant corruption that plagued American society. This prophetic critique extended beyond individual actions to encompass social structures and institutions. The Social Gospel theologians recognized that social problems were not simply the result of individual failings but were often rooted in systemic injustices. Therefore, they advocated for social and political reforms to address the root causes of poverty, inequality, and oppression.

Dorrien's work offers a valuable reassessment of the Social Gospel, rescuing it from historical obscurity and demonstrating its continuing relevance for contemporary social ethics. He argues that the Social Gospel's emphasis on the immanence of God's Kingdom, its prophetic critique of social injustice, and its commitment to social Christianity provide a powerful framework for addressing the social challenges of our own time.

Dorrien also acknowledges the internal tensions and complexities within the Social Gospel movement. He points out that the movement was not monolithic and included a variety of perspectives on social issues. Acknowledging that some Social Gospel theologians—typically Black proponents of the movement—were more radical than others, Dorrien demonstrates the advocacy of these visionaries for greater social and economic changes that advanced the spirit of progressivism during their era despite the groundswell of religious fundamentalism that would challenge the struggle for social justice. Others were more moderate, focusing on incremental reforms. Despite these differences, however, the Social Gospel theologians were united in their commitment to social justice and their belief that Christian faith had a crucial role to play in the transformation of society. In an era marked by increasing inequality, environmental degradation, and social division, the Social Gospel's call for social transformation remains as urgent as ever. Dorrien's interpretation helps us to see the Social Gospel not as a relic of the past, but as a living tradition that continues to inspire and challenge us to work for a more just and compassionate world. It reminds us that faith is not simply a matter of personal belief but a call to action, a commitment to building a world that reflects the values of God's Kingdom.

Social Activism as Organizing Insurgent Pedagogy

*[God] has told you, O mortal, **what is good, and what does the Lord require of you** but to do justice and to love kindness and to walk humbly with your God?*

—Micah 6:8

As an ethicist, Gary Dorrien provides a compelling vision of social activism as an intrinsic and enduring element of American Christianity. He argues that Christian faith, rightly understood, is not a privatized affair concerned solely with individual salvation, but rather a potent force for social transformation. Dorrien's perspective emphasizes the inherent social implications of Christian belief, highlighting the responsibility of Christians to actively engage with the world and work toward a more just and equitable society. He positions social activism not as an optional add-on to Christian faith, but as a central and indispensable expression of its core principles. In his book *What Should the Left Propose?* Brazilian progressive politician and scholar Roberto Mangabeira Unger gives a full-throated endorsement for a new vision of leftist politics by arguing that "the world suffers under a dictatorship of no alternatives. Although ideas all by themselves are powerless to overthrow the dictatorship, we cannot overthrow it without ideas."[16]

Dorrien's interpretation draws heavily from the legacy of the Social Gospel movement, recognizing its profound influence on the trajectory of American Christianity. The Social Gospel theologians, as Dorrien emphasizes, rejected the notion that Christianity's primary focus was on personal salvation, arguing instead for a holistic understanding of faith that

---

[16] Roberto Mangabeira Unger, *What Should the Left Propose?* (London: Verso, 2005).

encompassed both individual and social transformation. They understood that the love and justice preached by Jesus demanded not only personal piety but also active engagement with the social structures that perpetuate inequality and oppression. This conviction fueled a wide range of social activism, from advocating for the rights of workers against the exploitative practices of industrial capitalism to challenging the deeply entrenched system of racial segregation.

Dorrien's work, however, goes beyond simply chronicling the historical contributions of the Social Gospel. He articulates a robust theological framework for understanding the imperative for social activism within contemporary Christianity. Most notably, in works like "Social Ethics for Social Justice," Dorrien emphasizes the crucial connection between faith and action, arguing that true faith necessitates a commitment to working for social justice. He highlights the importance of "putting God in the life of the community," not as a form of religious imposition, but as a call to embody the values of love, compassion, and justice within the public sphere.[17] This involves a prophetic imperative—"speaking truth to power"—incumbent to contemporary Christianity's need to challenge oppressive systems and advocate on behalf of the marginalized and vulnerable.

Dorrien's vision of social activism is not limited to individualistic acts of charity or isolated protests. He emphasizes the necessity of collective action and systemic change. He recognizes that individual agency, while important, is insufficient to address deeply rooted social problems. True social transformation, according to Dorrien, requires a collective effort to reshape the "collective condition of citizens."[18] This involves working to dismantle unjust social structures and advocating for policies that promote equality and equity for all. He stresses the importance of empowering those who have been historically marginalized and downtrodden, ensuring that their voices are heard, and their needs are addressed.

Dorrien's emphasis on social activism within American Christianity offers a powerful counterpoint to more individualistic and pietistic

---

[17] Gary Dorrien, "Understanding Liberal Theology: An Interview with Gary Dorrien," August 15, 2023, https://adfontesjournal.com/interview/understanding-liberal-theology-an-interview-with-gary-dorrien/.

[18] Gary Dorrien, "Social Ethics for Social Justice: The Legacies of the Social Gospel and a Case for Idealistic Discontent," in *Ethics and Advocacy: Bridges and Boundaries*, ed. Harlan Beckley, Douglas Ottati, Matthew Petrusek, and William Schweiker (Eugene, OR: Cascade Books, 2022), xii.

interpretations of faith. He reminds us that the Christian call to love our neighbors as ourselves extends beyond personal relationships to encompass a commitment to building a more just and compassionate society. He challenges us to move beyond mere words of faith and to embody our beliefs through concrete actions that promote social transformation. His work serves as a call to reclaim the prophetic tradition within Christianity, to speak truth to power, and to work tirelessly for the liberation and empowerment of all. In Dorrien's vision, social activism is not simply one aspect of Christian life, but rather an essential expression of its very essence. It is the outworking of faith in the public sphere, a commitment to making the Kingdom of God through acts of justice, compassion, and solidarity.

Christian Socialism Optimizing Insurgent Pedagogy

I will stand at my watchpost
and station myself on the rampart;
I will keep watch to see what he will say to me
and what he will answer concerning my complaint.
Then the LORD answered me and said:
Write the vision;
make it plain on tablets,
so that a runner may read it.
For there is still a vision for the appointed time;
it speaks of the end and does not lie.
If it seems to tarry, wait for it;
it will surely come; it will not delay.
Look at the proud!
Their spirit is not right in them,
but the righteous live by their faithfulness.

—Habakkuk 2:1–4

Finally, Gary Dorrien's vision of Christian socialism offers a compelling framework for understanding the intersection of faith and social justice within our current political economic order (or lack thereof). Decades ago Martin Luther King Jr. diagnosed the US crisis quite succinctly: "The problem is that we all too often have socialism for the rich and rugged free enterprise capitalism for the poor. That's the problem."[19] It is a vision deeply rooted in the profound and prolonged tradition of prophetic American Christianity, one that seeks to create a society where true democracy serves as the engine for social progress, not for impoverished rugged individualism but for real integrity wherein human freedom and flourishing are prioritized over profligate profit and power. Yet, as his mentee Aaron Stauffer attests, it is important to note that Dorrien's Christian socialism is not simply a nostalgic yearning for a bygone era, but a dynamic and evolving project informed by a keen understanding of historical injustices and a commitment to build a more just and equitable future.[20]

A key influence on Dorrien's thought, particularly in shaping his understanding of democratic socialism, is the work of Michael Harrington. As a prominent democratic socialist and author of *The Other America*, Harrington profoundly influenced Dorrien's thinking by illuminating the persistent reality of poverty and inequality within affluent societies.[21] Harrington's analysis of systemic poverty, rather than simply attributing it to individual failings, resonated deeply with Dorrien's own emphasis on the social and structural dimensions of injustice. In thought, word, and deed, Dorrien notes how Harrington's work demonstrated the ways in which economic and political systems can be designed to perpetuate inequality, creating a permanent underclass of marginalized and vulnerable individuals. This understanding of systemic injustice is central to Dorrien's Christian socialist perspective. He argues that true social transformation requires not only individual acts of charity but also a fundamental restructuring of social and economic systems.

Dorrien's own vision of Christian socialism, informed by Harrington's insights, prioritizes "people over property." This means challenging the primacy of private property rights when they come at the expense of human well-being. It involves advocating for policies that redistribute wealth and

---

[19] Martin Luther King Jr., "The Minister to the Valley," February 23, 1968, retrieved from the archives of the SCLC as quoted in Andrew J. Douglas and Jared A. Loggins, *Prophet of Discontent: Martin Luther King Jr. and the Critique of Racial Capitalism* (Athens: University of Georgia Press, 2021), 48.

[20] Aaron K. Stauffer, "'American Democratic Socialism' by Gary Dorrien," *Tikkun*, July 19, 2022, https://www.tikkun.org/review-american-democratic-socialism-history-politics-religion-and-theory-by-gary-dorrien/.

[21] See Michael Harrington, *The Other America: Poverty in the United States* (New York: Simon and Schuster, 1962).

power, ensuring that all members of society have access to the resources they need to thrive. This emphasis on social and economic equality is not simply a matter of fairness; it is a fundamental expression of Christian love and justice. Dorrien's vision draws on the biblical tradition's concern for the poor and marginalized, recognizing that God's preferential option for the vulnerable demands a commitment to dismantling systems of oppression.

Furthermore, Dorrien's Christian socialism emphasizes "collaboration over domination." It envisions a society where power is shared and decisions are made democratically, rather than being concentrated in the hands of a few. This commitment to democratic participation is essential for ensuring that the needs and voices of all members of society are heard and addressed. It also requires challenging hierarchical structures of power that perpetuate inequality and marginalization. Dorrien's vision is not simply about redistributing wealth; it is about empowering individuals and communities to participate fully in the decisions that affect their lives.

Dorrien's Christian socialism is also deeply concerned with creating "equal and equitable opportunities" for all. This means not only providing access to basic necessities like food, housing, and healthcare, but also ensuring that all individuals have the opportunity to develop their full potential. It requires addressing systemic barriers to opportunity, such as discrimination based on race, gender, or other social categories. Dorrien's vision is one of a society where everyone has the chance to flourish, regardless of their background or circumstances. In our current era of Trump-induced trauma and tragedy, this particular observation by Dorrien's student, Aaron Stauffer, is vital:

> The left needs people who have a deeper faith, and a deeper spiritual and ethical commitment to sustain us. Without it, our political imaginations remain wedded to the ways of this world. Religious socialists work for democratic socialism not to just improve this world, but to repair it, transform it, and redeem it—not for heaven's sake, but for our own. Christian democratic socialism teaches me how to be a better human and how to engage in the very creaturely project of politics. Dorrien's story is one of the traditions that define my Christian commitments and it's a legacy we desperately need to pass down.[22]

---

[22] Stauffer, "'American Democratic Socialism' by Gary Dorrien."

Without question, Dorrien's Christian socialism is "historiographically cognizant" of the particularly vulnerable communities for which such pursuits have been systemically inhibited. This means recognizing the historical legacy of oppression and acknowledging the ongoing impact of systemic racism, sexism, and other forms of discrimination. It requires a commitment to reparative justice, working to address the historical injustices that continue to shape contemporary inequalities. Dorrien's vision is not simply about creating a level playing field; it is about actively working to dismantle the structures of oppression that have historically disadvantaged certain communities.

In sum, Dorrien's Christian socialism, carrying out the work of Gramsci's organic intellectuals, deeply influenced by Harrington's analysis of poverty and inequality, and in the moral leadership of MLK, offers a powerful vision for social transformation. It is a vision that prioritizes people over property, collaboration over domination, and equal and equitable opportunities for all. It is a vision rooted in the prophetic tradition of American Christianity, one that seeks to create a society where justice and compassion prevail.

The Faithful Aims of the Ethical Scholar

When all is said and done, to be an optimal Christian ethicist is to be at one's watch post in the brave yet safer space than the left out and left behind. Even more, to do this sort of work can often entail being a scribe who writes the vision, making it accessible to many audiences. As Dorrien has shown us, this entails that we must know the fateful role of history, understand the faithful pursuit of philosophy, and seek with our whole souls an understanding that undergirds our faithfulness. In her classic novel, *Their Eyes Were Watching God*, celebrated author and patron saint of womanist thought, Zora Neale Hurston, reminds us that doing the work of the scribe, whether as a novelist, anthropologist, historian, or moral leader at their watch post, like Habakkuk and Dorrien, is to know that "there are years that ask questions and years that answer."[23] Dorrien's work, often characterized as the work of American religious history because he attends with archivist detail, notating, and inundating us with not only the

---

[23] Zora Neale Hurston, *Their Eyes Were Watching God* (London: Virago Press, 2018).

horrors of history but its hallmarks and heroes, not simply retelling and but re-membering the lives and legacies of looming figures of moral fortitude like Reverdy Ransom, Mary Daly, W. E. B. Du Bois, Alexander Crummell, Richard R. Wright Jr., Ida B. Wells-Barnett, George W. Woodbey, Adam Clayton Powell Sr., Beverly W. Harrison, Michael Harrington, and Jim Wallis, and most often Rev. Dr. Martin Luther King Jr. Whether noting King's landmark March on Washington speech in which he heralded for the whole world to hear that "I have a dream," a dream that refused to be trampled underfoot into the red clay dirt of Georgia and Alabama or noting King's assassination in Memphis, where he had the holy boldness to stand in solidarity with Black sanitation workers who had the audacity to insist that they were humans even as they made their living disposing of trash, Dorrien has shown that the work of watching is not merely waiting. It is faithful action, even when met with fateful ends, that holds on to hope, which keeps us true to the faith.

Separated as we are by so many decades, Dorrien reminds us that we now have countless volumes filling up library shelves worldwide desperately trying to find a deeper understanding and greater relevance to those two biographic pinpoints of King's eventful yet all-too-brief life. But much like Hurston's musings suggest, *How does the interplay of time and opportunity combine so that we can ever truly make meaning out of these often bittersweet and bewildering things we call memories?* When we take the occasion of the recent 2025 King holiday to commemorate the life of possibly the most influential and important faith leader this nation has ever produced, does it make sense to focus on his highest heights such as the sunlit August day, where he spoke his truth loudly and proudly before God and everyone at the National Mall, without also processing the pain *and* loss we all suffered as a people, a nation, and even a world, when, only a few years later, he also experienced his lowest low as he was slain by a gunman on the balcony of the Lorraine Motel for the crime and misdemeanor of being a voice for the voiceless? Or even the greater insult and irony that Donald Trump, a convicted felon, was granted immunity from his crimes and literally inaugurated on the holiday of the observance of King's birthday. Trump refused to place his hand on the Bible as he took the oath office, which conferred upon him the unmerited grace to forgo a possible prison sentence and whose first act in office was to abolish everything that King fought so hard for and for which the nation stood in reckoning, if not reconciliation for its original sin. To discredit, defund, and denounce all federal and public DEI (Diversity, Equity, and Inclusion) initiatives, institutions, and individuals as well as putting a moratorium on the observance of King's birthday and any other aligned holidays that sought to affirm and resurrect the idea and ideal that to be made in the *imago Dei*, the image of God, is actually an affirmation of diversity, equity, and inclusion.

Much like the tumultuous era through which King and his compatriots lived, we now once again find ourselves in perilous and peculiar times. All of us recall the global COVID-19 pandemic that engulfed all of humanity in 2020 that forced us to stay at home while we couldn't turn a blind eye to the police killings of Breonna Taylor and George Floyd. There is a fierce urgency to find answers to the questions that this history poses for the work of hermeneutics and hope. The death-dealing ravages of COVID-19, alongside the deadening blows of police violence and political unrest, have created an unrelenting search for clarity and certainty amid the increasing complexity of the world around us. The truth of the matter is we can neither survive nor flourish if many of these questions remain unresolved and if the lessons to be drawn from these all-consuming crises go unlearned. We, as colleagues, collaborators, community organizers, and citizens, try to negotiate a world, amid the racist continuum of honorary whiteness and dishonorable Blackness. We as intellectuals, children of God, or ordained clergy, and citizens on the brink of a resegregated America, must be scribes like Dorrien, taking Kelly Brown Douglas's query seriously by asking ourselves, "What's faith got to do it?"

Here the oft-quoted pithy profundity of Hebrews 11:1, "Now faith is the substance of things hoped for and the evidence of things not seen" cannot go without our critical analysis. This rhetorical badge and brand of our religious platform rarely takes note of the fact that faith and lies share an epistemic root here in this verse (and in, perhaps, our "incarnation" of it). Lies that present themselves as FEAR-mongering—that is, False Evidence Appearing Real—are also the substance of things hoped for and the evidence of things not seen. Likewise, the adage "Hindsight is 20/20" is a hopeful sentiment rather than an established truth. Søren Kierkegaard's theological inflection on this aphorism extols that "life can only be understood backwards; but it must be lived forwards."[24] Predicated on a never-ending future, it presupposes the privileged position that we are

---

[24] Søren Kierkegaard, *Søren Kierkegaards Skrifter* (Copenhagen: Søren Kierkegaard Research Center, 1997), *Journalen* JJ:167 (1843), vol. 18, 306.

always moving ahead in a logical and linear manner with the added benefit that time is always on one's side. This perspective denotes the opportunities afforded to someone who routinely has the luxury of reflecting on time gone by to chart one's future. Yet what about those who must incessantly look back and peripherally process, as they are compelled to move forward in real time—particularly in times of devastation, despair, or distress? And even more so, as Columbia University professor Saidiya Hartman thoughtfully posits, "How might we understand mourning, when the event has yet to end?"[25] Truly, we are exasperated with our mourning and the enormous toll it has taken on so many lives: the Black ones that don't matter, the brown ones that are deported after doing our dirty work, the children placed into cages, the women whose bodies are governed, policed, and never their own.

We realize that, for those on the margins of society, faith from "hindsight" does not simply refer to learning from one's past but also living with one's past in such a way as to gain immediate insight that is crucial for instantaneous foresight for those who are on their watch post, engaging the troubles of our current era while also enduring them yet doubling down on that most tender and tendentious human endeavor: hope. In his groundbreaking text *Pedagogy of the Oppressed*, Brazilian educator Paulo Freire states that the precursor to such hope is only found in the neologism of conscientization (a term derived from the Portuguese word *conscientização*), which embodies the concept of cultivating, fortifying, and transforming one's consciousness or awareness. Sociologist of religion Peter Berger's classic text *The Sacred Canopy* contends that such a society, made up of such conscientized people, affords the only hope for human flourishing, which must be engaged in a dialectical relationship wherein we create society as much as society creates in us.[26] Berger asserts that this "religion is the human enterprise by which a sacred cosmos is established.... By sacred is meant here a quality of mysterious and awesome power, other than [humans] and yet related to [them], which is believed to reside in certain objects of experience."[27] "To be in 'right' relationship with the sacred cosmos," Berger asserts, "is to be protected against the nightmare threats of

---

[25] Saidiya V. Hartman, "The Time of Slavery," *South Atlantic Quarterly* 101, no. 4 (2002): 757–77, https://muse.jhu.edu/article/39111.

[26] Peter L. Berger, *The Sacred Canopy: Elements of a Sociological Theory of Religion* (Garden City, NY: Doubleday, 1967), 1–10.

[27] Berger, *The Sacred Canopy*, 25.

chaos. To fall out of such a 'right' relationship is to be abandoned on the edge of the abyss of meaninglessness."[28] Herein, the aims of the Christian liberationist ethics scholar must be the work of bringing to bear processes of liberative understandings in order to really achieve a world that is not only affirming humanity of all, but also cultivating a culture that affords all the rights to be free acting and responsible.

A world in which, philosophically or theologically, bodies are marked, oppressed, and marginalized based on categorizations and classifications of the past, or of the present, necessitates skilled scholars who are able to, first, do the deep listening of cultural centrism, to center on the agent that is in crisis, at the crosshairs of their dilemma and the constructs in such a way that the agent is heard, seen, and affirmed in the midst of their experience. Ethnocentrism, the often coercive and corrosive belief in the inherent superiority of one's own culture, creates an ethical minefield that does not allow for either evidence or empathy. Often rooted in a lack of knowledge and experience with other cultures, this perspective assumes one's own cultural norms and values are not only the standard but also occupy the highest position in a perceived hierarchy. This assumption fuels expressions of cultural supremacy, where one culture seeks to dominate others. While ethnocentrism in particular and cultural centrism more generally may be a universal human tendency, white supremacy goes both further and farther than the norm by actively leveraging economic, military, ideological, practical, institutional, academic, and even spiritual power to maintain this dominance, often with a willful disregard for the values and perspectives of other cultures. This disregard raises serious ethical concerns about freedom, justice, equity, flourishing, respect, and human dignity. Furthermore, the concept of white supremacy intersects with other forms of cultural dominance, such as those based on religion, nationality, and origin, in addition to that of race, creating complex systems of oppression. In a contemporary context that is undergirded by white supremacy, misogyny, and Christian nationalist hegemony, culture can become a dangerous proxy for biological justifications of inequality, echoing harmful and discredited theories. As historian Peter Gran notes,

> Upholders of the present variant [of white supremacy and cultural imperialism] frequently equate historical analysis with an account of progress; they note in their works achievements in science,

---

[28] Berger, *The Sacred Canopy*, 27.

weaponry, in the standard of living, or in the growth of knowledge. But ... the utility of such an approach is limited, for there has been continuity as well as change throughout the twentieth century.[29]

The ethical implications of such hierarchical thinking, quantification, and ranking of cultures are profound, particularly within fields like psychology. Combating white supremacy requires not only individual acts of resistance but also a systemic shift toward solidarity and *agape* (unconditional love), addressing the interpersonal, societal, and economic conditions that perpetuate these harmful power dynamics.[30]

A *JUST*ethics is an insurgent pedagogy that calls us to quote bell hooks's important text in *Teaching to Transgress*; hooks's clarion call stands true: "All of us in the academy and in the culture as a whole are called to renew our minds if we are to transform educational institutions—and society—so that the way we live, teach, and work can reflect our joy in cultural diversity, our passion for justice, and our love of freedom."[31] The great pedagogue Parker Palmer reminds us in his important text that having the *Courage to Teach* is essential for us as moral leaders, in our Social Gospel-Orienting, Social Activism-Organizing, and Christian Socialism-Optimizing, to remember that our responsibility becomes tangible for us and palpable pedagogies of possibility if and only when we focus on introspection—understanding ourselves as individuals and educators. This process involves examining not only our strengths but also acknowledging our weaknesses and limitations. This insurgent pedagogy of *JUST*ethics echoes Parker. Nothing that the greatest book we teach, read, or write is our biotext:

> We teach who we are.... Good teaching comes from the identity and integrity of a teacher.... I do not mean only our noble features, or the good deeds we do, or the brave faces we wear to conceal our

---

[29] Peter Gran, *Beyond Eurocentrism: A New View of Modern World History* (Syracuse, NY: Syracuse University Press, 1996), 6.

[30] Thomas Teo, "Culture-Supremacy: Expressions, Sources, and Resistance to a Psychology of Motivated Ignorance," *Research in the Social Scientific Study of Religion* 32 (2022); Franz Martin Wimmer, "Cultural Centrisms and Intercultural Polylogues in Philosophy," *International Review of Information Ethics* 7 (September 2007): 82–89.

[31] hooks, *Teaching to Transgress*, 34.

confusions and complexities. Identity and integrity have as much to do with our shadows and limits, our wounds and fears, as with our strengths and potentials.[32]

Whether we are faith scribes at our watch post on the ramparts of the classroom, church, or community, we know what God has commanded of us as mere mortals. We know that, if the Spirit of the Lord is truly upon us, it will see and free us indeed. And because we are human, a part of a less than perfect union, and history seems to be repeating itself, our faith claims are fretful; like the father in Mark 9:22–24 who was afraid and unsafe in his home as he stood watch over his demon-possessed child; having nowhere else to look, the father cried out to Jesus, making his desire plain, and casting his hope that Jesus has the ability to relieve his son of this horror. Jesus assures him that it is not Jesus's ability but rather, "All things can be done for the one who believes." Hoping against hope yet vulnerable and clear in the power of his own confession, the father struggles yet proclaims, "I do believe; help me overcome my unbelief." This *JUSTethics* is the corrective that includes the insurgent pedagogy of the scribe: urgent, prophetic, and done within the house of theological education.

In conclusion, *JUSTethics* is both scriptural and sociopolitical. It draws its inspiration and guidance from the sacred texts of our traditions, while simultaneously engaging with the concrete realities of the social and political world. It is a dynamic and evolving process, requiring ongoing reflection, dialogue, and action. By integrating the wisdom of scripture with the demands of social justice, we can create a more just and compassionate world for all. To me, what it means to be foils and not fooled emphasizes the importance of being a contrast to others, rather than being deceived by them. This phrase highlights the idea that it's better to stand out and be different, than to conform and be easily fooled. Furthermore, it suggests that being a foil, or a counterpoint to someone else, can be a strength, as it allows us to challenge and question conventional ideas, rather than blindly accepting them and being held captive or captivated in the caves of ignorance and insolence from which we could easily free ourselves.

---

[32] Parker J. Palmer, *The Courage to Teach*, 20th ed. (San Francisco: Jossey-Bass, 2017), 13.

Conclusion

Aaron Stauffer

IN THE EARLY 1980S, ROBERT FISHER WROTE *Let the People Decide: Neighborhood Organizing in America,* in which he argued that the future of community organizing in the United States depends on whether or not organizers and leaders can incorporate political education into their strategies.[1] Without political education—that is, without education and analysis around the structural roots of broader social ills that organizers are fighting against—organizing will constantly be stuck in issue cycles. In an environment where money dominates politics, the highest bidder directs the tide. Fisher isn't the only one who has made this point: more recently Mark Santow reminded readers that this challenge sits at the heart of Saul Alinsky's organizing legacy around racial injustice.[2] Santow's claim is that the strategy of building local power built through a territorial strategy of mobilizing and organizing local institutions cannot meet the power exercised by federal or regional power structures. Neighborhood community organizing cannot scale up to meet federal or state power.

This challenge goes to the heart of broad-based community organizing strategy—the tradition and strategy most closely identified with Alinsky's legacy currently found in the Industrial Areas Foundation, Faith in Action, the Gamaliel Foundation, and Direct Action and Research Training. Alinsky and neo-Alinskyite organizing has long been touted as non-ideological. But Fisher and Santow and many of the chapters in this book raise critical questions for organizers and scholars who are deeply committed to social justice fights today. Can organizing scale up? Are we organizing leaders or training technocrats? How do we teach organizing in new ways, in new classroom formats? Though the lessons in the preceding chapters are many,

---

[1] Robert Fisher, *Let the People Decide: Neighborhood Organizing in America* (Boston: Twayne Publishers, 1984).

[2] Mark E. Santow, *Saul Alinsky and the Dilemmas of Race: Community Organizing in the Postwar City* (Chicago: University of Chicago Press, 2023).

a critical one is the importance of the *why* in organizing. As long as issues dominate the strategy of community organizing, those fighting for economic and political democracy will lack a broader vision of what it is we are inviting people into. This is a question that scholar-organizers consistently find themselves wrestling and that Christian Social Ethics has debated since its inception. It takes for granted that organizing itself is rigorous intellectual and theoretical work, so the chapters in this book have sought to convene a conversation on the state of Christian social ethics so that a future direction of the field might be more closely aligned with the future of organizing.

We need conceptually clear accounts as to what we are up against and how we can build a more just world. Most important, we need clear pathways on how we can get there. In my previous writing, I have advocated that community organizers need to double down on the relational and value basis of their strategy.[3] Without such a basis, leaders will burn out, lose interest, or fail to adequately grasp how power is structured in US political and economic life. The promise of community organizing is that it teaches people to enact political and economic agency and build radically democratic communities. Organizing is really about building a democratic culture: a collective sense of meaning and action where working people have power over the conditions that affect their lives. It invites people into the public work of building transitionary structures away from racial capitalism and to a more just world. This does not happen overnight. Organizing asks different things of different people. What this means is that we need to spend as much time building and creating movements that people can fall in love with and see themselves in as we do developing strategies to win campaigns. The work of theology and social ethics here is key—we need thinkers who help us talk well about the visions of the communities we are creating and what those communities are grounded in. The work of building real alternatives and bridging the gap from the way the world is to what it ought to be will not be sustainable without an adequate vision of why we are called to this work in the first place and why the road we're trodding is the right one. People organize to protect and fight for what they hold most dear. Building strong organizations that can protect and fight for working people will require

---

[3] Aaron Stauffer, *Listening to the Spirit: The Radical Social Gospel, Sacred Value, and Broad-Based Community Organizing*, AAR Academy Series (New York: Oxford University Press, 2024).

Conclusion

building relationships grounded in mutual recognition and understanding between working people who are doing the organizing in the first place. Democratic cultures ask us to reweave our relationships, to reconnect with what it is we care most about, what threatens them, and how we can most adequately build a world where the goods we hold most dear will never be violated, desecrated or destroyed again.

The chapters in this book have explored the stakes of this work and the tools that are available to Christian social ethicists and scholar-organizers who take the work of organizing as theoretically rigorous and politically and economically serious work. The first section of this conclusion will focus on the role that issues and values play in organizing strategies. The second section turns to the importance of relational power-building. In closing, I will reflect briefly on what this all means for the future of Christian social ethics and community organizing.

Issues or Values?

When issues dominate organizing strategies, the political imagination of the organizing constituency is restricted to a particular political opportunity structure and time frame.[4] For organizers or scholars who front issues over values, wins or losses are limited to terms of individual issue agendas. A conception of power that is surprisingly thin undergirds this approach to organizing. Here, power is conflated to exertion and force. The power it takes for groups to change and adapt with fluctuating political and economic circumstances is missed.[5] My contention is that organizing strategies need to double down on the relational and value basis of their organizing strategy. Those who prioritize issues fail to see that organizing often includes tactics like negotiation, compromise, even losses in order to attack the root issues at the heart of our democratic culture. What plagues our democracy is not merely partisan polarization that forestalls legislation; the root of the problem has to do with how we conceive of democratic politics.

---

[4] The material in this section builds on previously published work, principally Stauffer, *Listening to the Spirit*.

[5] Arguably, even Marshall Ganz's conception of power as revolving around resources falls prey to this tendency within scholarship on organizing. Marshall Ganz, *People, Power, Change: Organizing for Democratic Renewal* (New York: Oxford University Press, 2024).

Broad-based organizers are institutional and relational organizers. Their work is to build strong institutions through cultivating the relational networks within and between these institutions. Four national networks and their local affiliates make up the field of broad-based community organizing. Each local affiliate is an organization of organizations, where local members of the constituency are organizations like churches, mosques, synagogues, unions, schools, and other organizations. Organizers work to build leadership of the member organizations that in turn strengthen the leadership of the entire affiliate. This is why the bread and butter of organizing are practices like the relational meeting and the listening campaign. The relational meeting is a public, time-limited, and value-directed conversation between two people. The listening campaign is a series of relational meetings within a single organization or institution. These practices prioritize culture work: work of tending to the values and stories that bring people into organizing in the first place, stories of pain and suffering that organizing promises to transform through public action. Institutions in this sense are normed collectivities of people who share rituals and meaning-making practices. The relational basis of organizing reweaves the relational fabric of these institutions to help identify the values and issues that sit at the heart of our personal narratives.

People organize to protect and fight for what they hold most dear. Although issues are crucial to pinpoint urgent action and focus individual and collective anger through strategic campaigns that are exercising political and economic power, issue agendas fade. Each new legislative season brings a host of new urgent issues. The 24-hour media news cycle and its coincident barrage of ever-present urgent issues is one of the hallmarks of our neoliberal racial capitalist age. Organizing is a slow and patient social practice grounded in building relational power. Sacred values, it turns out, are a key part of those organizing relationships. We get angry when things or people we hold most dear are threatened, violated, or destroyed. People get into the fight in the first place because what they hold sacred is threatened, violated, or destroyed. The drive to protect those goods and people keeps us in the fight when the going gets tough. Getting clear on why you're in the fight in the first place helps clarify and prioritize the issues that need to be taken up first regardless of the chaos that characterizes politics.

By "sacred values" I do not mean the "sacred." Sacred value is a value attributed to goods or people. When people attribute sacred value to something, they make a judgment about the world and people in it. Certain evaluative attitudes set apart this judgment from others in our daily lives. Recognizing this changes how we act and talk about these particulars. We attribute sacred value to the things we hold most dear, and so our behaviors and attitudes treat them as such. We revere the goods and people we hold sacred; we mourn and grieve their loss. We set up protections and prohibitions so that what we hold sacred is treated appropriately.[6] Because politics is about the contestation and negotiation of the goods a community holds in common, judgments of sacred value and the protections and prohibitions we establish in response to this attribution of value are political.

In the philosophical literature on sacred value, it has most often been characterized by innate value, objectivity, and inviolability. By innate value, scholars mean the location of the value.[7] In this sense, humans are accorded sacred value not because of their status or membership of a group; instead, it has more to do with their very being, their social ontology as humans.[8] Abolitionists claim that mass incarceration violates human dignity because of what keeping people in cages does to humans. Indigenous activists claim that certain lands are of sacred worth because recreational uses disregard their innate value. Objectivity, then, helps illustrate that the judgment of sacred value is not dependent on my recognizing it—I could be mistaken, misinformed, ignorant, or prejudiced in my judgment of some thing's or person's worth.[9] My failure in recognition does not change the status of a thing's value. This entails, however, two additional minor complications: First, sacred values are typically non-incremental goods—having more of them does not change my attitude to the others. Finding a cellar full of Rembrandt's paintings does not change the value we accord those we

---

[6] I take leave from Jeffrey Stout's work on sacred value and community organizing in terms of reverence, protections, and prohibitions. See Jeffrey Stout, *Blessed Are the Organized: Grassroots Democracy in America* (Princeton, NJ: Princeton University Press, 2010).

[7] See Christine M. Korsgaard, *Creating the Kingdom of Ends* (New York: Cambridge University Press, 1996), 250.

[8] This sense of ontology is best outlined in Robert Merrihew Adams, *Finite and Infinite Goods: A Framework for Ethics* (New York: Oxford University Press, 2002), 36–37.

[9] For more on this notion of objectivity, see Ronald Dworkin, "Objectivity and Truth: You'd Better Believe It," *Philosophy & Public Affairs* 25, no. 2 (1996): 87–139.

currently have.[10] Objectivity helps make sense of the claims that the value we accord does not depend on one's preferences or attitudes and having more or less of what we deem sacred does not change the value we attribute to that which we hold most dear. Second, objectivity of sacred value also lends itself to the sense that goods or people accorded sacred value are typically seen as incommensurable—meaning both that these goods or people are not measurable to others and that rival goods are not comparable.[11] Finally, inviolability helps illustrate the protections and prohibitions one might set up to safeguard the good or person held sacred.[12]

In my own experience in organizing circles, attitudes of sacred value have been thought to splinter group solidarity. It is almost as if valuing some as sacred is too uncontrollable, untidy, and unfit for political life. The response has been to build relationships on shared ethics, values, beliefs, or issues. In this frame of mind, organizers have sought to build solidarity through sameness, either in ideology or politics. Issues that are typically grounded in judgments of sacred value have been claimed as unwinnable, so that the strategy of organizing prioritizes winnable issues over a relational strategy that prizes value-work in the organizing practice. An organizing strategy that centers judgments of sacred value, however, helps surface the stories that form and shape our deepest identity. These are the stories that help draw others to us, form collectives, and help move us into action. When we encounter attitudes of sacred value, we are moved, physically and emotionally. Embracing the political role of sacred value allows our different judgments to manifest and form relationships. Crucial, here, is the recognition that difference is a deep relationship.

This is a point that philosophical theologians inspired by G. W. F. Hegel had made well, and my work takes leave from Gary Dorrien's post-Hegelian religious philosophy that accentuates idealistic discontent with the world.[13]

---

[10] The Rembrandt example stems from Dworkin's work on the non-incremental nature of sacred value. See Ronald Dworkin, *Life's Dominion: An Argument about Abortion, Euthanasia, and Individual Freedom* (New York: Vintage Books, 1994), 70–72.

[11] This sense of incommensurability is built on Ruth Chang's work. See Ruth Chang, Introduction to *Incommensurability, Incomparability, and Practical Reasoning*, ed. Ruth Chang (Cambridge, MA: Harvard University Press, 1997).

[12] Stout, *Blessed Are the Organized*, 210–11.

[13] Gary Dorrien, *In a Post-Hegelian Spirit: Philosophical Theology as Idealistic Discontent* (Waco, TX: Baylor University Press, 2020).

This philosophy accentuates *Spirit* as a key to individual and collective ethical life. Dorrien's work on Hegel first pointed me in this direction, helping me see—along with Peter Hodgson and Robert Williams—the theological and religious themes in Hegel's thought. The upshot here is that we can see how differences of judgment that stem from attitudes of sacred value—most often found in political, ethical, and religious difference, say—require deeper relational work for organizers and leaders to build a constituency. Differences need to be worked in and through—not out and away. In this organizing strategy, we get a clearer picture on the role of theology in the practice of organizing itself. We see that theology is deeply concerned with power and has a lot to say about politics as the contestation and negotiation of the goods that a community holds in common.[14] Our theological imagination can push our political imagination, so that our organizing strategy itself changes in response. In this way, organizing strategically unleashes the theological and Christian social ethical energies to protect and fight for what we hold most dear.

Nothing of what I've said above makes sacred value a distinctly religious concept—it is meant to be capacious enough to capture value in religious or nonreligious senses.[15] Religion itself is a deeply constructed and contested reality; religion is "lived" and practiced, something people take up, innovate, and experiment with.[16] Religion is not only about beliefs but also social ethics. My account here fronts a social practical framework of religious practices and practical reasoning. Sacred value is a concept that

---

[14] This sense of politics is indebted to the tradition of radical democrats and grassroots democracy, but also holds similarities with Luke Bretherton's consociationalism. See Jeffrey Stout, *Democracy and Tradition* (Princeton, NJ: Princeton University Press, 2004); Sheldon S. Wolin, *Fugitive Democracy: And Other Essays* (Princeton, NJ: Princeton University Press, 2016); Luke Bretherton, *Christ and the Common Life: Political Theology and the Case for Democracy* (Grand Rapids: Eerdmans, 2019).

[15] This is a point made by Dworkin, *Life's Dominion*; Adams, *Finite and Infinite Goods*; and Stout, *Blessed Are the Organized*.

[16] The field of "lived religion" is large and growing, but key texts remain. See Courtney Bender, *Heaven's Kitchen: Living Religion at God's Love We Deliver* (Chicago: University of Chicago Press, 2003); David D. Hall, ed., *Lived Religion in America: Toward a History of Practice* (Princeton, NJ: Princeton University Press, 1997); Robert A. Orsi, *The Madonna of 115th Street: Faith and Community in Italian Harlem, 1880–1950* (New Haven, CT: Yale University Press, 2002).

helps us track the diversity within the social practice of organizing and decide whether nor not they occur in the way or under the conditions we typically understand as "religious." Once we figure the role of sacred values in our social practical reasoning, we see how attributing such a value to certain goods or people brings along with it different behaviors and attitudes. We can see that certain actions within organizing, like the relational meeting and listening campaign, can be seen as religious practice.

Social practices are shared activities that are governed by collective norms and evaluative standards that individuals take up and live into. Social practices can scale up and be nested in larger social structures and institutions.[17] Social practical reasoning is itself a social practice, collectively possible and governed, yet individually innovated and creatively deployed. Through repetition, innovation occurs as contexts shift and people move through time. Similarly, organizing is a social practice that is open to individual style. Take the relational meeting for an example. As a social practice, it is made possible through the associational context that constitutes a group. In this public value-directed conversation between two people, new things happen even when old questions are asked, like: "What issues are you most concerned about in your community?" Or "Who taught you that standing up for justice is important?" New things happen because mutual recognition—an ethical relationship in which participants take their counterpart as an authority of knowledge and value—is possible here. But, crucially, a third thing is moving: the Spirit. As individuals engage in the social practice of practical reasoning, they tend to the ethical life of a group, cultivating new stories, tending to one another, and discerning the movement of God's Spirit.

Broad-based organizing claims that the root of our modern democratic problems has to do with our democratic life. To counter this, broad-based organizing aims to build political and economic relational power in order to gain wins for working people. But this relational power is built in constituencies—counterpublics—that exemplify the sort of radical democracy they are seeking to instill in the broader society. Broad-based organizing is deeply concerned about our democratic life. The work of organizing is about developing people into powerful agents in a time when radically democratic leaders are sorely needed. You cannot build powerful

---

[17] This point on nesting comes from Molly Farneth, *The Politics of Ritual* (Princeton, NJ: Princeton University Press, 2023), chap. 1. The point on social practices fitting into larger social structures is from Sally Haslanger, "What Is a Social Practice?" *Royal Institute of Philosophy Supplement; London* 82 (July 2018): 231–47.

organizations—organizations that can win on a range of issues that broadly appeal to working people; organizations that can adapt and absorb campaign losses in the midst of a larger political and economic vision of radical democracy—if you do not build strong leaders who understand relational power. Broad-based organizing aims to cultivate and tend the Spirit of its counterpublics so their members speak and act in a radically democratic way. Building and protecting this sort of radically democratic culture involves weaving relationships of mutual recognition. Recognition involves taking others as epistemic authorities with accountability, but it also means realizing that the other *counts* in a politically and economically important sense.[18] Recognition, here, is about political and economic status and less about self-realization.[19] Building this sort of culture requires a politics that tends to the Spirit of the counterpublic.

For Christians, this work of tending to one another, of listening to their neighbor's stories of justice and concern, involves listening to how God is calling us into deeper relationships with one another and moving us out into public action for power. As we encounter stories of sacred value, in which people share insights and commentary on how they protect and fight for what they hold most dear, we are pulled together—perhaps even pulled together because of our different stories of sacred value—and pushed into public. The Spirit moves in a spiral fashion, weaving us together in deeper ethical life, making reciprocal recognition possible. This is how organizing reweaves the social fabric of our communities and builds relational power. For relational organizers and for Christians committed to building a more just world, power is a crucial concept.

Power

For BBCO (broad-based community organizing) organizers there have long been two dominant understandings of power, which Bernard Loomer outlined in his 1976 article, "Two Conceptions of Power": unilateral and

---

[18] For more on reciprocal recognition see Robert R. Williams, *Hegel's Ethics of Recognition* (Berkeley: University of California Press, 1997), 57; Molly Farneth, *Hegel's Social Ethics: Religion, Conflict, and Rituals of Reconciliation* (Princeton, NJ: Princeton University Press, 2017), 57.

[19] See Nancy Fraser and Axel Honneth, *Redistribution or Recognition? A Political-Philosophical Exchange* (London: Verso, 2003).

relational power.[20] For Loomer, too much has been said and written about unilateral power. This definition presumes that power is defined "as the ability to produce an effect, or as the capacity to bring into being, to actualize or to maintain what has been actualized."[21] This is a "demonic" view of power in its "destructiveness."[22] It is "nonrelational" and "nonmutual." In this view, the agent who is exercising the influence, control, manipulation, or so on, is unaffected by this action. Even if the agent is somehow affected by the power relationship, it is "external" to the actor. As Loomer says, "But the main thrust of this kind of power is to produce a desired effect on the other in accordance with one's own purposes. Ideally, its aim is to create the largest effect on the other while being minimally influenced by the other."[23] In this view of power, the agent who acts over against the other gains in power while the one being acted upon diminishes in power.

Relational power, by contrast, is as much about reception as it is about exertion. Power in this sense involves the "strength" it takes to absorb or undergo an effect.[24] The basic difference between unilateral and relational power has to do with the manner in which relational power has a clearer understanding of how power is a value-term. Attributing power to an agent signals their value; calling someone powerless diminishes their value. In relational power terms, the ability to be influenced by another without losing one's sense of self or one's agency involves a significant degree of power more than unilateral power, which cordons off the agent from the outside world. Power in this sense includes the capacity to undergo influence without being overwhelmed, dominated, oppressed, or exploited by the other.

A relational understanding of power, while still maintaining that power is innately a capacity, positions this capacity in a larger scene and situation, unveiling hidden and structural forms of power that otherwise fade into the background. Here, power is more than exertion or mere force, including relationships that influence political and economic conditions

---

[20] Bernard Loomer, "Two Conceptions of Power," *Process Studies* 6, no. 1 (April 1, 1976): 5–32. This paragraph and the following on relational power adapts material from Aaron Stauffer, "Power in the Social Gospel: Howard Kester, Claude Williams, and the Southern Tenant Farmers Union," *Religions* 15, no. 9 (September 1, 2024).

[21] Loomer, "Two Conceptions of Power," 6.

[22] Loomer, "Two Conceptions of Power," 8.

[23] Loomer, "Two Conceptions of Power," 8.

[24] Loomer, "Two Conceptions of Power," 17.

that constitute our daily lives but often go unnoticed.[25] More than this, a relational view of power provides deeper insights into how power is generated and sustained, rather than confining the examination of power to decisions by individual agents. This understanding of power also helps to distinguish power from like concepts, such as influence, manipulation, coercion, force, and authority. Power is generated and sustained through relationships that enable (or prevent) action.[26]

Power, as a capacity of one agent (individual or group) to act meaningfully with another, is always in relationships. Power is generated through relationships and is equally about reception as it is about exertion. This capacity to act happens in a myriad of ways, through imposition, force, influence, conviction, manipulation, negotiation, or compromise, but the action is meaningful and significant only in relationship. Long-standing community organizer of the Industrial Areas Foundation (IAF), Ernesto Cortes talks of the difference between unilateral and relational power:

> Unilateral power tends to be coercive and domineering. It is the power of one party treating another as an object to be instructed and directed. Relational power is more complicated. Developed subject-to-subject, it is transformative, changing the nature of the situation and of the self. The IAF has spent fifty years teaching people to develop such relational power, mastering the capacity to act, and the reciprocal capacity to allow oneself to be acted upon.[27]

This view of relational power is the sort of power that feminists and people of color have long cherished and claimed as their own, and it is the framework that grounds the value-based approach of broad-based community organizing that I am advocating for here. It is built through the daily spadework of relational organizing that revolves around the politics of sacred values, and it can sustain campaigns that seek wins on

---

[25] Steven Lukes expands on these "unnoticed" aspects of power in Steven Lukes, *Power: A Radical View* (London: Bloomsbury Academic, 2021).

[26] Lukes helpfully illustrates how power is just as much about agenda-setting as it is about accomplishing agenda items, so to speak.

[27] Ernesto Cortes Jr., "Justice at the Gates of the City: A Model for Shared Prosperity," in *Back to Shared Prosperity: The Growing Inequality of Wealth and Income in America*, ed. Ray Marshall (New York: Routledge, 2015), 366.

issues that are vitally important for working people's communities.[28] The politics of tending, of attending to one another, of building relationships of mutual recognition that care about whether people count politically and economically in our society, requires the day-in-and-day-out grind of relational organizing.

What Lies Ahead for Scholar-Organizers

When Gary, Charlene, and I first came together to form Social Ethics Energizing Democracy (SEED), we kept saying the same statement over and over: There have got to be people out there like us—scholar-organizers hungry for collaboration, networking, friendship, and Spirit. SEED is a formation meant to be such a community and space of conversation. As the chapters in this book give testament to: The best of theological education is grounded in broad-based solidarity activist organizing. Strife, Moe-Lobeda, Baker and Wessel-McCoy, Snarr, and Floyd-Thomas illustrate this best. The best experiments in teaching come from there, too. It turns out, as Strife, Hayes-Mota, Ringer, and my own chapter illustrate, studying these movements is the original move of social ethics as a scholarly enterprise. The chapters in this book help us see how vital organizing is to the future of social ethics and how crucial the tools of social ethics are to successful organizing.

This statement matters because, as Gary Dorrien outlines in the Introduction, although the field of social ethics started with grassroots movements building relational power, it has not stayed that way. Many in the field have never heard of organizing, let alone consider it a theoretically rigorous political and economic practice. This book offers a counternarrative that offers a different way of thinking about the individual and interrelated work of social ethics and organizing.

The most exciting horizons in theological education are those that are found at its intersection with community organizing.[29] In the last decade

---

[28] "Spadework" refers to the organizing strategy of Ella Baker. See Barbara Ransby, *Ella Baker and the Black Freedom Movement: A Radical Democratic Vision*. Electronic resource. Gender & American Culture (Chapel Hill: University of North Carolina Press, 2003).

[29] I first made similar points as I make in the next few paragraphs in Aaron Stauffer, "The Theologically Trained Organizer," *Christian Century*, February 2024. Accessed February 15, 2024. https://www.christiancentury.org/features/theologically-trained-organizer.

or so, many schools have engaged the topic of community organizing, either in their curriculum or in their lifelong learning programs. This shift suggests a recognition that the dominant model of theological education is ill-suited for our time. But much is still unsettled: In the times of crisis for schools and congregations—as schools close or merge, congregations and denominations face smaller membership rolls and budgets; as in-residence student bodies get smaller and virtual student bodies grow, pastors and congregations face questions about hybrid worship and deep questions about what it means to be a member—the new models of theological education that prize the values and strategies of communities organizing are not clear. There is the real danger that broad-based solidarity activism will be viewed as a tilling ground for enrollments, without establishing real relationships of accountability and responsibility to movements. If social ethicists and theological educators are to continue to offer a field of inquiry and reflection that draws from and seeks to give life back to organizing movements, important shifts in the institutional life of the academic institutions and the role of professors will need to take place.

There are changes and challenges for organizing, too, as these chapters illustrate. Let me highlight just one that centers the future of value-based organizing.

In my work with congregations and people of faith, I continually return to the importance of relationships and values to organizing. People organize to protect and fight for what they hold most dear—it is the love that throws them in the fight, keeps their feet steady and their heads clear. Organizing is a transformative process, one that asks people to grow and develop in relationship around specific action.[30] The relational and value-basis of organizing leads to an issue-focused action agenda. But this process cannot be instrumentalized. As my colleague Joerg Rieger often says, you cannot "rent-a-collar" your way to a win.[31] Building power is the slow and patient work of building political, economic, and religious democratic relationships. Allowing leaders to explore the discomfort of being agitated in relationship with others who hold different sacred values

---

[30] Ganz names this approach to leadership, "developmental leadership." See Ganz, *People, Power, Change*, 176–201.

[31] See Joerg Rieger and Rosemarie Henkel-Rieger, *Unified We Are a Force: How Faith and Labor Can Overcome America's Inequalities* (St. Louis, MO: Chalice Press, 2016).

will deepen the relational bonds within the constituency, even if this means being uncomfortable. Such work is not only theologically and politically generative; it also allows our leaders to be honest and whole persons in the work of organizing.[32]

Organizing is about values, relationships, and the stories we use to explain ourselves and the work. When these values or relationships are threatened or violated, we react in fear, anger, even horror—this is the basis on which specific issues are selected for political action. As I argued in *Listening to the Spirit*, social practical reasoning helps us navigate the political and religious waters of our life together. We hold each other accountable and responsible based on this social practice of reasoning together—of giving and asking for reasons, of holding each other accountable to what we say and what we take others to mean. We weave stories about who we are individually and collectively and what it will take to uphold those narratives. We use such narratives to explain our past, present, and future actions and help us discern where we ought to start organizing and where we are going. Organizing in relationships that are grounded in sacred values includes agitating and tension-ridden moments. But the Spirit moves: pushing and pulling us into relationships with our neighbors and into the work of building God's cooperative commonwealth and the hope for a better day.

I came to seminary and pursued a doctorate there because I needed a deeper theological and social ethical vocabulary that would aid my organizing work. I came to Union because Gary took my questions about power and the Spirit seriously. This book has brought together a collection of fellow traveling scholar-organizers who see a fruitful and wise pairing between organizing and social ethics. Their best mutually respective futures are connected, and this book illustrates how and why that is the case.

---

[32] I make similar arguments to these in Stauffer, *Listening to the Spirit*, 75–77.

Afterword

Rev. Peter Laarman

Many of us steeped in the culture of the Left have spent much of our lives repeating Joe Hill's injunction: "Don't mourn! Organize!" I want to propose, however, that taking time for what might be called *constructive mourning* will serve us well in this moment. Grief and loss, and, in this case, reckoning with the power of real evil, can bring clarity and a degree of realism about the work that will need to be done over many generations to come.

For what we contend with now is not, as some have argued, merely a new instantiation of the same old racial capitalism that has inflicted so much pain and disfigured so many institutions over the course of four centuries. The new regime brings with it more than its share of this poison, naturally, but its harm goes farther and deeper. It seeks to obliterate all traces of accurate historical memory; it seeks to disable the capacity to separate fact from fiction; it seeks to eviscerate every system of measurement that might help us to see and gauge the damage being done; it seeks to trivialize and discredit any motivation or activity related to something other than naked self-interest; it seeks to *dislocate* and *relocate* all of us into a wilderness of unmeaning.

I imagine that every reader of this book understands how the core operating system of the old order was corrupted and contaminated by white supremacy, patriarchy, corporate rapacity, and toxic religion. But the new operating system will prove to be far worse, as Timothy Snyder and many other scholars of totalitarianism have warned. Several central figures in Trump's wrecking crew have eagerly imbibed the abhorrent and deadly political theology of Nazi enabler Carl Schmitt. *Sovereignty* is their watchword, and by that they most definitely do not mean popular sovereignty. Their goal is not merely to undo twentieth- and twenty-first-century gains in human and civil rights; it is not merely to uproot the institutions of the New Deal and to extirpate the labor movement once and for all; it is in fact to extinguish the idea of popular sovereignty altogether: to prevent any possibility of a new rising from below.

We can and should remind ourselves of the many developments that brought us to this sorry pass: the atomization and loneliness introduced by so-called "social" media; the capture of so much of US Christianity by dominionists lacking even a vague interest in the teachings of Jesus of Nazareth; the deplorable arrogance and sheer flat-out ignorance of many ostensibly progressive philanthropies; the smugness and self-righteousness of upper-middle-class culture scolds; the unabashed determination of ethically bereft tech bros and hedge funders to dominate both the economy and the common culture; the perfect willingness of higher education leaders to surrender to the grip, even strengthen the grip, of corporate values; and (last but not least) the lingering effects of the Reagan Revolution in discrediting the very idea of collective thriving while systematically sabotaging the capacity of public entities to serve the public effectively.

My purpose, however, is not to rehearse the multiple sources of present injury but to take stock of resources that can help us do more than survive the current onslaught: resources that can build up the power and spirit needed to bring to birth a new world from the ashes of the old.

Organizing Visions is replete with such resources, making it a bright testament of hope in a very dark time. This is a book about the theory and practice of Christian social ethics, but it is also about much more. It is about the excruciating loneliness of the prophetic calling. It is about the ambiguities facing congregations and pastors who seek to support broad-based community organizing. It is about where we might actually *find* church when "The Church" has lost its way. It is about the moral authority and dignity of everyday people: those so often ignored, if not actively oppressed, by this era's much-esteemed and highly compensated "knowledge workers."

Crucially, no fewer than five of the essays in this volume deal directly and powerfully with the kind of history our new overlords seek to erase: social history, in the best sense of *social*. Gary Dorrien shares the origin story of Christian social ethics and its relationship to political theology. Aaron Stauffer takes us on deep dive into the little-known roots of the Southern Tenant Farmers Union while also exposing the poison pill in civic republicanism. Joe Strife offers a panoptic view of both the settlement house movement and the radical urban ministries of the 1960s. Nicholas Hayes-Mota reminds us of the lasting significance of social Catholicism and how it remains embedded in today's Alinsky-descended community organizing projects. Carolyn Baker and Colleen Wessel-McCoy team up to paint a compelling portrait of a compelling prophet: the National Welfare Rights Organization's Beulah Sanders.

This history is life-giving to us now because the thinkers and leaders of these earlier eras exhibited both remarkable insight and remarkable shortsightedness, often at the same time. We can learn from their experiences. We can be in real conversation with the past. We can, with God's grace, avoid some of the limitations of vision, the failures of nerve, and the pitfalls of a false bravado.

Other essays problematize the organizing challenge in a helpful way. Such critical analysis is immensely valuable now, when many broad-based community organizing efforts have been professionalized and regularized. Structure and focus are important, obviously, especially at a time when many younger activists seem to be unclear about the difference between self-expression and the building of actual power. But is it possible that long-accepted structures and techniques leave something out? What happens institutionally and spiritually when middle-class congregations seize the opportunity to outsource their entire social justice ministry to the neighborhood Faith-Based Community Organization (FBCO)? What are the dangers of locating poverty "out there" somewhere, rather than understanding how middle-class security is significantly purchased through the exploitation of our working-class and poor neighbors: the very people the churches claim to want to help?

All of these hard issues are thoughtfully and thoroughly interrogated in this volume. The SEED project as a whole holds enormous promise precisely because it places passionate academics and organizers into productive dialogue and active collaboration. It recognizes that ideas about God, and even more, actual *experiences* of divinity, are sources of unimaginable strength and renewal for persons actually engaged in direct organizing. SEED co-founder Charlene Sinclair, when she was already an effective and accomplished organizer, became a theologian and much-beloved teacher/mentor precisely because she understood this power and wanted other organizers to be able to experience it. Bless you, Charlene, for showing the way.

In this vein, I wish to end my appreciation of the good work of this book's authors and editors. I believe all of us must now root ourselves in the experience of divinity and the experience of church, however we define it.

If I might pick up on a 1937 remark of Howard Kester (cited by Aaron Stauffer): *We must keep hammering away in the church, at the church, with the church, in the knowledge that we stand on solid ground and with the ages and not on the sand which already slips away as the rains descend and the winds of a new day blow with might.*

We are in wilderness now. We even tread upon sinking sands. I believe it will really help us to identify with how our ancestors in faith, both ancient and modern, engaged the experience of wilderness. Identify with ancestors who held fast to the rock of salvation and the wellsprings of deliverance despite their tribulations. Relate to interpreters of the deeper meaning of *church*.

I take no joy in mentioning that, during my undergraduate years of many years ago, I was introduced to a triumphalist understanding of liberal Christianity and its inevitable success in seeding a lasting principled ethic into a secularizing world. I might name the influence of scholars like Harvey Cox, Peter Berger, Robert Bellah, and others, in shaping this perspective, not to mention frontline exposure in my youth to the public witness of William Sloane Coffin Jr., Eugene Carson Blake, and other marquee clergy figures in that era's confident activism. Most of these men—and they were mainly white men with expensive names—routinely cited Dietrich Bonhoeffer, but I now doubt that they really understood what Bonhoeffer was about. They shared an underlying and unshakable belief in the ultimate success of the liberal project.

It was only later—and really much later, during and after a second-career ministry—that I began to appreciate the theology of brokenness and exile. I will not claim to understand it fully now. But I find balm for my broken heart in the anguished witness of W. E. B. Du Bois and Ida B. Wells-Barnett; in the tightly coiled rage of Mary McLeod Bethune; in the mournful mysticism of Howard Thurman; in the clear-eyed critical consciousness of James Baldwin and James Cone and Toni Morrison; in the constancy and courage of Fannie Lou Hamer and Ella Baker and James Lawson and Martin King and all who walked with them during times of terror.

Among the more widely acknowledged white Christians who have traversed desolate places, I found and still find grace in the plenitude and power of the "Two Walters" (Wink and Brueggemann); in the poetic precision of William Stringfellow; in the rigorous rectitude of dear old Bill Webber; in the feisty fearlessness of the Berrigan brothers; and in the steely spirituality of Dorothee Soelle.

These are wilderness voices I sometimes hear in the depths of the night. These great souls, and others like them within God's great cloud of witnesses, still keep me going. (I date myself with these references; I do realize that there are many others now witnessing and writing along the same lines.)

And so I leave us with questions about our readiness for the journey ahead: Can we sophisticated twenty-first-century people bring ourselves to understand and feel that there are, in fact, "principalities and powers" at loose in the world? Even more critically, can we align with, and root ourselves in, the only truly divine power, which is revolutionary love?

This is where the practical need for real church comes in, as we cannot do the aligning and rooting by ourselves, in isolation. We need both the *participation* and the *formation* that only a real church experience, with its grace in gathering and its liberatory opening up of sacred texts, both ancient and modern, can supply. To state the matter plainly, we need to break bread together. We need spirit, we need prayer, and we need song.

The late, great Vincent Harding liked to recall that, in the face of police dogs and KKK terrorists, the courageous freedom fighters of the 1960s would be "singing so loud we couldn't hear our knees knocking." In our time, most of the merchants of fear and death don't wear white robes or brandish clubs or release vicious dogs to tear flesh from the limbs of children. They, too, have learned from the past. But they are no less bent on our destruction. It is for this reason that we need each other desperately. We need, in our desperation, the presence and guidance and solace of the Holy Spirit. We need much deeper communion with the prophets and martyrs who have gone before. We need, even now, to be able to sing out *glory hallelujah* in the face of the evil oppressor.

Come what may, God's truth marches on. We have not been forsaken.

Contributors

Carolyn Baker is an organizer in Detroit, Michigan, whose work with The General Baker Institute preserves the legacy of her father, General Gordon Baker Jr., and her mother's advocacy, while also honoring other legends in the fight for Black social justice.

Malinda Elizabeth Berry is an associate professor of theology and ethics and director of the Faith Formation Collaborative at Anabaptist Mennonite Biblical Seminary in Elkhart, Indiana.

K. B. Brower is the organizing director for Bargaining for the Common Good at the Action Center on Race & the Economy.

Gary Dorrien teaches theology and social ethics at Union Theological Seminary in New York.

Stacey Floyd-Thomas is the E. Rhodes and Leona B. Carpenter Professor of Ethics and Society at Vanderbilt University in Nashville, Tennessee.

Nicholas Hayes-Mota is an assistant professor at Santa Clara University in Santa Clara, California, where he teaches courses in Christian social ethics and Catholic theology.

Peter Laarman is a United Church of Christ minister who has served as senior minister of New York's Judson Memorial Church and as executive director of Los Angeles–based Progressive Christians Uniting.

Cynthia Moe-Lobeda is the professor of theological and social ethics, with a joint appointment at Pacific Lutheran Theological Seminary and Church Divinity School of the Pacific. She is a member of the Core Doctoral Faculty of the Graduate Theological Union in Berkeley, California.

Christophe D. Ringer is an associate professor of theological ethics and society at Chicago Theological Seminary in Chicago, Illinois.

Charlene Sinclair is a consultant, trainer, and strategic advisor for leading social change organizations and leaders. She received her PhD in social ethics from Union Theological Seminary in 2017.

C. Melissa Snarr is the E. Rhodes and Leona B. Carpenter Chair of Ethics and Society, associate professor of ethics and society, director of the Doctor of Ministry program, on the faculty of the Graduate Department of Religion, and an affiliated faculty member in community research and action and women and gender studies at Vanderbilt University in Nashville, Tennessee.

Aaron Stauffer is the associate director of the Wendland-Cook Program in Religion and Justice at Vanderbilt Divinity School in Nashville, Tennessee.

Joseph Strife has taught courses at Fordham University and has worked at the Kairos Center for Religions, Rights, and Social Justice in New York City.

Colleen Wessel-McCoy is the assistant professor of peace and justice studies and director of the Masters of Peace and Social Transformation program at Earlham School of Religion in Richmond, Indiana.

Bibliography

Abell, Aaron. *The Urban Impact on American Protestantism, 1865–1900.* Cambridge, MA: Harvard University Press, 1943.

Accetti, Carlo Invernizzi. *What Is Christian Democracy? Politics, Religion and Ideology.* Cambridge: Cambridge University Press, 2019.

Adams, Robert Merrihew. *Finite and Infinite Goods: A Framework for Ethics.* New York: Oxford University Press, 2002.

Addams, Jane. *Democracy and Social Ethics.* Urbana: University of Illinois Press, 2002.

Aho, James A. *The Politics of Righteousness: Idaho Christian Patriotism.* Seattle: University of Washington Press, 1990.

Alicea, Benjamin. "Christian Urban Colonizers: A History of the East Harlem Protestant Parish in New York City, 1948–1968." PhD diss., Union Theological Seminary, 1989.

Alinsky, Saul. "Community Analysis and Organization." *American Journal of Sociology* 46, no. 6 (1941).

Angelou, Maya. "These Yet to Be United States." In *Complete Collected Poems of Maya Angelou.* Norwalk, CT: Easton Press, 2005.

Ansfield, Bench. "Unsettling 'Inner City': Liberal Protestantism and the Postwar Origins of a Keyword in Urban Studies." *Antipode* 50, no. 5 (2018).

Azaransky, Sarah. *This Worldwide Struggle: Religion and the International Roots of the Civil Rights Movement.* New York: Oxford University Press, 2017.

Baker, Gen. Gordon. Untitled talk. US Social Forum, Detroit, 2010. General Baker Institute.

Baltodano, Marta, Antonia Dardar, and Rodolfo Torres. "Critical Pedagogy: An Introduction." In *Critical Pedagogy Reader*, ed. Maria Baltodano, Marta, Antonia Dardar, and Rodolfo Torres, 1–23. New York: Routledge, 2017.

Behr, Thomas C. *Social Justice and Subsidiarity: Luigi Taparelli and the Origins of Modern Catholic Social Thought.* Washington, DC: Catholic University of America Press, 2019.

Bender, Courtney. *Heaven's Kitchen: Living Religion at God's Love We Deliver.* Chicago: University of Chicago Press, 2003.
Benford, Robert D., and David A. Snow. "Framing Processes and Social Movements: An Overview and Assessment." *Annual Review of Sociology* 26, no. 1 (2000): 611–39. https://doi.org/10.1146/annurev.soc.26.1.611.
Berger, Peter L. *The Sacred Canopy: Elements of a Sociological Theory of Religion.* Garden City, NY: Doubleday, 1967.
Berlin, Isaiah. *Liberty: Incorporating Four Essays on Liberty.* Edited by Henry Hardy. Oxford: Oxford University Press, 2002.
Beyer, Gerald J. "The Meaning of Solidarity in Catholic Social Teaching." *Political Theology* 15, no. 1 (2014): 7–25.
Blake, Eugene Carson. "The Church in the Next Decade." *Christianity and Crisis* 26, no. 2 (1966).
Bohlen, Casey. "The Politics of Conscience: Religious Activism and Social Change in Postwar America." PhD diss., Harvard University, 2016.
Bonnett, Alastair. *Anti-Racism: Key Ideas.* London: Routledge, 2000.
Boto, Carlota. "The Age of Enlightenment and Education." *Oxford Research Encyclopedia of Education.* February 23, 2021. Accessed January 28, 2025. https://oxfordre.com/education/view/10.1093/acrefore/9780190264093.001.0001/acrefore-9780190264093-e-1469.
Braunstein, Ruth. *Prophets and Patriots: Faith in Democracy across the Political Divide.* Oakland: University of California Press, 2017.
Braunstein, Ruth, Todd Nicholas Fuist, and Rhys H. Williams. *Religion and Progressive Activism: New Stories about Faith and Politics.* New York: NYU Press, 2017.
Bretherton, Luke. *Christ and the Common Life: Political Theology and the Case for Democracy.* Grand Rapids: Eerdmans, 2019.
Bretherton, Luke. *Hospitality as Holiness: Christian Witness amid Moral Diversity.* Burlington, VT: Ashgate, 2006.
Bretherton, Luke. *Resurrecting Democracy: Faith, Citizenship, and the Politics of a Common Life.* New York: Cambridge University Press, 2015.
Brown, Bréne. *The Gifts of Imperfection.* Center City, MN: Hazelden, 2022.
Brown, Dorothy, and Elizabeth McKeown. *The Poor Belong to Us: Catholic Charities and American Welfare.* Cambridge, MA: Harvard University Press, 2000.
Brown, Stewart. *Thomas Chalmers and the Godly Commonwealth in Scotland.* Oxford: Oxford University Press, 1983.

Bureau of Labor Statistics, "Union Members—2024." January 28, 2025. https://www.bls.gov/news.release/pdf/union2.pdf.

Burns, David. *The Life and Death of the Radical Historical Jesus*. New York: Oxford University Press, 2013.

Camarillo, Emmanuel. "Lawsuit Seeks to Stop Former South Shore High School from Being Turned into Shelter for Migrants: 'We were forced to do this,'" *Chicago Sun-Times*, May 11, 2023.

Cannon, Katie G. *Black Womanist Ethics*. Atlanta: Scholars Press, 1988.

Cannon, Katie G. *Katie's Canon: Womanism and the Soul of the Black Community*. Rev. and exp. 25th anniv. ed. Minneapolis: Fortress Press, 2021.

Carter, Heath. *Union Made: Working People and the Rise of Social Christianity in Chicago*. New York: Oxford University Press, 2015.

Casanova, José. *Global Religious and Secular Dynamics: The Modern System of Classification*. Brill Research Perspectives. Boston: Brill, 2019.

Casanova, José. *Public Religions in the Modern World*. Chicago: University of Chicago Press, 1994.

Chang, Ruth. Introduction to *Incommensurability, Incomparability, and Practical Reasoning*, edited by Ruth Chang. Cambridge, MA: Harvard University Press, 1997.

Chappel, James. *Catholic Modern: The Challenge of Totalitarianism and the Making of the Church*. Cambridge, MA: Harvard University Press, 2018.

Cloward, Richard, and Frances Fox Piven. "The Weight of the Poor: A Strategy to End Poverty." *The Nation*, May 2, 1966.

Cobb, William H. *Radical Education in the Rural South: Commonwealth College, 1922–1940*. Detroit: Wayne State University Press, 2000.

Coleman, John A. *An American Strategic Theology*. New York: Paulist Press, 1982.

Coleman, John A. "The Future of Catholic Social Thought." In *Modern Catholic Social Teaching: Commentaries and Interpretations*, edited by Kenneth R. Himes, 522–44. Washington, DC: Georgetown University Press, 2005.

Coleman, John A. "Neither Liberal nor Socialist: The Originality of Catholic Social Teaching." In *One Hundred Years of Catholic Social Thought: Celebration and Challenge*, edited by John A. Coleman, 25–42. Maryknoll, NY: Orbis Books, 1991.

Coley, Jonathan S. *Gay on God's Campus: Mobilizing for LGBT Equality at Christian Colleges and Universities*. Chapel Hill: University of North Carolina Press, 2018.

Cone, James H. *Black Theology and Black Power*. New York: Harper & Row, 1969.
Cortes, Ernesto, Jr. "Justice at the Gates of the City: A Model for Shared Prosperity." In *Back to Shared Prosperity: The Growing Inequality of Wealth and Income in America*, edited by Ray Marshall, 361–73. New York: Routledge, 2015.
Cox, Harvey. "The 'New Breed' in American Churches: Sources of Social Activism in Religion." *Daedalus* 96, no. 1 (1967).
Dalton, Frederick John. *The Moral Vision of César Chavez*. Maryknoll, NY: Orbis Books, 2003.
Daniel, Meghan. "The Social Movement for Reproductive Justice: Emergence, Intersectional Strategies, and Theory Building." *Sociology Compass* 15, no. 8 (2021): 1–13.
The David Seaton Show. WVON March 15, 2024, at 45:00, https://www.facebook.com/share/v/1AqyXnscMp/.
Davis, Allen. *Spearheads for Reform: The Social Settlements and the Progressive Movement, 1890–1914*. New York: Oxford University Press, 1967.
Day, Keri. *Azusa Reimagined: A Radical Vision of Religious and Democratic Belonging*. Stanford, CA: Stanford University Press, 2022.
Day, Keri. *Religious Resistance to Neoliberalism: Womanist and Black Feminist Perspectives*. New York: Palgrave Macmillan, 2016.
De La Torre, Miguel A. *The US Immigration Crisis: Toward an Ethics of Place*. Eugene, OR: Cascade Books, 2016.
DiAngelo, Robin. *White Fragility: Why It's So Hard for White People to Talk about Racism*. Boston: Beacon Press, 2018.
Dixie, Quinton Hosford, and Peter R. Eisenstadt. *Visions of a Better World: Howard Thurman's Pilgrimage to India and the Origins of African American Nonviolence*. Boston Beacon Press, 2011.
Dochuk, Darren. *From Bible Belt to Sunbelt: Plain-Folk Religion, Grassroots Politics, and the Rise of Evangelical Conservatism*. New York: W. W. Norton, 2012.
Doering, Bernard, ed. *The Philosopher and the Provocateur: The Correspondence of Jacques Maritain and Saul Alinsky*. Notre Dame, IN: University of Notre Dame Press, 1994.
Dorr, Donal. *Option for the Poor and for the Earth: From Leo XIII to Pope Francis*. Maryknoll, NY: Orbis Books, 2016.

Dorrien, Gary. *American Democratic Socialism: History, Politics, Religion, and Theory*. New Haven, CT: Yale University Press, 2021.

Dorrien, Gary. *Breaking White Supremacy: Martin Luther King Jr. and the Black Social Gospel*. New Haven, CT: Yale University Press, 2018.

Dorrien, Gary. *A Darkly Radiant Vision: The Black Social Gospel in the Shadow of MLK*. New Haven, CT: Yale University Press, 2023.

Dorrien, Gary. *In a Post-Hegelian Spirit: Philosophical Theology as Idealistic Discontent*. Waco, TX: Baylor University Press, 2020.

Dorrien, Gary. *The New Abolition: W. E. B. Du Bois and the Black Social Gospel*. New Haven, CT: Yale University Press, 2015.

Dorrien, Gary. *Over from Union Road: My Christian-Left-Intellectual Life*. Waco, TX: Baylor University Press, 2024.

Dorrien, Gary. "The Radical Social Gospel as Broad-Based Community Organizing." *Interventions*, April 5, 2024.

Dorrien, Gary J. *Reconstructing the Common Good: Theology and the Social Order*. Maryknoll, NY: Orbis Books, 1990.

Dorrien, Gary. *Social Democracy in the Making: Political and Religious Roots of European Socialism*. New Haven, CT: Yale University Press, 2019.

Dorrien, Gary. *Social Ethics in the Making: Interpreting an American Tradition*. Hoboken, NJ: Wiley-Blackwell, 2010.

Dorrien, Gary. "Social Ethics for Social Justice: The Legacies of the Social Gospel and a Case for Idealistic Discontent." In *Ethics and Advocacy: Bridges and Boundaries*, edited by Harlan Beckley, Douglas Ottati, Matthew Petrusek, and William Schweiker, 106–30. Eugene, OR: Cascade Books, 2022.

Dorrien, Gary. *The Spirit of American Liberal Theology: A History*. Louisville, KY: Westminster John Knox Press, 2023.

Dorrien, Gary. "Understanding Liberal Theology: An Interview with Gary Dorrien." August 15, 2023, https://adfontesjournal.com/interview/understanding-liberal-theology-an-interview-with-gary-dorrien/.

Dorrien, Gary, Nicholas Hayes-Mota, Charlene Sinclair, and Aaron Stauffer. "Organizing Visions: The Past, Present, and Future of Christian Social Ethics and Organizing Movements." Presented at the Society of Christian Ethics Annual Meeting, Chicago, January 5, 2023.

Drake, Janine Giordano. *The Gospel of Church: How Mainline Protestants Vilified Christian Socialism and Fractured the Labor Movement*. New York: Oxford University Press, 2024.

Du Bois, W. E. B. "The African Roots of the War." *Atlantic Monthly* 115 (May 1915): 707–14.

Dubler, Joshua, and Vincent Lloyd. *Break Every Yoke: Religion, Justice, and the Abolition of Prisons*. New York: Oxford University Press, 2019.

Dunbar, Anthony P. *Against the Grain: Southern Radicals and Prophets, 1929–1959*. Charlottesville: University Press of Virginia, 1981.

Dworkin, Ronald. *Life's Dominion: An Argument about Abortion, Euthanasia, and Individual Freedom*. New York: Vintage Books, 1994.

Dworkin, Ronald. "Objectivity and Truth: You'd Better Believe It." *Philosophy and Public Affairs* 25, no. 2 (1996): 87–139.

Eguizábal, Cristina, Matthew C. Ingram, Karise M. Curtis, Aaron Korthuis, Eric L. Olson and Nicholas Phillips. "Crime and Violence in Central America's Northern Triangle: How US Policy Responses are Helping, Hurting, and Can Be Improved." Woodrow Wilson Center Reports on the Americas, December 18, 2014.

Ely, Richard. *The Social Aspects of Christianity*. London: Thomas Y. Crowell, 1889.

Engel, Lawrence J. "The Influence of Saul Alinsky on the Campaign for Human Development." *Theological Studies* 59, no. 4 (1998): 636–61.

Engel, Lawrence J. "Saul Alinsky and the Chicago School." *Journal of Speculative Philosophy*, new series, 16, no. 1 (2002): 50–61.

Evans, Curtis J. *A Theology of Brotherhood: The Federal Council of Churches and the Problem of Race*. New York: New York University Press, 2024.

Evans, Maxwell. "Closed South Shore School Will Become Police Training Center as City Council Approves Controversial Plan." Block Club Chicago. April 24, 2020. https://blockclubchicago.org/2020/04/24/closed-south-shore-school-will-become-police-training-center-as-city-council-approves-controversial-plan/.

Ewing, Eve L. *Ghosts in the Schoolyard: Racism and School Closings on Chicago's South Side*. Chicago: University of Chicago Press, 2018.

Farneth, Molly. *Hegel's Social Ethics: Religion, Conflict, and Rituals of Reconciliation*. Princeton, NJ: Princeton University Press, 2017.

Farneth, Molly. *The Politics of Ritual*. Princeton, NJ: Princeton University Press, 2023.

Ferguson, Robert Hunt. *Remaking the Rural South: Interracialism, Christian Socialism, and Cooperative Farming in Jim Crow Mississippi*. Athens: University of Georgia Press, 2018.

Fetner, Tina. *How the Religious Right Shaped Lesbian and Gay Activism*. Minneapolis: University of Minnesota Press, 2008.

Finks, P. David. *The Radical Vision of Saul Alinsky*. New York: Paulist Press, 1984.

Fisher, Robert. *Let the People Decide: Neighborhood Organizing in America*. Boston: Twayne Publishing, 1984.

Floyd-Thomas, Stacey M. *Mining the Motherlode: Methods in Womanist Ethics*. Cleveland: Pilgrim Press, 2006.

Floyd-Thomas, Stacey M. *When the Good Life Goes Bad: The US and Our Seven Deadly Sins*. Forthcoming 2026.

Floyd-Thomas, Stacey M., ed. *Deeper Shades of Purple: Womanism in Religion and Society*. New York: New York University Press, 2006.

Fraser, Nancy. "Behind Marx's Hidden Abode." *New Left Review*, no. 86 (April 1, 2014): 55–72.

Fraser, Nancy, and Axel Honneth. *Redistribution or Recognition? A Political-Philosophical Exchange*. New York: Verso, 2003.

Freire, Paulo. "The 'Banking' Concept of Education." In *The Pedagogy of the Oppressed*. New York: Herder and Herder, 1970.

Freire, Paulo, and Antonio Faundez. *Learning to Question: A Pedagogy of Liberation*. New York: Continuum, 1989.

Frisbie, Margery. *An Alley in Chicago: The Life and Legacy of Monsignor John Egan*. Franklin, WI: Sheed & Ward, 2002.

Fulton, Brad, and Richard L. Wood. "Interfaith Community Organizing: Emerging Theological and Organizational Challenges." In *Yours the Power: Faith-Based Organizing in the USA*, edited by Katie Day, Esther McIntosh, and William Storrar, 17–40. Leiden: Brill, 2013.

Ganz, Marshall. *People, Power, Change: Organizing for Democratic Renewal*. New York: Oxford University Press, 2024.

Giddings, Paula. *When and Where I Enter: The Impact of Black Women on Race and Sex in America*. New York: Morrow, 1984.

Givan, Rebecca Kolins, Kenneth M. Roberts, and Sarah A. Soule. *The Diffusion of Social Movements: Actors, Mechanisms, and Political Effects*. Cambridge: Cambridge University Press, 2010.

Givens, Jarvis. *Fugitive Pedagogy: Carter G. Woodson and the Art of Black Teaching*. Cambridge, MA: Harvard University Press, 2021.

Gonzalez, Juan. "The Current Migrant Crisis: How US Policy toward Latin America Has Fueled Historic Numbers of Asylum Seekers." Great Cities Institute, October 2023.

Gould, Elise, and Josh Bivens. "There's No Debate: Measurable Income Inequity Has Skyrocketed in Recent Decades." Economic Policy Institute, January 18, 2024. https://www.epi.org/blog/theres-no-debate-measurable-income-inequality-has-skyrocketed-in-recent-decades/.

Gourevitch, Alexander. *From Slavery to the Cooperative Commonwealth: Labor and Republican Liberty in the Nineteenth Century*. New York: Cambridge University Press, 2015.

Gramsci, Antonio, et al. *Selections from the Prison Notebooks of Antonio Gramsci*. 1st ed. New York: International, 1971.

Gran, Peter. *Beyond Eurocentrism: A New View of Modern World History*. Syracuse, NY: Syracuse University Press, 1996.

Greene, Alison Collis. *No Depression in Heaven: The Great Depression, the New Deal, and the Transformation of Religion in the Delta*. New York: Oxford University Press, 2016.

Grubbs, Donald H. *Cry from the Cotton: The Southern Tenant Farmers' Union and the New Deal*. Chapel Hill: University of North Carolina Press, 1971.

Gushee, David P. *Defending Democracy from Its Christian Enemies*. Grand Rapids: Eerdmans, 2023.

Gutiérrez, Gustavo. *A Theology of Liberation: History, Politics, and Salvation*. Translated by Caridad Inda and John Eagleson. Maryknoll, NY: Orbis Books, 1973.

Hall, David D., ed. *Lived Religion in America: Toward a History of Practice*. Princeton, NJ: Princeton University Press, 1997.

Harrington, Michael. *The Other America: Poverty in the United States*. New York: Simon & Schuster, 1962.

Hart, Stephen. *Cultural Dilemmas of Progressive Politics: Styles of Engagement across Grassroots Activists*. Chicago: University of Chicago Press, 2001.

Hartman, Saidiya V. "The Time of Slavery." *South Atlantic Quarterly* 101, no. 4 (2002): 757–77. https://muse.jhu.edu/article/39111.

Haslanger, Sally. "What Is a Social Practice?" *Royal Institute of Philosophy Supplement, London* 82 (July 2018): 231–47.

Hayes-Mota, Nicholas. "Partners in Forming the People: Jacques Maritain, Saul Alinsky, and the Project of Personalist Democracy." *Journal of Moral Theology* 13, special issue no. 1 (2024): 121–45.

Hayes-Mota, Nicholas. "Practicing the Common Good: Catholic Tradition, Community Organizing, and the Virtues of Democratic Politics." PhD diss., Boston College, 2023.

Hayes-Mota, Nicholas. "Principle in Practice: A MacIntyrean Analysis of Community Organizing and the Catholic Social Tradition." *Journal of Catholic Social Thought* 21, no. 2 (2024): 207–28.

Hedge Clippers, "Hedge Papers No. 43: Connecticut Billionaires and Their Lucrative Loophole," *Hedge Papers*, no.43, February 7, 2017, https://hedgeclippers.org/hedge-papers-no-43-connecticut-billionaires-and-their-lucrative-loophole/.

Heineman, Kenneth. *A Catholic New Deal: Religion and Reform in Depression Pittsburgh*. University Park: Pennsylvania State University Press, 1999.

Heyer, Kristin E. *Kinship across Borders: A Christian Ethic of Immigration*. Washington, DC: Georgetown University Press, 2012.

Higginbotham, Evelyn. *Righteous Discontent: The Women's Movement in the Black Baptist Church, 1880–1920*. Cambridge, MA: Harvard University Press, 1993.

Hollenbach, David. *The Common Good and Christian Ethics*. Cambridge: Cambridge University Press, 2002.

Holm, Charles. "'To Be Free from the Slavery of Capitalism' : David Walker, Peter H. Clark, and George Washington Woodbey's Black Socialist Thought." PhD diss., University of Texas, Austin, 2021.

Hondagneu-Sotelo, Pierrette. *God's Heart Has No Borders: How Religious Activists Are Working for Immigrant Rights*. Berkeley: University of California Press, 2008.

hooks, bell. *All About Love: New Visions*. New York: Harper Collins, 2001.

hooks, bell. *Teaching Critical Thinking: Practical Wisdom*. Teaching Trilogy, vol. 3. New York: Routledge, 2010.

hooks, bell. *Teaching to Transgress: Education as the Practice of Freedom*. New York: Routledge, 1994.

Horton, Myles, and Paulo Freire. *We Make the Road by Walking: Conversations on Education and Social Change*. Philadelphia: Temple University Press, 1990.

Horwitt, Sanford D. *Let Them Call Me Rebel: Saul Alinsky—His Life and Legacy*. New York: Vintage, 1989.

Hull House Maps and Papers. New York: Crowell, 1895.

Hurston, Zora Neale. *Their Eyes Were Watching God*. London: Virago Press, 2018.

Jasper, James M., and Jeff Goodwin, eds. *The Social Movements Reader: Cases and Concepts*. Malden, MA: Wiley-Blackwell, 2015.

Jennings, Willie James. *After Whiteness: An Education in Belonging*. Grand Rapids: Eerdmans, 2020.

Katz, Michael. *In the Shadow of the Poorhouse*. New York: Basic Books, 1996.

Kester, Howard. "Ceremony of the Land." Folder 214 in the Howard Kester Papers #3834, Southern Historical Collection, Wilson Special Collections Library, University of North Carolina at Chapel Hill.

Kester, Howard. *Revolt among the Sharecroppers*. New York: Covici, Friede, 1936.

Kierkegaard, Søren. *Søren Kierkegaards Skrifter*. Copenhagen: Søren Kierkegaard Research Center, 1997. *Journalen* JJ:167 (1843), vol. 18, 306.

King, Martin Luther, Jr. "I Have a Dream." March on Washington for Jobs and Freedom, August 28, 1963, Lincoln Memorial, Washington, DC.

King, Martin Luther, Jr. "The Minister to the Valley." February 23, 1968, retrieved from the archives of the SCLC as quoted in Andrew J. Douglas and Jared A. Loggins, *Prophet of Discontent: Martin Luther King Jr. and the Critique of Racial Capitalism*. Athens: University of Georgia Press, 2021.

Kirschner, Don. *The Paradox of Professionalism: Reform and Public Service in Urban America, 1900–1940*. New York: Greenwood Press, 1986.

Korsgaard, Christine M. *Creating the Kingdom of Ends*. New York: Cambridge University Press, 1996.

Lambelet, Kyle B. T. *¡Presente!: Nonviolent Politics and the Resurrection of the Dead*. Washington, DC: Georgetown University Press, 2020.

LeFevre, Perry D. *Challenge and Response: The Chicago Theological Seminary Story, 1960–1980*. Chicago: Exploration Press, 1999.

Liboiron, Max. *Pollution Is Colonialism*. Durham, NC: Duke University Press, 2021.

Lisi, Gabriella, and George Schmidt. "Counter Memory with Wilson Dickinson." *Religion and Justice*. Accessed June 5, 2024. https://www.buzzsprout.com/2237315/14373019-counter-memory-with-wilson-dickinson-grant-series.

Lloyd, Vincent W. *Black Dignity: The Struggle against Domination*. New Haven, CT: Yale University Press, 2022.

Loomer, Bernard. "Two Conceptions of Power." *Process Studies* 6, no. 1 (April 1, 1976): 5–32.

Luecke, Richard Henry. "Protestant Clergy: New Forms of Ministry, New Forms of Training." *Annals of the American Academy of Political and Social Science* 387 (1970).

Lukes, Steven. *Power: A Radical View*. London: Bloomsbury Academic, 2021.
MacIntyre, Alasdair. *After Virtue: A Study in Moral Theory*. Notre Dame, IN: University of Notre Dame Press, 1984.
MacIntyre, Alasdair. *Ethics in the Conflicts of Modernity: An Essay on Desire, Practical Reasoning, and Narrative*. Cambridge: Cambridge University Press, 2016.
MacIntyre, Alasdair. "Politics, Philosophy, and the Common Good." In *The MacIntyre Reader*, edited by Kelvin Knight, 235–54. Oxford: Polity Press, 1998.
MacIntyre, Alasdair. *Whose Justice? Which Rationality?* Notre Dame, IN: University of Notre Dame Press, 1988.
Mainwaring, Scott, and Timothy Scully, eds. *Christian Democracy in Latin America*. Stanford, CA: Stanford University Press, 2003.
Martin, Robert F. *Howard Kester and the Struggle for Social Justice in the South, 1904–1977*. Charlottesville: University Press of Virginia, 1991.
Maxwell, Carol J. C. *Pro-Life Activists in America: Meaning, Motivation, and Direct Action*. Cambridge: Cambridge University Press, 2002.
McAdam, Doug. *Political Process and the Development of Black Insurgency, 1930–1970*. Chicago: University of Chicago Press, 1999.
McAlevey, Jane. *A Collective Bargain: Unions, Organizing, and the Fight for Democracy*. New York: Ecco, an imprint of HarperCollins Publishers, 2020.
McAlevey, Jane. *No Shortcuts: Organizing for Power in the New Gilded Age*. New York: Oxford University Press, 2016.
McCarraher, Eugene. *Christian Critics: Religion and the Impasse in Modern American Social Thought*. Ithaca, NY: Cornell University Press, 2000.
McGiffert, Arthur Cushman. *No Ivory Tower: The Story of the Chicago Theological Seminary*. Chicago: Chicago Theological Seminary, 1965.
McKnight, John. "Professionalized Service and Disabling Help." In *The Disabling Professions*, edited by Ivan Illich, 69–91. London: Marion Boyars, 1977.
McIntosh, Alastair, and Matt Carmichael. *Spiritual Activism: Leadership as Service*. Cambridge: Green Books, 2016.
McLaren, Peter. "Critical Pedagogy: A Look at the Major Concepts." In *The Critical Pedagogy Reader*, edited by Antonia Darder, Rodolfo D. Torres, and Marta P. Baltodanao. New York: Routledge, 2017.
McWhorter, John. *Woke Racism: How a New Religion Has Betrayed Black America*. New York: Portfolio, 2021.

Mendoza, S. Lily. "Transdiasporic Indigeneity and Decolonizing Faith." In *Decolonizing Ecotheology: Indigenous and Subaltern Challenges*, edited by S. Lily Mendoza and George Zachariah, 155–78. Eugene, OR: Pickwick, 2022.

Metz, Johann Baptist. *Theology of the World*. Translated by William Glen-Doepel. New York: Seabury, 1969.

Minus, Paul. *Walter Rauschenbusch: American Reformer*. New York: Macmillan, 1988.

Misner, Paul, *Catholic Labor Movements in Europe: Social Thought and Action, 1914–1965*. Washington, DC: Catholic University of America Press, 2015.

Misner, Paul. *Social Catholicism in Europe: From the Onset of Industrialization to the First World War*. London: Darton, Longman, and Todd, 1991.

Moe-Lobeda, Cynthia. "Faith and #BlackLivesMatter: Future Directions and Current Directives for White Folk." *Currents in Theology and Mission* 49, no. 1 (January 2022).

Moltmann, Jürgen. *Religion, Revolution, and the Future*. Translated by M. Douglas Meeks. New York: Charles Scribner's Sons, 1969.

Monahan, Michael J. "Emancipatory Affect: bell hooks on Love and Liberation." *CLR James Journal* 17, no. 1 (Fall 2011): 102–11.

Moore, Natalie Y. "Black Chicago, Let's Check Our Attitudes on Migrants." *Chicago Sun-Times*, October 19, 2023, sec. Columnists. https://chicago.suntimes.com/columnists/2023/10/19/23923937/black-chicago-lets-check-our-attitudes-on-migrants.

Morris, Aldon D. *The Origins of the Civil Rights Movement*. New York: Free Press, 1984.

Morris, Viki. "The Woman from Welfare Rights." *World Magazine*, n.d., Beulah Sanders family collection.

Munson, Ziad W. *The Making of Pro-Life Activists: How Social Movement Mobilization Works*. Chicago: University of Chicago Press, 2010.

Murakawa, Naomi. "The Origins of the Carceral Crisis: Racial Order as 'Law And Order' in Postwar American Politics." In *Race and American Political Development*, edited by Joseph E. Lowndes, Julie Novkov, and Dorian Warren. New York: Routledge, 2008.

National Council of Churches. "About the National Council of the Churches of Christ in the USA," https://nationalcouncilofchurches.us/about-us/.

Nepstad, Sharon Erickson. *Convictions of the Soul: Religion, Culture, and Agency in the Central American Solidarity Movement*. New York: Oxford University Press, 2004.

Niebuhr, Reinhold. *Moral Man and Immoral Society: A Study in Ethics and Politics*. London: C. Scribner's, 1932.

Niebuhr, Reinhold. *Reflections on the End of an Era*. New York: C. Scribner's Sons, 1934.

Niemonen, Jack. "Antiracist Education in Theory and Practice: A Critical Assessment." *American Sociologist* 38, no. 2 (June 2007): 159–77. https://www.jstor.org/stable/27700497.

Nutt, Rick. *The Whole Gospel for the Whole World: Sherwood Eddy and the American Protestant Mission*. Macon, GA: Mercer University Press, 1997.

Nyquist, Mary. *Arbitrary Rule: Slavery, Tyranny, and the Power of Life and Death*. Chicago: University of Chicago Press, 2013.

O'Brien, David J., and Thomas A. Shannon, eds. *Catholic Social Thought: Encyclicals and Documents from Pope Leo XIII to Pope Francis*. Maryknoll, NY: Orbis Books, 2016.

Orsi, Robert A. *The Madonna of 115th Street: Faith and Community in Italian Harlem, 1880–1950*. New Haven, CT: Yale University Press, 2002.

Owens, Ernest. "Mazzoni Staff Forced Firing of Alt-Right-Supporting Anti-Union Consultants." *Philadelphia*, September 11, 2017. https://www.phillymag.com/news/2017/09/11/mazzoni-center-anti-union-consultants/.

Palmer, Parker J. *The Courage to Teach*. San Francisco: Jossey-Bass, 2017.

Payne, Charles M. *I've Got the Light of Freedom: The Organizing Tradition and the Mississippi Freedom Struggle*. Berkeley: University of California Press, 2007.

Peabody, Francis. *Jesus Christ and the Social Question*. New York: Macmillan, 1900.

Peters, Rebecca Todd. *Trust Women: A Progressive Christian Argument for Reproductive Justice*. Boston: Beacon Press, 2018.

Pettit, Philip. *Republicanism: A Theory of Freedom and Government*. Oxford: Oxford University Press, 1997.

Pew Research Center. "2023–24 US Religious Landscape Study Interactive Database," 2025.

Pew Research Center. "The Future of World Religions: Population Growth Projections, 2010–2050." April 2, 2015. https://www.pewresearch.org/religion/2015/04/02/religious-projections-2010-2050/.

Pharo, Zoe. "South Shore Residents Blast City's Plan to House Migrants at Repurposed School." *Hyde Park Herald*, May 5, 2023. https://www.hpherald.com/evening_digest/south-shore-residents-blast-city-s-plan-to-house-migrants-at-repurposed-school/article_c88111c0-eb95-11ed-9d16-47da2eaed89f.html.

Phillips [Maparyan], Layli. "Introduction: Womanism—On Its Own." In *The Womanist Reader*, ed. Layli Phillips [Maparyan]. New York: Taylor and Francis, 2006.

Phillips, Paul T. *A Kingdom on Earth: Anglo-American Social Christianity, 1880–1940*. University Park: Penn State University Press, 1996.

Piven, Frances Fox, and Richard A. Cloward. *Poor People's Movements: Why They Succeed, How They Fail*. New York: Vintage Books, 1977.

Pontifical Council for Justice and Peace. *Compendium of the Social Doctrine of the Church*. 2004. https://www.vatican.va/roman_curia/pontifical_councils/justpeace/documents/rc_pc_justpeace_doc_20060526_compendio-dott-soc_en.html.

Pope Francis. *Laudato Si'*. 2015. https://www.vatican.va/content/francesco/en/encyclicals/documents/papa-francesco_20150524_enciclica-laudato-si.html.

Pope John Paul II. *Sollicitudo Rei Socialis*. 1987. https://www.vatican.va/content/john-paul-ii/en/encyclicals/documents/hf_jp-ii_enc_30121987_sollicitudo-rei-socialis.html.

Pope John XXIII. *Pacem in Terris*. 1963. https://www.vatican.va/content/john-xxiii/en/encyclicals/documents/hf_j-xxiii_enc_11041963_pacem.html.

Pope Leo XIII. *Rerum Novarum: The Condition of Labor*. 1891. In *Catholic Social Thought: The Documentary Heritage*, edited by David J. O'Brien and Thomas A. Shannon, 14–39. Maryknoll, NY: Orbis Books, 1992.

Pope Paul VI. *Gaudium et Spes*. 1965. https://www.vatican.va/archive/hist_councils/ii_vatican_council/documents/vat-ii_const_19651207_gaudium-et-spes_en.html.

Pope Pius XI. *Quadragesimo Anno*. 1931. https://www.vatican.va/content/pius-xi/en/encyclicals/documents/hf_p-xi_enc_19310515_quadragesimo-anno.html.

Ramsay, Edmund. "WVON Radio and the Black Public Sphere," n.d. https://communication.depaul.edu/academics/digital-communication-and-media-arts/student-resources/complete-your-degree/Documents/Project%20Examples/EdRamsay_WVON%20Radio%20and%20the%20Black%20Public%20Sphere.pdf.
Ransby, Barbara. *Ella Baker and the Black Freedom Movement: A Radical Democratic Vision*. Chapel Hill: University of North Carolina Press, 2003.
Rieger, Joerg. *Theology in the Capitalocene: Ecology, Identity, Class, and Solidarity*. Minneapolis: Fortress Press, 2022.
Rieger, Joerg, and Rosemarie Henkel-Rieger. "Deep Solidarity: Broadening the Basis of Transformation." *HTS Teologiese Studies / Theological Studies* 73, no. 3 (November 24, 2017).
Rieger, Joerg, and Rosemarie Henkel-Rieger. *Unified We Are a Force: How Faith and Labor Can Overcome America's Inequalities*. St. Louis, MO: Chalice Press, 2016.
Riggs, Marcia, ed. *Can I Get a Witness? Prophetic Religious Voices of African American Women: An Anthology*. Maryknoll, NY: Orbis Books, 1997.
Ringer, Christophe Darro. *Necropolitics: The Religious Crisis of Mass Incarceration in America*. Religion and Race. Lanham, MD: Lexington Books, 2021.
Ringer, Christophe Darro. "Tangle of Perils: The Eschatological Dilemma of Black Families in America." *Concilium: International Journal of Theology* 2 (2016).
Robert, Nikia. "Not Meant to Survive: Black Mothers Leading beyond the Criminal Line." In *Walking through the Valley*, edited by Emilie Townes et al., 107–22. Louisville, KY: Westminister John Knox Press, 2022.
Robnett, Belinda. *How Long? How Long? African American Women in the Struggle for Civil Rights*. New York: Oxford University Press, 1997.
Rogers, Mary Beth. *Cold Anger: A Story of Faith and Power Politics*. Denton: University of North Texas Press, 1990.
Rogers, Melvin L. *The Undiscovered Dewey: Religion, Morality, and the Ethos of Democracy*. New York: Columbia University Press, 2009.
Roll, Jarod. *Spirit of Rebellion: Labor and Religion in the New Cotton South*. Urbana: University of Illinois Press, 2010.
Ross, Loretta J. "Reproductive Justice as Intersectional Feminist Activism." *Souls: A Critical Journal of Black Politics, Culture, and Society* 19, no. 3 (2017): 286–314.

Rowlands, Anna. *Towards a Politics of Communion: Catholic Social Teaching in Dark Times*. London: T&T Clark, 2022.
Roy, Diana. "Do US Sanctions on Venezuela Work?" *Council on Foreign Relations* online, November 4, 2022. Accessed April 4, 2025. https://www.cfr.org/in-brief/do-us-sanctions-venezuela-work.
Ryan, John A. *A Living Wage*. New York: Macmillan, 1906.
Sanders, Beulah. "Speech to NCC, Houston, December 1972." *Guida West Papers*, Smith College Archives, box 11, folder 1, transcript.
Santow, Mark. *Saul Alinsky and the Dilemmas of Race: Community Organizing in the Postwar City*. Chicago: University of Chicago Press, 2023.
Schutz, Aaron, and Mike Miller, eds. *People Power: The Community Organizing Tradition of Saul Alinsky*. Nashville: Vanderbilt University Press, 2015.
Scott, James C. *Seeing Like a State: How Certain Schemes to Improve the Human Condition Have Failed*. New Haven, CT: Yale University Press, 1998.
Sen, Rinku. *Stir It Up*. San Francisco: Jossey-Bass, 2003.
Shannon, Thomas A. "Commentary on *Rerum Novarum* (The Condition of Labor)." In *Modern Catholic Social Teaching: Commentaries and Interpretations*, edited by Kenneth R. Himes et al. Washington, DC: Georgetown University Press, 2005, 127–50.
Shapiro, Karin A. *A New South Rebellion: The Battle against Convict Labor in the Tennessee Coalfields, 1871–1896*. Chapel Hill: University of North Carolina Press, 1998.
Shelby, Tommie. *Dark Ghettos: Injustice, Dissent, and Reform*. Cambridge, MA: Harvard University Press, 2016.
Shelby, Tommie. "Justice, Work, and the Ghetto Poor." *Law and Ethics of Human Rights* 6, no. 1 (2012).
Smith, Christian. "Correcting a Curious Neglect, or Bringing Religion Back In." In *Disruptive Religion: The Force of Faith in Social-Movement Activism*, 1–13. New York: Routledge, 1997.
Smith, Christian. *The Emergence of Liberation Theology: Radical Religion and Social Movement Theory*. Chicago: University of Chicago Press, 1991.
Smith, Christian, ed. *Disruptive Religion: The Force of Faith in Social-Movement Activism*. New York: Routledge, 1996.
Smith, Linda Tuhiwai. *Decolonizing Methodologies: Research and Indigenous Peoples*. London: Zed Books, 2021.

Smith, Ted. *The End of Theological Education*. Grand Rapids: Eerdmans, 2023.
Snarr, C. Melissa. *All You That Labor: Religion and Ethics in the Living Wage Movement*. New York: New York University Press, 2011.
Snow, David A. *A Primer on Social Movements*. New York: W. W. Norton, 2010.
Soja, Edward W. *Postmodern Geographies: The Reassertion of Space in Critical Social Theory*. New York: Verso Books, 1989.
Soja, Edward W. *Seeking Spatial Justice*. Minneapolis: University of Minnesota Press, 2010.
Sölle, Dorothee. *Beyond Mere Obedience: Reflections on a Christian Ethic for the Future*. Minneapolis: Augsburg Press, 1970.
Stassen, Glen H. *A Thicker Jesus: Incarnational Discipleship in a Secular Age*. Louisville, KY: Westminster John Knox Press, 2012.
Stauffer, Aaron K. "'American Democratic Socialism' by Gary Dorrien." *Tikkun*, July 19, 2022/ https://www.tikkun.org/review-american-democratic-socialism-history-politics-religion-and-theory-by-gary-dorrien/.
Stauffer, Aaron. *Listening to the Spirit: The Radical Social Gospel, Sacred Value, and Broad-based Community Organizing*. New York: Oxford University Press, 2024.
Stauffer, Aaron. "Power in the Social Gospel: Howard Kester, Claude Williams, and the Southern Tenant Farmers Union." *Religions* 15, no. 9 (September 1, 2024).
Stauffer, Aaron. "Sacred Roots: Exploring the Social Gospel in the Southern United States (Grant Series)." *Religion and Justice*. Accessed June 5, 2024. https://open.spotify.com/show/0ejqgxSgGGfCdPc20wGBoZ.
Stauffer, Aaron. "The Theologically Trained Organizer." *Christian Century*, February 2024. Accessed February 15, 2024. https://www.christiancentury.org/features/theologically-trained-organizer.
Stout, Jeffrey. *Blessed Are the Organized: Grassroots Democracy in America*. Princeton, NJ: Princeton University Press, 2010.
Stout, Jeffrey. *Democracy and Tradition*. Princeton, NJ: Princeton University Press, 2004.
Taylor, Graham. *Chicago Commons through Forty Years*. Chicago: Chicago Commons Association, 1936.
Taylor, Graham. *Pioneering on Social Frontiers*. Chicago: University of Chicago Press, 1930.
Taylor, Graham. *Religion in Social Action*. New York: Dodd, Mead, 1913.
Teo, Thomas. "Culture-Supremacy: Expressions, Sources, and Resistance to a Psychology of Motivated Ignorance." *Research in the Social Scientific Study of Religion* 32 (2022).

Thompson, Michael G. *For God and Globe: Christian Internationalism in the United States between the Great War and the Cold War*. Ithaca, NY: Cornell University Press, 2015.

Thurman, Howard. *Meditations of the Heart*. Boston: Beacon Press, 2023.

Todd, George, and Trey Hammond. *Exposure and Risk: The Great Coming Church*. CreateSpace Independent Publishing Platform, 2016.

Townes, Emilie Maureen. *In a Blaze of Glory: Womanist Spirituality as Social Witness*. Nashville: Abingdon Press, 1995.

Trolander, Judith Ann. *Professionalism and Social Change: From the Settlement House Movement to Neighborhood Centers, 1886 to the Present*. New York: Columbia University Press, 1987.

Tuck, Eve, and K. Wayne Yang. "Decolonization Is Not a Metaphor." *Decolonization: Indigeneity, Education, and Society* 1, no. 1 (September 8, 2012).

Unger, Roberto Mangabeira. *What Should the Left Propose?* London: Verso, 2005.

Verstraeten, Johan. "Re-Thinking Catholic Social Thought as Tradition." In *Catholic Social Thought: Twilight or Renaissance?* edited by J. S. Boswell, F. P. McHugh, and J. Verstraeten, 59–78. Leuven, Belgium: Leuven University Press, 2000.

Walker, Alice. *In Search of Our Mothers' Gardens: Womanist Prose*. San Diego: Harcourt Brace Jovanovich, 1983.

Walker, Keith. "Transformational and Enduring Vision of Aimé Césaire." *PMLA* 125, no. 3 (May 2010): 756–63.

Warren, Mark R. *Dry Bones Rattling: Community Building to Revitalize American Democracy*. Princeton, NJ: Princeton University Press, 2001.

WBEZ and *Chicago Sun-Times*. "Chicago's 50 Closed Schools." Accessed April 4, 2025. https://www.wbez.org/chicagos-50-closed-schools.

Weir, Robert E. *Beyond Labor's Veil: The Culture of the Knights of Labor*. University Park: Pennsylvania State University Press, 1996.

Welfare Fighter. *The Welfare Fighter* 3, no. 5 (June 1972). Microform. Columbia University.

West, Cornel. *Race Matters*. New York: Vintage Books, 1995.

West, Guida. Interview of Beulah Sanders. July 9, 1983. New York City. Guida West Papers, Smith College Archives, box 11, folder 2, audio file and transcript.

West, Guida. *The National Welfare Rights Movement: The Social Protest of Poor Women*. New York: Praeger, 1981.

West, Traci C. *Disruptive Christian Ethics: When Racism and Women's Lives Matter*. Louisville, KY: Westminster John Knox Press, 2006.
Whitmore, Todd David. "Catholic Social Teaching: Starting with the Common Good." In *Living the Catholic Social Tradition: Cases and Commentary*, edited by Kathleen Maas Weigert and Alexia K. Kelley, 59–85. Lanham, MD: Rowman & Littlefield, 2005.
Wild, Mark. "Liberal Protestants and Urban Renewal." *Religion and American Culture: A Journal of Interpretation* 25, no. 1 (2015).
Williams, Delores S. "The Color of Feminism: Or Speaking the Black Woman's Tongue." In *Feminist Theological Ethics: A Reader*, edited by Lois K. Daly. Louisville, KY: Westminster John Knox Press, 1994.
Williams, Robert R. *Hegel's Ethics of Recognition*. Berkeley: University of California Press, 1997.
Wimmer, Franz Martin. "Cultural Centrisms and Intercultural Polylogues in Philosophy." *International Review of Information Ethics* 7 (September 2007): 82–89.
Wink, Walter. *Engaging the Powers: Discernment and Resistance in a World of Domination*. Powers Trilogy, vol. 3. Minneapolis: Fortress Press, 1992.
Winter, Gibson. *The Suburban Captivity of the Churches: An Analysis of Protestant Responsibility in the Expanding Metropolis*. Garden City, NY: Doubleday, 1961.
Wolin, Sheldon S. *Fugitive Democracy: And Other Essays*. Princeton, NJ: Princeton University Press, 2016.
Wolterstorff, Nicholas. *Justice in Love*. Grand Rapids: Eerdmans, 2015.
Wood, Richard L. *Faith in Action: Religion, Race, and Democratic Organizing in America*. Chicago: University of Chicago Press, 2002.
Wood, Richard L., and Brad R. Fulton. *A Shared Future: Faith-Based Organizing for Ethical Democracy*. Chicago: University of Chicago Press, 2015.
Woodruff, Nan Elizabeth. *American Congo: The African American Freedom Struggle in the Delta*. Cambridge, MA: Harvard University Press, 2003.
Woods, Clyde Adrian. *Development Arrested: The Blues and Plantation Power in the Mississippi Delta*. New York: Verso, 2017.
Wynter, Sylvia. "Unsettling the Coloniality of Being/Power/Truth/Freedom: Towards the Human, After Man, Its Overrepresentation—An Argument." *CR: The New Centennial Review* 3, no. 3 (2003): 257–337.

Younger, George. *From New Creation to Urban Crisis: A History of Action Training Ministries, 1962–1975*. Chicago: CSSR, 1987.

Yukich, Grace. *One Family under God: Immigration Politics and Progressive Religion in America*. New York: Oxford University Press, 2013.

Zalzman, Nell. "Two Years after Migrants Began to Arrive, Many Have Settled in Chicago Even as Some Continue to Struggle." *Chicago Tribune*, September 13, 2024. https://www.chicagotribune.com/2024/09/02/two-years-after-migrants-began-to-arrive-many-have-settled-in-chicago-even-as-some-continue-to-struggle/.

Zeitz, Josh. "How Trump Is Recycling Nixon's 'Law and Order' Playbook." *Politico Magazine*, July 18, 2016. https://www.politico.com/magazine/story/2016/07/donald-trump-law-and-order-richard-nixon-crime-race-214066.

Zimmerman, Yvonne C. *Other Dreams of Freedom: Religion, Sex, and Human Trafficking*. New York: Oxford University Press, 2013.

Index

Abbott, Greg, xxxiii, 149
abortion, 89–90, 127
Addams, Jane, 26–28, 30, 31, 32, 37
After Virtue (MacIntyre), 44, 48
After Whiteness (Jennings), 115, 136
agitation, role in organizing, 60, 105, 107, 108–9, 201–2
Agricultural Adjustment Act (AAA), 14–15
Aho, James, 122
Alden, John, 12
Alicea, Benjamin, 39–40
Alinsky, Saul, 36, 40, 41
   BYOC, launching, 37–38
   IAF, as founding, 47, 58, 61, 62–63, 66
   organizational legacy of, 42, 57, 58, 64, 189, 205
   social Catholicism, alignment with, 43, 58–66, 67–68
All You That Labor (Snarr), xxxi
American Economic Association, xv
American Exceptionalism, xii
American Federation of Labor, xx, 11
Angelou, Maya, 170
Azusa Reimagined (Day), 41
Azusa Street revival, 41

Back of the Yards Neighborhood Council (BYNC), 59, 60, 61
Back of the Yards Organizing Council (BYOC), 37–38
Baker, Carolyn, xxvii, 205, 206
Baker, Ella Jo, 42, 81, 200
Barbour, J. Pius, xix
Baril, Rob, 94
Barnett, Samuel, 25–26

Barry, David, 35
Baumann, John, 64
Belafonte, Harry, 69
Benedict, Don, 23, 34–35
Berger, Peter, 184–85, 206
Berry, Malinda Elizabeth, xxxii
Black community, 8, 9, 81, 130, 153, 183
   African Americans, 34, 156–57, 172–73
   Black churches, 16, 92, 125
   Black education, 172–73
   Black Power movement, 150
   Black Protestants, 58, 62, 64
   Black sanitation workers, 182
   Black social gospellers, 120, 175
   Black-led organizing, 42, 81
   enslavement of, 13, 74
   NWRO, Black membership in, 71, 78
   as oppressed, 78, 125
   poor Black women, 69, 78, 79
   sharecropping, Black nationalists on, 5–6
   womanist writings, Black women in, 81, 140–41
Black Lives Matter movement, 129, 135–36
Bliss, W. D. P., xiv, xvii, xxvi
Bonhoeffer, Dietrich, 206
Bonnett, Alastair, 143–44, 146
Booth, Charles, 28
Bourdieu, Pierre, xxxviii
Braunstein, Ruth, 122, 126
Bretherton, Luke, 62, 123
broad-based community organizing (BBCO), 197–98
Brower, K. B., xxix–xxx

Burgess, Ernst, 37
Burke, Edmund, 44
Bush, George W., xii

Cahill, Lisa Sowle, xxvi
Cain and Abel narrative, 70, 77–78
Can I Get a Witness? (Riggs), 81
Cannon, Katie, 81, 131–32
capitalism, 4, 87, 95, 114, 120
  anti-capitalism, 3, 51
  challenging capitalism, 96
  Christian capitalist nationalism, 125
  commodification under, 86
  free enterprise capitalism for the poor, 179
  individual character, corroding, 25
  industrial capitalism, 22, 50, 174, 177
  plantation capitalism, 6, 12–13
  predatory capitalism, 101–2, 104, 109, 116
  racial capitalism, 5–6, 11, 74, 190, 192, 203
  Sanders on historical development of, 79
  under-waged workers, dependence on, 74, 75
Carrasco, José, 64
Carver, George Washington, 10
Casanova, José, 121
Catholic Action, 55–56, 57, 62
Catholic Campaign for Human Development (CCHD), 65
Catholic labor unions, 55, 57
Catholic Social Teaching, 51, 65, 68
  American Catholics' non-familiarity with, 57
  Catholic women religious trained in, 64
  Christian Democracy and, 56, 62
  common good, on the primacy of, 52, 53–54
  dignity of the human person, on the principle of, 52–53
  faith-based organizing, influence on, 65, 68

Rerum Novarum, as traced back to, 49
United Farm Works as incorporating, 63
Catholic social tradition
  Alinsky as linked with, 58–66, 67, 204–5
  organizing, as impacting, 43, 68
  Social Catholicism as a tradition, 49–57
  as unfamiliar in the US context, 42–43
Catholic Worker movement, xx, xxvii, 57
Catholic Youth Organization (CYO), 59
"Ceremony of the Land" litany, 3–4
Césaire, Aimé, 113
Chalmers, Thomas, 25
Chambers, Ed, 62, 63, 64
Charities and the Commons (journal), 31
charity, 50, 177, 179
  "my brother's keeper" injunction and, 70, 78
  new breed of American Churches as working beyond charity, 38
  the poor as not objects of charity, 73, 79
  Sanders as rejecting charity, 70, 73, 80
  scientific charity, 25, 27
  settlement houses as more than charity, 26
  social justice ministries as charitable services, 103
Charity Organization Society (COS), 25–26, 27, 28, 31
Chavez, César, 63
Chicago, 26, 31, 36, 41, 69
  Back of the Yards neighborhood, 58–60, 62
  Chicago Commons, 30, 150
  Chicago Freedom Movement, 40
  Chicago sociology, 28, 38, 61
  Hull House social settlement, 28
  South Side, 150, 152, 155, 157, 158
  University of Chicago, 31, 35, 37, 150
  Venezuelan asylum seekers in, 149–59

Index

Chicago Theological Seminary (CTS), 30–31, 149, 150–51
Christian Critics (McCarraher), 32
Christian Democracy, 51, 56, 57, 60, 61, 62
Christian ethics, 103, 136, 181
  of Beulah Sanders, 70–71
  community organizing, study of, 119, 123
  fullness of Christian social ethics, 131–32
  Society of Christian Ethics, 131, 133
  womanist scholars contributing to, 81
Christian nationalism, 85–86, 88, 98, 185
Christian socialism, 26, 162, 186
  Delta Cooperative Farm as an experiment in, 19
  freedom, Christian socialist vision of, 6, 17
  insurgent pedagogy, optimizing, 178–81
  justice, Christian socialist vision of, 3, 16
  Kester as a Christian socialist, 11, 21
  Social Catholicism, as a political expression of, 51
civil disobedience, 94, 97
civil rights, 36, 76, 203
  Black Civil Rights Movement, 125, 127–28
  civil rights activity, 81, 120, 137, 150, 168
  civil rights violations, 72
  religious support for, 40
Cloward, Richard, xxvii
Cold War, xviii
Coleman, John, 50–51
common good, 52, 65, 163
  Alinsky in pursuit of, 59–62
  bargaining for, 92
  defining and describing, 53–54
  eschatology and spatial justice, engaging, 157–59
  the good in common, 164
  intermediary institutions, promoting through, 54–55

particularity, discerning common good through, 68
Common Good and Christian Ethics (Hollenbach), 158
Communities Organized for Public Service (COPS), 63–64
Cone, James, 101, 206
Congregation of the Divine Providence (CDP), 64
conscientization, 119, 124, 127, 184
constructive mourning, 203
cooperative commonwealth, 3, 5, 6, 8, 17–19, 21, 202
"Correcting a Curious Neglect" (Smith), 121–22
Cortés, Ernesto, Jr., 63–64, 199
Courage to Teach (Palmer), 186–87
COVID-19 pandemic, 105, 183
Cox, Harvey, 23, 36, 38, 39, 206
critical consciousness, 156, 159, 171, 172, 206
cultural centrism, 185
Curran, Charles, xxvi

Daly, Mary, xxvi, 182
Daniel, Meghan, 130
Day, Dorothy, xx, xxvi, xxvii, 57
Day, Keri, 41, 123
D'Azeglio, Luigi Taparelli, 52
De La Torre, Miguel, 151, 152
decolonial theory, 109, 112–16
Deeper Shades of Purple (Floyd-Thomas), xxxiv, xxxv
Delta Cooperative Farm, 19
Democracy and Social Ethics (Addams), 26–28
democratic organizing movements, 20
democratic socialism, 5, 6, 42, 179, 180
demonarchy, 139–40
dignity of the person, principle of, 52–53
Direct Action Research and Training (DART), 58, 64–65, 189
discernment, 5, 68, 159, 170, 196, 202
disruptive religion, 122
Domination System, 134, 137

Dorrien, Gary, 80, 120, 202, 204
　on advocacy of social ethicists, 133–34
　as a Christian social ethicist, 160, 162, 181–82, 183, 200
　Christian social ethics, defining, 163–64
　Christian socialism, vision of, 178–81
　Hegel, as inspired by, 194–95
　pedagogical impact of, 168–70, 171–73
　social Gospel movement, interpreting, 174–76, 176–78
Du Bois, W. E. B., 28, 120, 182, 206

East Harlem Protestant Parish (EHPP), 23, 35, 37, 39–40, 41
Eddy, Norman, 39
Eddy, Sherwood, 15, 18, 19
Egan, Jack, 62
Ely, Richard T., 33, 120
Emanuel, Rahm, xxxiii, 153
the Enlightenment, 50, 162, 165, 169
eschatology, 19, 157, 159, 175
ethnocentrism, 29
Eurocentrism, 165, 167, 185
Evangelical Lutheran Church in America (ELCA), 100, 104–5

faith, 75, 85, 98, 173, 178
　action, faith as interconnected with, 160, 177
　democratic faith, 28, 30, 40
　ethical scholar, faithful aims of, 181–87
　faith-based organizing, 47, 58, 63–66, 99, 100, 101, 107
　labor partnerships and the power of faith, 93–95
　nurses and their faith, 89, 92–93
　social change, people of faith working for, 139, 148, 170
　social justice as a component of, 171, 175–76, 178
　workers, addressing on matters of faith, 90, 91

Faith in Action, 58, 189
Faundex, Antonio, 103
Federal Council of Churches, 72
Fellowship of Reconciliation, xxiii, 11
feminism, 109, 110, 112, 116, 199
Field, Marshall, III, 60
Fisher, Robert, 29, 189
Flexner, Abraham, 31
Floyd, George, 183
Floyd-Thomas, Stacey, 138, 200
Francis, Pope, 51
freedom, 3, 57, 61, 162
　1960s freedom fighters, 207
　Black freedom struggles, 74, 81
　Chicago Freedom Movement, 40
　Christian socialist versions of, 5, 6, 17
　in cooperative commonwealth, 5, 8, 19, 21
　education as a practice of freedom, 163, 171–72
　republican vision of freedom, 5–6, 7, 18
Freire, Paulo, 103, 111, 134, 163, 172, 184
Fromm, Eric, 155
fugitive pedagogy, 172–73
Fugitive Pedagogy (Givens), 172

Galluzzo, Greg, 64
Gamaliel Foundation, 58, 64, 105, 189
Gaudette, Tom, 62, 64
Givens, Jarvis, 172–73
Gladden, Washington, xiv, xv, 24
Goldwater, Barry, 76
Gonzales, Mary, 64
Gourevitch, Alex, 5, 7, 19
Graham, Barney, 11
Gramsci, Antonio, 162, 181
Gran, Peter, 185–86
Greene, Alison Collis, 14
Gushee, David, 169

Hamer, Fannie Lou, 81, 206
Harding, Vincent, 207
Hargraves, Archie, 23, 34–35, 41, 150

Harrington, Michael, 179, 181, 182
Harris, Kamala, 93
Harrison, Beverly W., 101, 131, 170, 182
Hart, Stephen, 65
Hartford Seminary, 30
Hartman, Saidiya, 184
Hayes-Mota, Nicholas, 200, 204–5
Hegel, G. W. F., 194, 195
Hill, Joe, 203
Hollenbach, David, 158
Hollinger, David, 33
Holy Spirit, 41, 108, 187, 196–97, 202, 207
hooks, bell, 111, 149, 159
   critical pedagogy of, 163, 171–72, 186
   engaged pedagogy of, 134, 142
   reciprocity in the works of, 154, 155–56
Hoover, Herbert, 14
Huerta, Dolores, 63
Hull House (social settlement), 26, 37
Hurston, Zora Neale, 181, 182

immigrants, 29
   Catholic immigrants, 57, 59
   immigrant labor, 24, 74
   undocumented immigrants, 89, 130, 152, 157
   Venezuelan migrants in Chicago, 149–59
immorality, 27, 76, 78, 79
In Search of Our Mothers' Gardens (Walker), 138, 141
Industrial Areas Foundation (IAF), 60, 126, 189
   Catholic organizers associated with, 62–63
   common good, as working for, 61
   faith-based organizing tradition growing out of, 47, 58, 66
   relational power, teaching people to develop, 199
   Southwest IAF, 64
injustice, 95, 151, 159, 164, 189
   colonial myths as foundation of, 114
   communion, as shredding, 104

historical injustices, 170, 179, 181
   Social Gospel's prophetic critique of, 174, 175
social structures and institutions, as embedded in, 162
social-injustice model, Shelby employing, 154
systemic injustice, 101, 102, 103, 107, 116, 175, 179
See also justice
inner cities, 24, 35, 36
Institutional Based Community Organizing (IBCO), 126
insurgent pedagogy, 171, 187
   Christian socialism as optimizing, 178–81
   resistance, expanding strategies of, 172–73
   social gospel as organizing, 176–78
   social gospel as orienting, 174–76
interfaith alliance, 58, 65, 92–93, 95
intermediary institutions, 54–55, 57, 60, 66
Interreligious Foundation for Community Organization (IFCO), 72
Irenaeus of Lyons, 104

Jennings, Willie James, 104, 115
Jesus Christ, 73, 104, 169, 177, 187, 204
   biblically sophisticated Jesus-Followers, 135
   as a community organizer, 101, 107
   Domination System, Jesus's message reverberating in, 137
   ethics of, 17, 21
   following Jesus through community organizing, 108
   on the Kingdom of God, 99, 138
   radical teachings on love and compassion, 161
   social injustice as incompatible with teachings of, 175
Johnson, Mordecai, xix
The Jungle (Sinclair), 58

JUSTethics, 160–61, 162, 170, 186–87
justice, 26, 92, 98, 162, 180
   Christian socialist visions of, 3, 16
   community organizing, enacting justice through, 109
   contributive and distributive justice, 158–59
   eschatology and spatial justice, 157–59
   ethical pursuit of, 160–61, 163, 164
   God's justice, 108, 114
   Jesus, justice preached by, 177
   justice-oriented ministries, 105, 106
   Kingdom of God, creating through, 178
   love as central to, 155, 157
   moral arc of the universe moving toward, 173
   racial justice, 10, 11, 18, 20, 33, 94–95, 120, 136, 177
   reparative justice, 181
   reproductive justice, 130
   spatial justice, 149, 157
   Sprong on what justice requires of us, 154
   See also social justice

Katz, Michael, 28, 29–30, 32
Kester, Alice, 10, 11
Kester, Howard
   racial and economic justice, commitment to, 10, 11, 18
   Revolt Among the Sharecroppers, 8–9, 11–12
   as a social gospeller, 3, 5, 18, 19, 21
   as a STFU member, 3–5, 16–17, 20, 206
Kester, Nannie, 9
Kester, William, 9
Kierkegaard, Søren, 183
King, Coretta Scott, 70
King, Martin Luther, Jr., 94, 166, 170
   civil rights movement scholarship and, 81
   critical consciousness of, 206
   holiday to commemorate birthday, 182–83
   moral leadership of, 181
   on the political economic order, 178
   Poor People's Campaign and, 69
   as a visionary, 173
Kingdom of God, 17, 33, 99, 133, 138, 150, 173, 174–76, 178
Knights of Labor, 7–8
Ku Klux Klan, xxiii, 9

Landless Workers' Movement (MST), 97
Learning to Question (Faundez/Freire), 103
Leo XIII, Pope, 49, 51, 52
Let the People Decide (Fisher), 189
Lewis, John L., 38
liberation theology, 56, 133, 168
listening campaign, 192
Listening to the Spirit (Stauffer), 202
A Living Wage (Ryan), xx
Loomer, Bernard, 197–98
luxocracy, 138, 141

Machiavelli, Niccolò, 7
MacIntyre, Alasdair, 44–49
Malthus, Thomas, 25, 26
Manifest Destiny, xii, xiv
Maparyan, Layli Phillips, 137–38, 140–41
Maritain, Jacques, 60–61, 62, 66, 67
Martinez, Isaiah, 94
Marx, Karl, xvi, 97
Mays, Benjamin, xix, 10
McAlevey, Jane, 85, 90–91, 93–94
McCarraher, Eugene, 32
McKnight, John, 32
Meegan, Joseph, 59
metis knowledge, 27–28, 30, 31
miners, 9, 10–11, 20
Mining the Motherlode (Floyd-Thomas), xxxiv–xxxv
Misner, Paul, xxvi, 50
mobilization, 5, 57, 85–86, 92, 98, 127, 189
Moe-Lobeda, Cynthia, xxx, 200
Monahan, Michael J., 156

Index

Moore, Natalie, 156
moral compass, 139, 161
Moral Man and Immoral Society (Niebuhr), xviii
Morris, Aldon, 122, 125
Morrison, Toni, 138, 206
Mother's Day March, 69–70
Munson, Ziad, 122, 127
Murray, John Courtney, xxvi, xxvii, 57

National Association for the Advancement of Colored People (NAACP), 8, 11, 16
National Catholic Welfare Council (NCWC), xx
National Conference on Charity and Corrections (NCCC), 31
National Council of Churches (NCC), 23, 70, 72–73, 73–74
National Welfare Rights Organization (NWRO), 23, 80, 205
  churches as partnering with, 78–79
  civil law, upholding, 80
  law and order, pushing back on the use of, 77
  National Council of Churches and, 72–73
  organizing skills of welfare mothers, 69–71
Nepstad, Sharon, 122, 126, 127
"The 'New Breed' in American Churches" (Cox), 38
new breed of activist clergy, 23, 36, 38–40
New Deal, 13, 14, 125, 203
New Sanctuary Movement, 127, 130
Niebuhr, Reinhold, 10–11, 20
Nixon, Richard, 73, 76, 78, 80, 82
No Shortcuts (McAlevey), 90
Nolden, Eliza, 15

Obama, Barack, xii, xiii
Occupy Wall Street, xiii
O'Grady, John, 62, 67
O'Sullivan, John, xii

Pacific Institute for Community Organization (PICO), 58, 64. *See also* Faith in Action
Pacific Lutheran Theological Seminary (PLTS), 101, 102, 104–5, 111
Padilla, Gilbert, 63
paideia, principle of, 128, 163
Palmer, Parker, 186
Park, Robert, 37
Paul VI, Pope, 61
Peabody, Francis Greenwood, xv–xvi, 120
Peacher, Paul D., 15–16
Peck, M. Scott, 155
Pedagogy of the Oppressed (Freire), 172, 184
Pentecostalism, 34, 41
Peraino brothers, 88–89
Peters, Rebecca Todd, 123, 130
Pickett, Ray, xxx, 101
Pius XI, Pope, 51, 55
Piven, Frances Fox, xxvii
plantations
  Peacher's plantation, 15–16
  plantation capitalism, 6, 12–13
  planter domination over sharecroppers, 3–4, 8–9
Plato, 165, 166
Poor People's Campaign, 69–70
Powell, Adam Clayton, Sr., xiv, 182
preferential option for the poor, 56, 161–62
Progressive Era, 23, 33, 41, 119
progressives, 15, 33, 60, 95, 98, 119, 176
pro-life movement, 127
prophetic activity, 160, 177, 204
  in American Christianity, 179, 181
  Hebrew prophets, 161, 175
  modern prophets, 26, 35, 37, 170, 205
  prophetic tradition, reclaiming, 178
  social injustice, prophetic critique of, 174, 175
Prophets and Patriots (Braunstein), 126
Protestant work ethic, 166

Quadragesimo Anno encyclical, 51

race and racism, 7, 128, 139, 172, 183, 189
  antiracism organizing, 135, 138, 143
  antiracism practices, 146–48
  antiracism training, 134, 137, 141, 143
  antiracism from a womanist worldview, 138, 146, 148
  antiracist critiques of community organizing, 109–10
  as a barrier to opportunity, 155, 180
  Beckley, racial tensions in, 9
  capacious antiracism and engaged pedagogy, 141–46
  cities as structured in racialized terms, 34, 35
  cross-racial organizing efforts, 6, 16
  CTS involvement in racial politics, 150
  divisions between workers based on, 86–87, 91
  domination and oppression of racism, 5–6, 13, 137, 185
  economy, race as a factor in, 74, 80, 157
  manipulation of the poor along racial lines, 74
  people of faith without racial power, 41
  as a persistent division in society, 158
  racial capitalism, 5–6, 11, 74, 190, 192, 203
  racial equity lens, 100, 105, 116
  racial justice efforts, 10, 18, 20, 33, 94–95, 120, 136, 177
  racialization of crime, 76, 135, 138
  racism as part of a deadly trajectory, 114
  racist fear-mongering of the far right, 89
  social control, racism as a mechanism of, 140
  social sin, racism as, 119–20
  systemic racism, 181
Ransom, Reverdy, 30, 120, 182
rational actor theory, 122, 125
Rauschenbusch, Walter, 22, 120

Read, Scott, 64
reciprocity, 153–54, 154–57, 159
relational meeting, practice of, 192
relational power, 191, 192, 196–97, 197–98, 199, 200
Rerum Novarum encyclical, 49, 51–52
resource mobilization theory, 124, 125, 126
Reveille for Radicals (Alinsky), 60–61, 62
Richmond, Mary, 32
Rieger, Joerg, 167, 169, 201
Riggs, Marcia, 81
righteousness, 166
Ringer, Christopher, xxxiii–xxxiv, 200
Robnett, Belinda, 122, 127–28
Rochdale Farms, 19
Rogers, Ward, 10, 17
Roll, Jarod, 13, 16, 17, 18
Roosevelt, Franklin Delano, 14
Ross, Fred, 63
Ross, Loretta, 130
Russell, Letty, xxv, 35
Ryan, John A., 57

The Sacred Canopy (Berger), 184
sacred values, 197
  agitation and, 201–2
  diversity, helping to track, 195–96
  judgments of sacred value, 193–94
  politics of, 199–200
salvation, 133, 176, 206
Sanborn, Richard, 120
sanctions, 152, 157
Sanders, Bernie, xiii
Sanders, Beulah
  as an ethicist, 79–80
  NWRO, as a leader of, 71–72, 205
  speech to the churches, 73–79, 81
  West Side Welfare Recipients League, founding, 70
Santow, Mark, 189
Schmitt, Carl, 203
Scott, James C., 27
Scudder, Vida, xiv, xvii, xxvi
Seaton, David, 156–57

INDEX 239

Second Vatican Council, 60, 61, 64
secularization theory, 121–22
Seeing Like a State (Scott), xxiv, 27
Seeking Spatial Justice (Soja), 157
SEIU 1199 (union), 93–94
Sen, Rinku, 110
settlement house movement, 31, 38, 204
   Alinsky, critique of the movement, 37
   casework methodology, use of, 32
   Chicago Commons as a settlement house, 150
   democratic power, failing to raise, 29
   early days of the movement, 25–26
   urban mission of settlement workers, 30, 34–35
   urban sociology arising from, 28
sharecropping, 17, 19
   AAA as promising relief for, 14–15
   in the Arkansas Delta, 5, 12, 13–14
   as a form of slavery, 5–6, 8, 12, 16
   planter domination over, 3–4, 8–9
Sheil, Bernard, 59–60, 61, 62, 66, 67
Shelby, Tommie, 149, 154–55
Sinclair, Charlene, 200, 205
Sinclair, Upton, 58
Slater, George, Jr., xvii, xviii
slavery, 18, 137, 140
   chattel slavery, 4, 5, 7, 8, 13
   Gourevitch's paradox of, 5, 19
   indentured slaves, 13, 74
   sharecropping as a form of slave labor, 3, 4, 5–6, 12, 16
   wage slavery, 4–5, 6, 8, 16, 17, 21
Smith, Christian, 121–22, 127
Smith, Linda Tuhiwai, 109, 112–16
Snarr, C. Melissa, 80, 200
Snyder, Timothy, 203
social Catholicism. *See* Catholic social tradition
Social Darwinism, xv, 25
Social Diagnosis (Richmond), 32
social ethics, 17, 130, 171, 191, 201
   advocacy, social ethicists conducting, 133–34
   Beulah Sanders as overlooked by social ethicists, 70
   at Chicago Theological Seminary, 150, 151
   Christian social ethics as rooted in Scripture, 160, 161
   democracy, as energizing, xxii–xxxviii
   Dorrien as defining Christian social ethics, 163–64
   establishment as a discipline, 23
   fullness of Christian social ethics, enacting, 131–32
   future direction of Christian social ethics, 190
   in higher education, 139, 149
   moral work of movements, analyzing, 124, 125, 131
   organizing as paired with, 200, 202
   political theology, relationship to, xxi–xxii, 204
   religion and social ethics, 123, 195
   SMT as a complement to Christian social ethics, 127, 131–32
   social Catholicism as a distinct tradition of, 43
   "Social Ethics for Social Justice," 177
   Social Gospel's relevance for, 175
   social movement theorists, offering insights to, 119
   social science, ceding authority to, 31
   sociology, as intertwined with, 120–21
   transformed society as goal of, 80–81
Social Ethics Energizing Democracy (SEED), 200, 205
Social Ethics in the Making (Dorrien), 133, 163
social gospel, 6, 33, 38, 42, 163, 177
   in *JUSTethics* framework, 162, 170
   Kester as a social gospeller, 3, 5, 18, 19, 21
   as orienting insurgent pedagogy, 174–76
   Sherwood Eddy as a social gospeller, 15, 19
   social ethics and, 10, 120, 133
   social gospel leaders, 22, 24, 32–33, 120, 186

social justice, 85, 89, 97, 135, 137, 147
  as boundary-crossing, 80–81
  Christian faith, as a component of, 171, 175–76, 178
  divine justice, linking to, 163
  education as oriented toward, 134, 151
  in *JUSTethics* framework, 187
  pastoral care, linking social justice work with, 107
  radical social justice movements, 17
  seminaries oriented toward, 136
  "Social Ethics for Social Justice," 177
  Social Gospel as striving for, 133
  social justice ministries, 102–3, 105, 117, 205
  in womanist framework, 141, 148
Social Movement Theory (SMT), 119, 120, 121–24, 126–27, 128, 130–32
social practice, 145, 163, 192, 196, 202
the social question, 22, 24, 31, 50–52, 55, 121
social salvation, 24–25
social sin, 120
social work, 23, 30–32, 39, 79
socialism. *See* Christian socialism; democratic socialism
sociology, 33, 119, 123
  Chicago school of sociology, 28, 37, 38, 61
  Christian sociology, 30–31, 121, 150
  empirical sociology, 28, 37
  redemption of the world expressed through, 24–25
  religious leaders as embracing, 22, 119
  SMT as a focus within, 124
  Social Darwinism, developing beyond, 25
  social ethics as intertwined with, 120, 133
  sociology of religion, 122
Soja, Edward, 149, 157
solidarity, 92, 158, 164, 182, 194
  Alinsky tradition, as part of, 68
  broad-based solidarity activism, 200, 201
  of Chicago Commons residents, 150
  to combat white supremacy, 186
  common good, building solidarity for, 65
  deep solidarity, 169
  in interdependent relationships, 80
  in *JUSTethics* framework, 162
  Kingdom of God as made through, 178
  among North Philadelphia nurses, 93
  principle of solidarity, 54
  of STFU members, 3, 17
  of working-class Catholics, 60, 87, 91
Southern Tenant Farmers Union (STFU)
  Kester as a member, 3, 11–12, 16–18, 20, 206
  plantation overlords, fighting against, 8–9, 15–16, 21
  sharecroppers, advocating for, 4, 12, 17, 19
Spencer, Herbert, xv, 26
spiritual activism, 139–40
Starr, Ellen Gates, 26
Stassen, Glenn, 169
Stauffer, Aaron, 179, 180, 204, 206
Stephens, Christine, 64
Stivers, Laura, 151
Strife, Joseph, 200, 204
Stringfellow, William, 35, 206
structural-functionalism, 122
struggle theology, 75–76
subsidiarity, principle of, 54–55, 60, 66
suburbanization, 34–41, 158
Sumner, William Graham, xv
The Survey (journal), 31

Taparelli, Luigi, 52
Taylor, Alva, xxiii, 10, 11, 20
Taylor, Breonna, 183
Taylor, Graham, 23, 24–25, 29, 30–31, 33, 37, 41, 120, 150
Teaching to Transgress (hooks), 171, 186
techne knowledge, 27–28, 31
Their Eyes Were Watching God (Hurston), 181
theological education, 102, 109, 187

community organizing, intersection
  with, 111, 116, 118, 200–1
decolonizing theological education,
  113–16
guidelines for the teaching of
  community organizing, 110
psychology as embraced by, 123
sociology as helping to advance, 150
sustained attention to the Spirit,
  developing, 41
theological presupposition regarding
  purpose of, 103–4
Thomas, Norman, 10–11
Thurman, Howard, 168–69, 206
Tillmon, Johnnie, xxvii, 69
Todd, George and Mary, xxv, 35
Townes, Emilie, xxxiv–xxxv
Toynbee Hall (settlement house), 25–26
traditions in community organizing, 23
  the Alinsky organizing tradition, 58–99
  MacIntyrean approach to organizing,
    44–49
  organizing and tradition, 42–43
  social Catholic organizing, 49–57
  traditions in conversation, 66–68
Trump, Donald, 86, 88, 98, 124, 152,
  157, 180, 182, 203
Tucker, William Jewett, 120
"Two Conceptions of Power" (Loomer),
  197–98

Unger, Roberto Mangabeira, 176
union busters, 88–90, 91, 93
Union Theological Seminary, 10, 34,
  101, 139
United Church of Christ, 65
United Farm Workers, 63
United Mine Workers of America
  (UMWA), 11, 20
urban life, 26, 32, 158
  Chicago school of urban
    sociology, 28, 38
  CTS involvement in, 24, 150
  EHPP in urban settings, 35, 40
  European urban innovators, 34

industrial capitalism and, 25, 50
urban ministry, 23, 30, 31, 34, 35,
  37, 204
urban neighborhoods, 23, 29, 36
urban planning, 30, 34
urban poverty, 36, 154
the urban social question, 22
Urban Training Center (UTC), 35

Vanderbilt School of Religion, 10, 11, 17
Vatican II, 60, 61, 64
Venezuelan asylum seekers, 149, 150–51,
  152, 153, 156, 159

wages, 28, 53, 74, 91, 97
  campaign for fair wages, 91
  living wages, 87, 129–30, 131
  low-wage employers, 75, 80
  low-wage labor, 79, 89, 95
  minimum wage, 129
  nurses, wages for, 90, 92
  poverty wages, 72, 75
  wage labor, 4, 7, 8
  wage slavery, 4–5, 6, 8, 16, 17, 21
Walker, Alice, 138, 141
Walker, Lucius, 72
Walters, Alexander, xiv, xviii
Ward, Harry F., xiv, xvii
Warren, Mark, 64, 122
Webber, George, 20, 34–35
welfare. *See* National Welfare Rights
  Organization
Wells-Barnett, Ida B., 30, 182, 206
Wen, Zhuang, 94
Wessel-McCoy, Colleen, 200, 205
West, Don, 10
West Side Recipients League, 70
What Should the Left Propose? (Unger),
  176
When the Good Life Goes Bad
  (Floyd-Thomas), 161
white supremacy, 11, 114, 116, 147,
  166, 203
  Black women as getting out from
    under, 140

white supremacy *(continued)*
  churches in support of, 6
  ecclesial structures, effect on, 115
  laws as buttressing, 16
  ministry confronting and countering, 102
  Peter Gran on, 185–86
  theological education to counter forces of, 109
  wealth-based supremacy, as linked with, 101, 104
  white supremacist rallies, 88–89
Whitfield Owen, 8
Wiley, George, xxvii, xxviii, 72
Williams, Claude, 10, 16–17, 19–20
Williams, Delores, 101, 138, 139–40
Wink, Walter, 134, 137, 142, 206
Winter, Gibson, xxvi, 35
womanism, 138, 160, 181
  antiracism stance, 142, 146, 148
  characteristics of womanist thought, 141
  critical pedagogy theory and, 109, 112
  on the Kin-dom of God, 174
  spiritual activism of, 139–40
  womanist ethics, 132, 168
  womanist scholars, work of, 81
The Womanist Idea (Maparyan), 141
Woodbey, George W., xvii, xxxvii, 182
Woodruff, Nan, 8, 13–14, 15–16
Woods, Clyde, 4
Woodson, Carter G., 173
Wright, Richard R., Jr., 120, 182
Wynter, Sylvia, 115

Young Men's Christian Association (YMCA), 9, 10, 18, 31
Younger, George, xxv, 35
Yukich, Grace, 122, 127, 130